PAPERS
FOR THE
MILLIONS

Recent Titles in
Global Perspectives in History and Politics
George Schwab, Editor

This is a Subseries to Contributions in Political Science.

PAPERS
FOR THE
MILLIONS

The New Journalism in Britain, 1850s to 1914

Edited by
Joel H. Wiener

Contributions to the Study of Mass Media and Communications,
Number 13

Global Perspectives in History and Politics

Greenwood Press
New York • Westport, Connecticut • London

Library of Congress Cataloging-in-Publication Data

Papers for the millions : the new journalism in Britain, 1850s to 1914
  / edited by Joel H. Wiener.
      p.   cm. — (Contributions to the study of mass media and
  communications, ISSN 0732-4456 ; no. 13. Global perspectives in
  history and politics)
    Based on the proceedings of the CUNY Conference on History and
  Politics, held at the Graduate Center of the City University of New
  York, Nov. 7-8, 1986.
    Bibliography: p.
    Includes index.
    ISBN 0-313-25939-9 (lib. bdg. : alk. paper)
    1. Journalism—Great Britain—History—19th century—Congresses.
  2. Journalism—Great Britain—History—20th century—Congresses.
  3. Newspaper publishing—Great Britain—History—19th century—
  Congresses. 4. Newspaper publishing—Great Britain—History—20th
  century—Congresses. 5. English newspapers—History—19th century—
  Congresses. 6. English newspapers—History—20th century—
  Congresses. 7. Press and politics—Great Britain—History—19th
  century—Congresses. 8. Press and politics—Great Britain—
  History—20th century—Congresses. I. Wiener, Joel H. II. CUNY
  Conference on History and Politics (1986 : Graduate Center of the
  City University of New York) III. Series: Contributions to the
  study of mass media and communications : no. 13. IV. Series:
  Contributions to the study of mass media and communications. Global
  perspectives in history and politics.
  PN5117.P37 1988
  072—dc19   88-25071

British Library Cataloguing in Publication Data is available.

Library of Congress Catalog Card Number: 88-25071
ISBN: 0-313-25939-9
ISSN: 0732-4456

First published in 1988

Greenwood Press, Inc.
88 Post Road West, Westport, Connecticut 06881

Printed in the United States of America

The paper used in this book complies with the
Permanent Paper Standard issued by the National
Information Standards Organization (Z39.48-1984).

10 9 8 7 6 5 4 3 2 1

For Paul, Debbie, and Jane

Contents

Preface

This volume is based on the proceedings of the CUNY Conference on History and Politics that was held at the Graduate Center of The City University of New York on November 7-8, 1986. The conference was also sponsored by the Research Society for Victorian Periodicals (its eighteenth annual conference), the CUNY Academy for the Humanities and Sciences, and the CUNY Center for European Studies. I am grateful to the latter two organizations for their financial support. The research for portions of this book was also supported (in part) by a grant from the City University of New York PSC-CUNY Research Award Program.

A book like this is dependent upon the contributions of many scholars. I am grateful to Professor George Schwab for his unstinting assistance and support. I wish to thank Professor Robert A. Colby for sharing so generously with me both his time and his impressive knowledge of the Victorian period. I also appreciate the important contributions to this book of the following scholars: Professor Vineta Colby, Dr. Merrill Distad, Ms. Linda Brandt Fritzinger, Professor Christopher Kent, Mr. David Linton, Professor Roy T. Matthews, Professor Peter Stansky, and Professor Anthony S. Wohl. My wife, Suzanne, has come to share my sometimes unrestrained enthusiasm for the press. She has also applied her many talents to making this a better book than it would otherwise have been.

Joel H. Wiener
Introduction

In May 1887 Matthew Arnold launched a cultural thunderbolt
against the New Journalism, which he characterized as "feather-
brained" and unworthy of emulation.[1] Then, eight months later,
T. P. O'Connor responded in kind with the publication of the
halfpenny evening *Star,* for a class of readers that welcomed
"animated, readable and stirring" accounts of "unpolitical
literature."[2] A century of popular journalism ensued, defined by
ceaseless change and what one historian of the press has referred
to as "the constant erosion of the tides of human feeling, so
imprecise, so incoherent, so fallible, yet so powerful and compelling."[3] Still, the press, "that boiling, bubbling, seething
cauldron,"[4] refuses to settle down. In London, as this is being
written (in April 1987), two press magnates, Lord Rothermere

and Robert Maxwell, are contending bitterly for control of the evening market, almost as their predecessors did ninety years ago. It is possible for a reader of the *Evening Standard* or the *London Daily News* to win a "dream house" or a trip to New York via Condorde, whereas, a century ago, the prizes for readers of *Tit-Bits* and *Answers* were slightly more modest: a staff position on the paper, a suburban villa, a pound a week for life. Meanwhile "Fleet Street," that seemingly impregnable touchstone of modern journalism (itself a product of the New Journalism), continues to crumble. It is being replaced by "Wapping," the docklands outpost of *The Times* and the *Sun,* where the muffled sounds of computer terminals bid fair to replace the clack of typewriters and the incessant buzz of human activity.

If British journalism is undergoing a profound transformation in the late 1980s, almost certainly a century ago the changes were at least as dramatic. Then a historic shift occurred: from a press limited by its own traditions and the modest demands of its readers to one whose capacity for change was, seemingly, without end. Technology was a crucial element of this New Journalism, for within a relatively short period of time (1860-1900), the electric telegraph, telephone, typewriter, high-speed rotary press, and half-tone block for the reproduction of photographs all came into regular use. Likewise, the economic basis of journalism was transformed. Profits replaced ideas as the motor force of the new industry of journalism, while, as an accompaniment to this shift, a market for journalism was located somewhere near that point on the social scale where the "man on the knifeboard of the onmibus" sat.[5] In readership terms, classlessness edged past class as the circulation of newspapers soared into the millions.

Innovation became commonplace: bold headlines, gossip columns, interviews, sports reporting, pictures, and "news stories" whose appeal derived from a subjective interest in the evolving human drama. Sandwichmen walked the streets of London,

Manchester, and other cities, loudly proclaiming the virtues of their cheap newspapers. And integral to this New Journalism, great newspaper personalities emerged; W. T. Stead, whose "nonconformist conscience" transplanted itself from Darlington to London in the early 1880s and whose efforts to combine political conversion with sensationalism caused it to be said of him that he was "too good a fanatic to be a real journalist, and too real a journalist to be a good fanatic"[6]; T. P. O'Connor, who published and edited the *Star,* which one penetrating critic described as "an odd mixture of culture and sport and char-women's cups of tea"[7]; and, most strikingly, Alfred Harmsworth (Lord Northcliffe), of whom it has been said that he was "the enthusiast, the explorer, and the adventurer, with the world's news as his uncharted seas."[8]

When about 75 specialists on the press assembled at the City University of New York in November 1986 to exchange ideas on the subject of the New Journalism, it soon became evident that the "celebrities" of the occasion were Arnold and Stead. Arnold stood on one side of a great cultural divide. He was the traditionalist, the arbiter of culture, clinging to a view of life that gave away little to the emerging "new democracy," of which journalism was a part. Stead, confronting Arnold, was determined to change the rules of the game by invoking "true journalism" (in place of "critical or paragraph quilting") as the "very soul . . . of national unity." In Stead's view, the function of the journalist was to give voice to the democratic culture of the people by holding forth to them an "inspiring ideal."[9] What underlay this tough battle of wills in the 1880s (and at the conference itself) were differing ideas about the notion of quality in culture. Could the latter, for example, be applied to a newspaper like the *Star,* which evinced an obsessional concern for ferreting out every last scrap of information about the Whitechapel murders in the autumn and winter of 1888 or, more presciently, to the *Daily Mirror,* which in 1904 began, for the first time in the history of the press, to create a constellation of pictures out of the printed text of the daily newspaper?

The enthusiasts gathered in New York could not agree completely, though the bulk of sentiment gravitated to Arnold rather than Stead. Yet, as one tough question after another emerged at the conference regarding content, readership, professionalism, distribution of news, editing, and so on, it became evident that notwithstanding the lively debate and discussion, most of the questions could not easily be answered. Yet an honest attempt was made to find answers, and had not the powers that be at the City University of New York abruptly decreed the closing of the Graduate Center as evening drew near at the end of the second day of the conference, it is possible that some of the participants might still be engaged in animated discussion of the finer points of the New Journalism.

This book cannot convey the full flavor of conference debate. But it does include the bulk of the essays presented in formal session, now slightly revised for publication, and an additional essay by Joel H. Wiener. The fourteen chapters are divided into four sections. Part One, "The Beginnings of the New Journalism," deals with the transitional period between the old and the new journalism, when conventional methods of putting together a newspaper for a limited market were being challenged. In the first of four essays, Laurel Brake emphasizes the continuities between the two kinds of journalism. She maintains that the mid-Victorian press was not monolithic and that the history of journalism is replete with cultural transformations. In her view, the *Pall Mall Gazette,* under the editorship of W. T. Stead, exemplified these continuities rather than (as is usually assumed) initiating a sharp break with the past. B. I. Diamond examines the career of Frederick Greenwood, who edited the *Pall Mall Gazette* for fifteen years before Stead arrived on the scene.

According to Diamond, Greenwood was an important precursor of the New Journalism who encouraged investigative journalism of the kind to be found in a series of articles written for the paper by his brother James under the title "A Night in the Workhouse." Joel H. Wiener discusses the changes ushered in by the New Journalism and concludes that many of them were anticipated by the old journalism. He suggests that prior episodes in the history of the press need to be more closely examined, including bohemian journalism, which spawned innovative pressmen such as George Augustus Sala, Frederick Greenwood, and Edmund Yates. In the final essay in Part One, Harry Schalck surveys the London press in the 1880s. He maintains that the New Journalism of this decade was transitional between the old journalism and the subsequent commercialization of the press. Yet what both new and old had in common, according to Schalck, was a serious interest in politics.

Part Two, "The Flowering of the New Journalism," deals with some of the innovations in late nineteenth-century journalism as well as several practitioners of these changes. Ray Boston focuses on Stead and his ideas concerning the relationship between government and journalism. Boston believes that Stead used the press for moral purposes and was an outstanding pamphleteer in the tradition of Daniel Defoe and such democrats as Thomas Paine and William Cobbett. In his essay on Stead and the *Pall Mall Gazette,* Joseph O. Baylen makes clear that Stead was very much a part of the intricate web that connects politics with journalism. Baylen explores Stead's close relationship with Lord Esher, who provided him with confidential information for use in the paper and helped to shape its policies. John Goodbody examines the early history of the *Star* and shows how its content and makeup represented facets of the New Journalism. He concedes that crime, sports, and gossip had much to do with the success of the paper but argues that in the first three years of its existence the *Star* was primarily a vehicle for radical politics rather than commericial enterprise. Aled Jones concludes the section on "The Flowering of the New Journalism" by demonstrating that similar changes occurred in Wales, particularly the creation of an undifferentiated market of readers that was not sectarian in its religious or cultural outlook. Jones maintains that the New Journalism accentuated differences between English- and Welsh-language newspapers and that it reflected the dynamism that coursed through Wales as it defined its nationhood.

Part Three, "Subjects and Audiences," illustrates the content of the New Journalism and the multiple interests of its readers. In the first of five essays, John M. Robson analyzes an extensive exchange of letters in the correspondence columns of the *Daily Telegraph* in 1868 on the subject of "Marriage or Celibacy." This was one of the earliest attempts to give full expression to readers' opinions in a popular context, and Robson concludes from it that there is much to be learned about the lives of ordinary people from papers like the *Daily Telegraph,* which were beginning to reflect the new mass journalism. Kate Flint discusses the debate over the New Art in the pages of the *Westminster Gazette,* focusing on John A. Spender, the paper's editor, who defended the traditional link between art and morality against the "art for art's sake" position. Flint suggests that the New Journalism, notwithstanding its innovative character, upheld conventional moral values and the intelligibility of culture. Deian Hopkin explores the relationship between socialism and the New Journalism. He shows how such left-wing papers as the *Clarion* and the *Labour Leader* successfully adopted some of the new journalistic ideas. At the same time, many socialist papers resisted elements of popular journalism in the belief that these could not be reconciled with political conviction. Using the failure of the *Daily Citizen* (1912-15) as a test case, Hopkin concludes that this oppositon to change hampered the left-wing press in its attempts to gain a large readership. Rosemary T. VanArsdel discusses the importance of the interview as a facet of journalism, especially in the women's press. She analyzes different kinds of interviews, including "Biographical Sketches" and "Character Sketches," and concludes that interviews made a lively addition to the New Journalism by combining popular appeal and political saleability. Finally, Martha Vogeler looks at the news-gathering aspect of journalism, especially the work of overseas correspondents. She casts light on the working conditions of these correspondents and shows how appointments to important positions on papers such as *The Times* (and, by implication, to popular papers as well) were often the result of personal influence.

Part Four, "An Assessment," contains a single essay by James D. Startt who argues that in the Edwardian period a symbiotic relationship existed between quality and popular journalism. Both kinds of journalism benefitted from this relationship, Startt contends, the former by incorporating liveliness and readability into its columns and the latter (in the case of the *Daily Mail* and other newspapers) by including serious news coverage and analysis in its pages. Startt asserts that "good journalism" was very much alive in the age of the New Journalism and that it is wrong to assume an incompatibility between the two.

Do any general observations about the New Journalism suggest themselves from these essays? First, it is necessary to issue the usual disclaimer about selectivity, all the more so in this case because of the sheer variety of the subject matter. It is clear that this book is a tentative one. It is meant to indicate the kind of research that remains to be done as well as what has been done. The holes in the fence marked "New Journalism" are admittedly large. There is, for example, no chapter in the book devoted to Harmsworth (almost certainly the most important personality in the history of popular journalism), although one possible justification is that a great deal has been written about him already. Less excusably, there is little about the American influence on the British press, which appears to have been decisive at times. Several aspects of working journalism are overlooked, including proprietary interference, "descriptive reporting," remuneration and conditions of work, and the development of professionalism. Sport does not receive satisfactory treatment, and there is little about gossip and crime. There are only scattered references to the financing of newspapers. Yet, overall, the essays in this volume, in some ways significantly, push forward the boundaries of exploration and analysis of a critical period in the history of the press. They make it easier to comprehend what the New Journalism was about and, by implication, what the shift from Fleet Street to Wapping portends in today's newspaper world.

As its title indicates, *Papers for the Millions: The New Journalism in Britain, 1850s to 1914,* is revisionist in its emphasis. Most of its contributors take a long view of the popular press. They are prepared to extend its chronology some distance on either side of the watershed years 1880-1900 and are willing to acknowledge its positive dimension. Few of them would agree with Lord Salisbury's caustic verdict on Harmsworth (which might be applied to the New Journalism as a whole): that he had "invented a paper for those who could read but could not think, and another for those who could see but could not read."[10] And although Stead and O'Connor in particular emerge as strong personalities in the book, it is the complexity of journalism, its multicolored aspect, above all, its capacity to excite "the busiest and poorest in the community,"[11] including, most emphatically, "the cabman's wife,"[12] that stand out.

Journalism reflects life in its full richness, and the New Journalism especially mirrors the disjointed, frenzied quality of life in the twentieth century. But further analysis is needed before such a relationship can be satisfactorily postulated. Here are some points to consider: Perhaps the New Journalism represents an uneasy compromise between oral and written culture.[13] Possibly elite and popular elements of culture are bound to clash with each other when forced to interact. Or it may be that Arnold and the contemporary critics were right after all: that, in the final analysis, amusement and enlightenment do not mix well together and that any attempt to fuse them, as was tried a century ago by the New Journalism, is doomed to failure. This book may stimulate readers to ask further questions about the relationship between the press and society. It is my hope that it contains a few of the answers hidden away among its pages.

NOTES

1. Matthew Arnold, "Up to Easter," XXI *Nineteenth Century* (1887), 638.

2. T. P. O'Connor, "Our Confession of Faith," *Star*, 17 January 1888.

3. Francis Williams, *Dangerous Estate: The Anatomy of Newspapers* (London, 1959), p. 246.

4. David Christie Murray, *Recollections* (London, 1908), p. 70

5. Raymond Williams, *The Long Revolution* (New York, 1961), pp. 194-195.

6. T. P. O'Connor, *Memoirs of an Old Parliamentarian* (London, 1929), I, p. 303.

7. Hamilton Fyfe, *Sixty Years of Fleet Street* (London, 1949), p. 68.

8. Philip Gibbs, *Adventures in Journalism* (London, 1923), p. 84.

9. Stead's views are summarized in two important essays: "The Future of Journalism," *Contemporary Review* L (1886): 663-679, and "Government by Journalism," *Contemporary Review* XLIX (1886): 653-674. Both are reprinted in W. T. Stead, *A Journalist on Journalism: Being a Series of Articles ... on Journals and Journalism,* edited by Edwin H. Stout (London, 1892).

10. J. L. Hammond, *C. P. Scott of the Manchester Guardian* (London, 1934), p. 95.

11. *Review of Reviews* (January 1890), 14.

12. Arthur Pearson stated: "Never forget the cabman's wife." (Sidney Dark, *The Life of Sir Arthur Pearson* [London, 1922], p. 17).

13. On this interesting point, see Larry D. Wilcox, "Hitler and the Nazi Concept of the Press in the Weimar Republic," *Journal of Newspaper and Periodical History* II (Winter 1985), 25.

PART ONE

THE BEGINNINGS OF THE NEW JOURNALISM

1

Laurel Brake

The Old Journalism and the New: Forms of Cultural Production in London in the 1880s

As a cultural form journalism may be seen as the commercial and ideological exploitation of the transient and the topical, a ceaseless generating or production of "news" and novelty, involving a plurality of discourses, including literary and political. It has normally been seen by critics, however, as "subliterary"; and the retrospective foregrounding of the novel as the dominant literary form of the nineteenth century must be predicated on the exclusion of the nonfictional prose that appeared so prodigiously in periodicals and newspapers in the forms of essays, reviews, leaders, and "correspondence." The "New" Journalism was named in an article in the *Nineteenth Century* in 1887 by Mathew Arnold, a practitioner for more than thirty years of what by implication was the "Old" Journalism, whose long-term project was to elevate his journalistic practice into "criticism" and thus to the authority of literature. He places unsurprisingly the New

Journalism at the bottom of a hierarchy of cultural forms, at the top of which is art, which, by his definition, outlives the specificities of history and is accessible only to the cultivated. In tainting the *Pall Mall Gazette* and journalism like it with the epithet *New* (a pejorative term for Arnold and much of his audience) and, by implication, designating a sector of the press Old and trustworthy, Arnold created a "history" and a tradition that posit a decisive and anomalous transformation in the nature of journalism associated with the *Pall Mall Gazette* in the 1880s. I argue that the Old Journalism was by no means monolithic or stable in character or forms, that the *Pall Mall Gazette* shared this instability of ideology and form, and that in none of its forms was it aimed at a mass readership. Nor was this phase of journalism founded in the 1880s in the expected form of the cheap daily morning newspaper but appeared in the relative freedom of a "quality" London evening paper and monthly and weekly periodicals, to some of which Arnold was a regular contributor. In short, transformations of journalism in the 1880s do not fit into the social, economic, and cultural hierarchies of Matthew Arnold's definition of the New Journalism. Nor do they accord with his apocalyptic notion of history, which posits sudden change.

The Old Journalism

To indicate the difficulties of the notion of an Old Journalism counterpart to the New, it may serve to look at the dialectical relation of pairs of journals in midcentury: on the one hand, the *Saturday Review* predicating its existence in its first number on the "autocracy" of *The Times,* and on the other, the "hatching" from one journal of a second, which in part derived its identity from its rivalry with and its appropriation of its parent, as in the case of the emergence of the *Nineteenth Century* from the *Contemporary Review.*

The circumstances of origin of both the *Saturday Review* (1855) and the *Nineteenth Century* (1877) are set out elsewhere; what I want to note is the way both present themselves as offering a serious alternative to the existing cultural hegemony, the alternative in both cases being perceived as an independence that suggests representation and service of a readership beyond the limits of the existing rivals.

In an early number of the *Saturday Review* appeared the following:

> Even the direct rivals of the *Times* in the daily press impliedly admit its autocracy. . . . Each of them has a small special following of Tories, Radicals, or old ladies, or footmen, and to these they sometimes appeal, but the greater part of their occupation consists in echoing the small cries of the *Times*. As for the weekly papers, they have degenerated into the toadies of the great daily journal . . . we don't much mind it ourselves. We would infinitely sooner live under the *Times* than under the French Empire, or the American democracy.[1]

It is clear from the acerbic tone and the conclusion of this paragraph, in which the new paper's antipathy to both the right and the left is indicated, that the *Saturday Review* is making a bid for existing readers of *The Times* as well as for new ones among the highly literate and cultured and for comparable status to *The Times*. What it did offer to both kinds of readers was serious attention to literature, science, and art as well as to politics, which was the plain focus of *The Times* and which was excluded from the *Athenaeum*, its main rival. The *Saturday* presents itself then as reformative, its innovations of wider subject matter and independence firmly associated with "the great daily journal" in the challenge to its autocracy.

The relation of the *Nineteenth Century* to its predecessor, the *Contemporary*, is similarly one of continuity and innovation, but both the initial and the final relationship of the one to the other is far closer than in the previous example. On the one hand, the new monthly "which will be conducted on the absolutely impartial and unsectarian principles which governed the *Contemporary*"[2] can be regarded as a clone of the old, having the same editor, price, size, and many of the most eminent contributors (including Gladstone) but a new publisher and title, whereas the new periodical is the parent that has refashioned itself to conform to the narrower interest (in theology) of its backers, publisher, and new editor. This is a pattern of transformation that was also to characterize the *Pall Mall Gazette* (only for a period the carrier of the New Journalism) in 1880, in 1889-1890, and again in 1893. James Knowles, former editor of the *Contemporary* and the new editor of the *Nineteenth Century*, calls attention to his previous connection in the advertisement for the latter, "Edited by James Knowles. Late of the *Contemporary Review*,"[3] but he also introduces in the second number a structure of debate, the Symposium, which enhances the controversial impartiality of debate, an important factor in his departure from the parent journal, and which serves to distinguish it further from its now narrow forebear.[4] It may be observed that both the *Nineteenth Century* and the *Saturday Review* twenty-two years before it sought intellectual readers from among the new clerisy for publications that stressed respectively a more erudite, broader, and impartial orthodoxy and a complementary exhaustive pluralism. Significant transformations and innovation are evident in these journals, which inscribe social and cultural change in generated formations.

Nor are these phenomena anomalous in the long history of the Old Journalism; they are common occurrences. The entire history of the press is characterized by markers, or transformations, of equal significance to the changes in the newspaper press of the 1880s to which Arnold attached the epithet *new*.

Another aspect of the Old Journalism of the 1860s and 1870s that is of interest in connection with the New Journalism is the relation between the advocacy of signature and the disruption of the monolithic authority of a periodical, its fictional "unity" such as that claimed by *The Times* and the earlier nineteenth-century quarterlies. Two anonymous writers of midcentury, in the weekly *Saturday Review* in 1855 and in the monthly *Cornhill* of 1862, and Leslie Stephen take pains to reveal the collective endeavor of the daily newspaper where, on the whole, a kind of anonymity was to continue far longer than in other sectors of the press.

The *Saturday* skeptically considers claims by *The Times* for its own unity.

The recent manifesto will have it that a daily journal, if not the labour of a single pen, is an emanation from a body of men, fused into the nearest possible approximation to unity. The most complete solidarité is suggested as existing between the producers of the leading articles—they have but one will, but one style, but one calibre of talent. A lively representative is provided for this mysterious entity in its Editor. He moves about in the world, and absorbs the intelligence which may be floating in the atmosphere of society; while the contributors are kept in bottles of smoke in the back-office, to be summoned forth like the genie in the *Arabian Nights* when the giant energies are required for service. . . . A very little common sense will show the most cursory observer that the leading articles of a great newspaper cannot be written by less then six or eight gentlemen, who, as it is, are probably a great deal overworked for the perfect accuracy of their reasoning, and the perfect felicity of their illustrations. The power of selecting some one member of a literary staff for the treatment of a particular topic, must of course be vested in some one person, and this it is which constitutes the unity of a newspaper. The conductors of a daily journal who should attempt to secure a closer uniformity than this would obtain it at the cost of the most important elements of intellectual power. There is no reason to believe the *Times* when it insinuates that such a blunder is committed in its own case. It strikes us that a man must have singularly little discrimination who cannot detect a variety of hands in the articles of the Leading Journal. The writers who rule us are clearly characterized by different degrees of ability, different degrees of taste, and, we must add, different degrees of morality. . . .

We are not for a *loi de la signature*, which, for the excessive protection afforded by the present system, would substitute an excessive proscription. Still less would we imitate Mr. Drummond in giving publicity to the names which gossip associates with the Leading Journal—a course to be avoided for this reason among others, that you may chase, like Mr. Drummond himself, egregiously to mistake your man. We say to a confiding public—do your best to resolve the 'we' into 'I'. . . . Consider, above all things, that each of your literary rulers has been selected to govern you, not for his Absolute Wisdom but for his peppery style and his fertility of allusion. Does Absolute Wisdom necessarily accompany these qualifications? Is Absolute Wisdom exactly compressible into a column and a bit, and does it assume those not less than three times per week.[5]

Leslie Stephen also comments on the editorial "we" in his biography of his brother, James Fitzjames Stephen; in connection with Stephen in the *Pall Mall Gazette* and G. S. Venables of the *Sat rday Review*. First Stephen:

The inexperienced person is inclined to explain it ['we'] as a mere grammatical phrase which covers in turn a whole series of contributors. But any writer in a paper, however free a course may be conceded to him, finds as a fact that the 'we' means something very real and potent. As soon as he puts on the mantle, he finds that an indefinable change has come over his whole method of thinking and expressing himself. He is no longer an individual but the mouthpiece of an oracle. He catches some inflection of style, and feels that although he may believe what he says, it is not the independent outcome of his own private idiosyncrasy. Now Fitzjames's articles are specially remarkable for their immunity from this characteristic . . . a large part of the 'Pall Mall Gazette' represented the individual convictions of a definite human being.[6]

It is clear that Stephen is divided. About Venables Stephen remarks:

One of his fancies was a prejudice against the editorial 'we'. His remarks would take the form of a series of political aphorisms not so much expressing personal sentiment as emanating from wisdom in the abstract. They seemed to be judicial utterances from the loftiest regions of culture, balanced, dignified, and authoritative, though of course edged by a sufficient infusion of scorn for the charlatan or the demagogue.[7]

Although Stephen is reluctant to cede the "we" (he writes as an autocratic editor himself), I conclude that that is what he is moving toward.

The *Cornhill* article that appeared anonymously in July 1862 makes a forceful effort to demystify journalism for a family audience that is assumed to be ignorant of the subject but, significantly, interested in it. Conceived as a family magazine — which epithet would appear to include women in its intended readership — *Cornhill* consequently barred religion and politics. Journalism, because of its heady sense of an expanding readership among the middle classes, however, is regarded as suitable for exposé and familiarization. This article offers a full, astute, and utilitarian analysis of the Old, higher journalism. Of leaders, or "intellectual mincemeat,"[8] the author opines

The best leading articles that are written are nothing more than samples of the conversation of educated men upon passing events, methodized and thrown into a sustained and literary shape. They seldom or never rise above this level. . . . The faculty of composing leading articles is merely a form of technical skill, like the handiness of a mechanic, the fluency and readiness of a barrister, or the delicate touch of a musician.[9]

and of leader writers:

They are, generally speaking, able and educated men, who, from some cause or other, have as it were been caught in some of the eddies of the main streams which are navigated in search of wealth and distinction, or have reached comparatively early secure shelves which connect them with the business of life, and leave them a certain degree of leisure, and an appetite for some additional income. Our leading journalists are barristers waiting for business, or resigned to the want of it; clergymen unattached, who regret their choice of a profession which their conscience or inclination forbids them to practice, and which the law forbids them to resign; Government officials whose duties are not connected with party politics, and do not occupy the whole of their time; and in a few cases men of independent means, who have a fancy for writing, and who wish to increase their incomes.[10]

Although the writer seems denigrating if ironic here, it is clear that leader writers, authors of the form of journalism that he most exalts and respects, are drawn from other, establishment, professions or are "independent." The contempt of the leisured wealthy for the working journalist is more explicit in the hierarchy of the profession, contempt that emerges in his account of "journalists, pure and simple" who are "men who have no other occupation or position in life than those which they derive from newspapers, and no other prospect than those which lie in their success." They are often of low beginning and without "much other education than the newspaper itself supplies."[11] For these periodicals and all three authors the monolithic authority of the newspaper press is absorbing and challengeable; that the fascinating anatomy of the formation is revealed and exposed and celebrated and belittled is the inscription of the dialectic of the nascent profession in the mid-Victorian period.

If anonymity gradually lost ground during this period, signature per se was not a form of personalizing that newspapers would readily adopt, although an increase in the personal in a different form was a characteristic that later came to be associated with the New Journalism in its use of interviews and personal detail. T. P. O'Connor writes

The main point of difference is the more personal tone of the more modern methods. There was a day when any allusion to the personal appearance, the habits, the clothes, or the home and social life of any person would have been resented as an impertinence and almost as an indecency . . . .[12]

The author, a Gladstonian Liberal M.P. and editor of the *Star*, writing in 1889, was particularly conscious of Parliamentary reporting in the past.

You had no information as to how the speech was delivered or how received. You were told nothing of the personality of the persons who made the speech. There the long lifeless even columns were before you; the speech delivered in the dread void of the dinner hour to a select audience of the speaker and the orator himself, filled the space in exactly the same kind of way as the speech that was punctuated by the ringing cheers of a crowded and deeply moved House. The words that came with fierce fluency of an impassioned speaker were given in exactly the same way as the speech that was interrupted by hems and haws, or mumbled from an inarticulate throat. It was the same of course with public men throughout their whole life.[13]

For the periodicals the argument for anonymity was often cast in terms of their desire to retain contributors from high places who without the protection of formal anonymity would no longer be at liberty to influence opinion covertly, if at all. And less eminent and more penurious contributors could use the system to write similar material for a variety of journals. But of course the implications for sales of named contributors also beckoned editors and proprietors. James Knowles's principled position of signature for his new *Nineteenth Century* later attracted the envious charge from the knowing perspective of a New Journalism publication, the *Review of Reviews,* that this was a policy of predatory "tuft-hunting," or attracting readers through names irrespective of the quality of their articles.

Editing of the tuft-hunting variety seldom had a more successful exponent than Mr. Knowles. While other editors have sought for articles he has sought for names, and he has made a golden harvest out of the quest. He absolutely refuses to publish any anonymous or pseudonymous articles. Lord Tomnoddy's trivial inanities, if so be that they be signed 'Tomnoddy,' on this system are welcome, while the letters of 'Junius' or 'Ecce Homo' would be shown to the door.[14]

And Frederick Greenwood, founder of the *Pall Mall Gazette,* regretted what he regarded as the imposition of anonymity on the new venture: "Anonymity was an inflexible rule for journalists then, and the public was slow to descry our galaxy of shining ones through the universal veil."[15]

It may be suggested that while the periodical press was moving, with reservations, toward signature and fragmented authority, the newspaper press came to occupy the middle ground between blanket anonymity and the vulgarity of named contributors: a kind of acknowledged collectivity that indicated the individuality of journalists by generic bylines (From our own Correspondent), regular columns, and occasionally outright signature; in the New Journalism these were supplemented with the foregounding of the editor and the personal details of individuals in the news as described by O'Connnor above. An enhancement of the editorial power over the individual journalist's is evident in the greater extent of subediting in papers associated with the New Journalism,[16] but at the same time, subediting attests to the collective nature of the enterprise. The entrepreneurial component of editing and publishing, the professionalization of journalists and journalism, and the transition from the wealthy, educated, leisured reader to the working, literate reader of the middle classes are inscribed in the changing cultural formations of the periodical and newspaper press throughout the period. T. P. O'Connor, in his signed article on the New Journalism in the monthly *New Review* in October 1889, shortly after he began his stint as editor of the *Star*, attests to the self-consciousness of journalists about these changes.

A journal, whatever its views, should express them with the greatest lucidity and in the strongest and most striking manner it can command. We live in an age of hurry and of multitudinous newspapers. The newspaper is not read in the secrecy and silence of the closet as is the book. It is picked up at a railway station, hurried over in a railway carriage, dropped incontinently when read. To get your ideas through the hurried eyes into the whirling brains that are employed in the reading of a newspaper there must be no mistake about your meaning . . . you must strike your reader right between the eyes. The daily newspaper often appears to me to bear a certain resemblance to a street piano: its music is not classical, nor very melodious, and perhaps there is a certain absence of soul, but the notes should come out clear, crisp, sharp.[17]

It is an excitement that Arnold recognizes, resists, and discredits in a paragraph on the New Journalism in an article that he wrote on politics and Parliament in early 1887.

If we look more closely at the two examples of midcentury anonymity cited above in the *Saturday Review* and the *Cornhill*, an understanding of the ways in which anonymity functioned may result. The author of the *Saturday Review's* "Our Newspaper

Institutions" (1855) is Henry Maine, a jurist and one of the founders, with J. D. Cook, of the new weekly; the author of the *Cornhill's* "Journalism" (1862) is James Fitzjames Stephen, also in law and a former student of Maine, who had introduced Stephen to Cook and professional journalism while Cook was editing the daily *Morning Chronicle.* Moreover, Stephen published three articles on journalism in 1859 in the *Saturday Review,* which he then abandoned between 1861-1863 for the *Cornhill,* enticed by better pay. But so closely was Stephen associated with the *Saturday Review* for most of his life that T. H. S. Escott wrote: "He *was* the *Saturday Review."* At the *Cornhill* Stephen was writing for Frederick Greenwood, the editor at that time but to found and edit the *PMG* in 1865. Stephen was a frequent contributor both to the early *Saturday Review* (from 1855 onward) and to the early *Cornhill.* The vigilant interest in the press maintained by the *Saturday Review* from its inception fostered Stephen's interest in it, led to the publication of his work about the subject, and directly contributed to the astute understanding of the press shown in the *Cornhill* article. My main interest here is to stress the continuities between different forms of journalism (a literary and political weekly, a monthly that eschewed politics, and two dailies); between the Old and New kinds, and between periodicals and newspapers; for in addition to the network of anonymous journalists revealed here, close links exist between the *Pall Mall Gazette* and the *Saturday Review* and the *Cornhill,* which Greenwood named as the daily *Pall Mall Gazette's* antecedents. And Stephen's frequent contributions to the *Saturday Review* and the *Cornhill* were succeeded by a significant commitment to the *Pall Mall Gazette* for which he wrote "middles" intensively between 1865 and 1874.

The New Journalism

In his *Cornhill* article Stephen wryly drew attention to the way in which the press in 1862 legitimized cultural and economic hegemony:

In almost all the most influential papers, their tone [of the leaders] is conservative in the extreme upon all essential points, however they may favour political liberalism. It is easy to trace in every one proof of the fact that its author has a strong interest in the maintenance of all the chief principles and institutions of society, and a general conviction that alterations in them are rash . . . in a rich and intelligent country, a perfectly free press is one of the greatest safeguards of peace and order. Under such circumstances it is nearly certain that the ablest newspaper will be both read and written by and for the most comfortable part of society, and will err rather on the side of making too much of their interest than on that of neglecting them.[18]

Fragmentation of this kind of complacency about the establishment press is signaled by, among other things, Greenwood's and W. T. Stead's challenges to the balance of the links between press and state in the *Pall Mall Gazette* and in "Government by Journalism,"[19] which appeared in the most outspoken and exposed of many articles written by Stead on aspects of this theme.

But the origins in 1865 of the *Pall Mall Gazette,* so closely associated with the development of the New Journalism in the 1880s, show the same alliance between the press and the status quo. Frederick Greenwood consciously modeled his new *Pall Mall Gazette* on the *Anti-Jacobin,* a weekly (fl.1797-1798), which appeared only when Parliament was sitting; founded by George Canning to combat radical views and initially edited by William Gifford, whose interest lay in literary parody and satire, it published the following considered view in 1801: "We have long considered the establishment of newspapers in this country as a misfortune to be regretted, but since their influence has become predominant by the universality of their circulation, we regard it as a calamity most deeply to be deplored."[20] The *Anti-Jacobin* attracted Greenwood through its liveliness and its "quaintly graceful . . . old-fashioned form," including its "old-faced type, the lettering of the title, the italic capital head-lines." Thus the *Pall Mall Gazette*, which was to develop some of the characteristics associated with the New Journalism and to occasion its denunciation, had its origins in a project that was in part regressive and conservative; the other principal model for Greenwood, more reformative than conservative but still looking to past achievements, was "to bring into Daily Journalism the full measure of thought and culture which is now found only in a few Reviews."[21] According to J. W. R. Scott[22], as well as Greenwood, these "Reviews" were the *Saturday Review* and the *Cornhill.* Looking back in the *Review of Reviews* in 1893, Stead saw this as an attempt to wed literature to journalism,[23] a project that echoed the position of Arnold who contributed frequently to Greenwood's *Pall Mall Gazette.* All three models—the *Anti-Jacobin,* the *Saturday Review,* and the *Cornhill*—point to the continuation of the aim for an educated readership for the new paper, which was later to be associated with a "clubland" readership as well as Arnold's "demos." Although various campaigns of the *Pall Mall Gazette* under Greenwood and Stead resulted in surges in readership figures, the normal figure lay between 20,000-30,000 of "the political and literary classes"[24] at its height, after the price had dropped from 2d to 1d in 1882 and during Stead's stint as editor.[25] It seem clear that many of the features (such as headlines, illustrations, and interviews) of this evening daily, which commentators other than Arnold (such as Greenwood, O'Connor, and Scott) came to associate with the New Journalism in their subsequent glosses on Arnold's epithet, did not as such enter into Arnold's definition. What seems to have triggered his alarm was the combination of the anomalous (and momentary) surge of the *Pall Mall Gazette's* circulation figures to

100,000 at the time of the week-long series of articles on "The Maiden Tribute of Modern Babylon" in July 1885 and the subsequent agitation and legislation and Stead's high-pitched claim from prison on "Government by Journalism" in May 1886. This momentary foray of the *Pall Mall Gazette* and its editor into the spheres of both mass readership and government in the face of Arnold's vehement opposition to the Gladstonian Liberals and Home Rule—the principal enemies in the article "Up to Easter" in which the comments on New Journalism appear—and habitual defense mounted by Stead and the *Pall Mall Gazette* occasioned Arnold's attack. Arnold objects here to T. H. Huxley's claim in the previous number of the *Nineteenth Century* that "the chief good is, in brief, freedom to say what he pleases"[26] and observes that in Ireland "we might need a much more thorough repression of disorder than any we have had hitherto, but that much more thorough medieval measures were needed as well . . . whoever obstructs the repression of disorder, obstructs remedial measures"[27]; in his glancing single long paragraph on the New Journalism, a transference of tone and anxiety concerning the populous in Ireland to the restless "demos" at home is evident. This is the group that Arnold inappropriately associates with the readership of the *Pall Mall Gazette,* which, under Stead, supported Home Rule. The passage, which follows in its entirety, shows the transference clearly and the origin of the association of the New Journalism with the masses before the publication of the halfpenny *Star* in 1888 and before the connection had in fact been made, although Stead's rhetoric in a number of articles had made the association. Whereas Arnold locates the "critic" (read "journalist") outside class and "interest", as an "alien" or part of the "remnant" poised against the majority, Stead in "Government by Journalism" writes provocatively from prison: "An editor must live among the people whose opinions he essays to express."[28] Arnold writes:

It has suited Mr. Gladstone and his friends to launch their new doctrine that no constraint must be put upon the Irish, and that there is no remedy for the disorder there until the national aspirations of the Irish are gratified. I have said that no reasonable man, who thinks fairly and seriously, can doubt that to gratify these aspirations by reconstituting Ireland as a nation politically, is full of dangers. But we have to consider the new voters, the *democracy* as people are fond of calling them. They have many merits, but among them is not that of being, in general, reasonable persons who think fairly and seriously. We have had opportunities of observing a new journalism which a clever and energetic man has lately invented. It has much to recommend it; it is full of ability, novelty, variety, sensation, sympathy, generous instincts; its one great fault is that it is *feather-brained*. It throws out assertions at a venture because it wishes them true; does not correct either them or itself, if they are false; and to get at the state of things as they truly are seems to feel no concern whatever. Well, the democracy, with abundance of life, movement, sympathy, good instincts, is disposed to be, like this journalism, feather-brained. . . .[29]

In replies to Arnold's definition of the New Journalism, the case for the *Pall Mall Gazette's* accuracy and self-correction is the one consistent note. But even the month before Arnold's allegation of "feather-brained" journalism, the *Saturday Review,* no friend of "democracy," in an article titled "The Old Journalist and the New," singles out the authority of the new press for praise:

Thanks to lavish expenditure and admirable management, the best of the contemporary journals are distinguished for their authority and impartiality. Partisans they are, no doubt, but, so far as facts go, they have found that frankness and honesty are the best policy. Indeed, they can hardly help themselves; should they decline the explanation of an aggrieved opponent, who asserts that he has been misrepresented, it is sure to find publicity elsewhere, and thus permanent injustice is made practically impossible.[30]

This article, which offers its own analysis of the New Journalism, puts its entire argument on the twin factors of technology and the cash to purchase it: "The marvellous inventions of modern science are all in favour of the moneyed journals." The cool regrets of this piece prompt me to suggest that one more factor might have contributed to Arnold's ire. It is that the *Pall Mall*

Gazette campaigns, principally under Stead but also Greenwood, concerned themselves not only with Irish politics but also with the unsalubrious such as divorce and child prostitution and slavery, subjects which, in their "coarseness," went beyond the Dickensian exposure of shallow graves, debtor's prison, and workhouses. The *Pall Mall Gazette* strain of investigative journalism invokes the world of naturalism—the absorption in low life or the sordid—found in contemporary French novels by Zola and English novels by Gissing, Moore, and Hardy. Realism was a mode that Arnold never accepted, fixed as his attention was on the best that was thought and said; for him Chaucer lacked "high seriousness." In correspondence in 1886 he refers revealingly to both the American and the British press: from the United States he writes to Miss Arnold: "The great relief will be to cease seeing the American newspapers . . . their badness and ignobleness are beyond belief," and he goes on immediately to link these qualities with the *Pall Mall Gazette:* "They are the worst feature in the life of the United States, and make me feel kindly even to the *Pall Mall Gazette* by comparison with them." To John Morley, former editor of the *Pall Mall Gazette,* he writes a terse P.S.: "Under your friend Stead, the *P.M.G.,* whatever may be its merits, is fast ceasing to be literature." In these remarks, with their invocation of nobility and literature in relation to the press, are inscribed the rhetoric and tenets of the high-culture hegemony now beginning to give way and the common contemporary identification of the New Journalism in Britain with American press methods. The increasing and public self-consciousness of journalists and journalism in the midcentury and after and the growth of a profession of journalism in the period highlight the confrontation between the hegemony of the clerisy and the competing ideologies of the emergent capital, electorate, and literate, which are significantly yoked by Arnold with the New Journalism. An alternative hegemony to that of Arnold and the clerisy is nascent here, promising alternative formations in the press. Moreover, although Arnold's besmirching of the New Journalism has dominated the tradition we know best, there existed at the time other critical discourses in which journalism was viewed more equitably.

The bouyancy and vigor of these groups in the period are manifest in the multiple forms that the *Pall Mall Gazette* took, the two look-alikes it generated, the *St. James's Gazette* in May 1880 when Greenwood was forced to leave the *Pall Mall Gazette* and the *Westminster Gazette* in January 1893 when E.T. Cook left; examination of the first issues of both shows similar and interesting claims to constitute the original publication under a new name, as in the case of the generation of the *Nineteenth Century* by the *Contemporary Review*. The most prodigious offspring, the lavishly illustrated monthly *Review of Reviews,* was created in 1890 when Stead left. A "Character Sketch" of the *Pall Mall Gazette,* unsigned but apparently by Stead, appeared there in February 1893. In it the successive positions of the *Pall Mall Gazette* to date are limned:

This composite personality ... has been almost Protean in its shapes. It has been a morning paper and an evening; it has been an eight-page, a twelve-page, and a sixteen-page paper. It began as a kind of a Whig, and developed into a Conservative Jingo. It has been Cobdenite under Mr. Morley; Imperialist under his successor [Stead]; Ruskinian under Mr. Cook, and now it is Unionist and socialist under Mr. Cust. It has been the organ of the most antagonistic movements. Originally projected in jest as a paper written by gentlemen for gentlemen, it was for some years the daily champion of the Socialists of Trafalgar Square. At one time the sworn defender of the medical priesthood, with all its shibboleths – vaccination, vivisection, and the C.D. Acts – it became the enthusiastic champion of all the crusaders against all the infamies of the doctors and of the police. It has been priggish with the culture of the classes, and sensational with the passions of the democracy. From being the cold cynical exponent of the gospel of those whose motto is 'above all things no enthusiasm' it became the eager and sympathetic exponent of every new fad and the apologist for every new craze.[31]

Other forms its multiplication took were the publication of a weekly distillation, the *Pall Mall Budget,* and of numerous "Extras" that consisted of reprints of single or successive articles associated with one of the *Pall Mall Gazette's* campaigns. These appear to provide a substantial additional income for the publisher and to amount to increased circulation of a kind. Even the format of the *Pall Mall Gazette* registers this consciousness of the proliferation of the press; from January 3, 1881, shortly after Stead arrived to aid Morley, a feature called "Ideas from the Reviews," which echoed in form the "Epitome of [Political] Opinion" occupying pp. 2-3, appeared on pp. 11-12 with the following rubric:

The multiplication of monthly magazines and reviews and the increasing importance attaching to them as vehicles for the responsible discussion of public questions and the ventilation of new ideas have frequently been remarked. So many readers, however, have neither time nor opportunity to master the contents of all the monthlies, that the following summary of the thoughts embodied in the more important papers of three leading periodicals may, perhaps, be found useful.[32]

The appropriation of this feature found commonly in weekly and monthly journals of the period illustrates how the *Pall Mall Gazette* had straddled the divide between the newspaper and the periodical press from its inception; moreover, it brings into play the subediting function to which producers of Victorian evening papers (which summarized the news and opinions of the morning papers) were accustomed. H. W. Massingham describes the process of producing an evening paper as putting into framework and focusing "in a strong clear light the whole loose body of news and opinion which the morning papers present."[33] This form of short, pithy summary or commentary is seen preeminently in the famous Occasional Notes columns of every *Pall Mall Gazette* number, the Notes consisting of a series of unheaded paragraphs, shapely and incisive, by different authors on various topics of the day. What these various forms—the Epitome, Ideas from the Reviews, and the Occasional Notes—share is the breaking up of the subject into short digestible units that contrast dramatically with the unbroken columns of type in morning dailies such as *The Times* and the *Daily Telegraph*. The incorporation of headlines of all kinds and of frequent illustrations in the form of maps, graphs, and line drawings also helped make the page accessible to less resolute reading at the end of the day and possibly by the family at home. These features suggest a potential readership that was to be articulated and pursued more fully later in the advertisements for *Review of Reviews* publications—"Reading for the Million" (1895)—and for the *Review* itself—"Best Magazine for Busy Men, Best for Busy Women" (1892). The conception and the format of the *Reviews of Reviews* as well are direct developments of the epitomizing and informing of busy readers, which came increasingly to characterize the project of the *Pall Mall Gazette*, although the circulation figures of the *Pall Mall Gazette* at 30,000 per day set against the figure of 100,000 per month claimed by Stead for the *Review of Reviews*[34] suggest that the 6d monthly's circulation was far wider.

The last feature of the *Pall Mall Gazette* to which I want to draw attention is the Index and the extent to which it is indicative of the conscious interest of Stead and more generally this phase of the New Journalism in a particular segment of the readership, the journalist and the profession of journalism. In the *Leisure Hour* articles on "The Great London Dailies" in 1892, Massingham singles out for special comment the archives of the *Pall Mall Gazette:*

[It] has not only a far better reference library than the 'Times', but it has a special kind of information bureau, presided over by a lady. In this a minute record is kept of notable events and speeches, and from it an army of facts and illustrations can be produced at a moment's notice to confound a political opponent, to show a statesman's record, and to instruct the public as to the progress of a great controversy. Out of this bureau has grown the series of 'PM' 'extras,' without which . . . no politician's library is complete.[35]

After Stead left the *PMG*, the index disappeared.

I want to look briefly at the *Review of Reviews*, which began in 1890, before the onset of the *Daily Mail* in 1896, and survived until 1936. It was published initially by George Newnes who, beginning in 1881, published the highly successful and downmarket *Tit-Bits*, which the *Review* resembled only in the units in which its material was presented. Appropriating and legitimizing the common practice of the day, *Tit-Bits* did not acknowledge the sources for its material, whereas Stead sought and obtained permission from his. The *Review* is notably oriented to the needs of the new profession of journalism and the exigencies of the methods of production for which rapid reference is essential. A paradigm of compilation, classification, and subediting, the *Review* manifests the same commitment to the improvement of access to sources as the *Pall Mall Gazette* indexes. Beginning in 1892, it published individual volumes of annual indexes to the periodical literature of the world, some of which included a Directory of Periodicals from which I quoted the account of James Knowles's "tuft-hunting"; these give an excellent overview of the opinions of the first phase of the New Journalism about its predecessors and contemporaries, and the index for 1893 includes an article by its compiler, Miss E. Hetherington, on the indexing of periodicals. For some years, until February 1897, the *Review* included monthly lists of the contents of current periodicals. At the end of the May issue of volume I, for example, is a fifteen-page section of information clearly aimed at journalists. It contains a Diary for April (events, utterances and dates, Parliamentary record, and obituary), a classified list of "The New Books and Blue Books of the Month," Contents of the Leading British Reviews, of the Current Quarterlies,

Proceedings of Societies, Art in the Magazines, Music Magazines, The More Notable Articles in the Magazines, American Periodicals for April, and an Index to Periodicals.

The other group among the millions of which the *Review of Reviews* takes special notice is its women readers. Early in the run, in June 1890, "Women and the Study of Contemporary History. A Scholarship of £100 per Annum for three years" appeared, which describes its project as an effort to add to the numbers of female politicians. In the course of explaining the terms of the contest and the grant, the author of the article regrets the dearth of women readers of newspapers and women journalists, and points to particular features of the *Review of Reviews*—its character sketches and the monthly resumé of the "Progress of the World"—which make it more suitable for women readers than *The Times* or *Spectator*. Knowledge of these two sections during six months is to constitute the subject of a scholarship examination, success at which will be rewarded by a three-year grant for study at Oxford or at home. More equitable staffing of newspapers is envisaged: "Some day, sooner or later, the great Daily will be born which will represent both sections of humanity in being staffed, from top to bottom, half by men, half by women. At present the supply of competent men for newspaper work is far in excess of that of competent women."[36] And the present situation of female readers of newspapers is detailed:

The value of the present offer lies not so much in the benefit which it will bring to the one successful competitor as in the stimulus which it will give to the minds of the multitude of girls who, but for such a competition, might never have looked in the newspaper for anything but births, marriages, and deaths, the *Court Circular,* and personal gossip.[37]

The two women who shared the prize were both working women—a journalist and a teacher.

Stead was not alone in believing that women were an untapped source of newspaper reader. The February 1893 "Character Sketch" of the *Pall Mall Gazette* in the *Review* included "Mr. [E.T.] Cook's Impressions" of the Magazine that he had just ceased editing. This piece coincided with the launching in January of the second offspring of the *Pall Mall Gazette,* the *Westminster Gazette,* to which Cook had moved. He writes:

A general newspaper should be made interesting to everybody. The evening newspaper is mostly consumed in railway trains; we want the *Westminster Gazette* to be taken home. We shall try and have something everyday to interest the city man; but we want him to say as he turns over some of its pages, "I must take this home to show my wife and children". And once taken home the *Westminster* will try and deserve to be read through.[38]

The identity of these two groups of readers, journalists and lower middle-class women, who lie within the compass of "busy men" and "busy women," perhaps offers the best gloss on the lower social and educational limits of the readership aimed at by this phase of the New Journalism.

It would seem that substantial continuities in cultural formations and transformations exist between the Old Journalism and this phase of the New and that the process of change is gradual rather than sudden. Applied to the journalism of the 1880s before the *Star,* it would seem that Arnold's definition is a misnomer. But this fear-inspired definition made by an establishment-based journalist did correctly anticipate the mass journalism to come in 1888, the year of Arnold's death. Moreover, discourses counter to Arnold's existed in the 1880s, which explicitly opposed distinterestedness and the impersonal—"impersonal journalism is effete,"[39] Stead writes—and commended rather than castigated the New Journalism's "crisp condensed laconic style of the telegraph."[40]

NOTES

1. "Our Newspaper Institutions," *Saturday Review* I (3 November 1855), 2-3.

2. Advertisement in the *Athenaeum* (10 February 1877), 205

3. Ibid.

4. Moreover, he retrospectively involves the first number in the Symposium format by following up Gladstone's review of a book on the influence of authority on matters of opinion with an article on the same subject in the second and a reply in the third and through the structure of the Contents page of volume one, which is organized by subject.

5. "Our Newspaper Institutions," p. 3; for an earlier metaphor of the press as government, see Walter Bagehot in the same year in "The First Edinburgh Reviewers" in the *National Review* I (October 1855), 253-284, and compare W. T. Stead's "Government by Journalism," *Contemporary Review* IL (May 1886), 653-674.

6. Leslie Stephen, *Life of Sir James Fitzjames Stephen (London, 1895), p. 216.*

7. Quoted by J. W. R. Scott, *The Story of the Pall Mall Gazette* (London, 1950), p. 27, where it is attributed to Stephen, *James Fitzjames Stephen,* in which I can find only an abbreviated version of the passage, p. 151.

8. James Fitzjames Stephen, "Journalism," *Cornhill* VI (1862), 53.

9. Ibid., 55-56.

10. Ibid., 56.

11. Ibid., 61.

12. T. P. O'Connor, "The New Journalism," *The New Review* I (1889), 423.

13. Ibid.

14. [*Review of Reviews*], *Index to the Periodical Literature [for 1892]* (London, 1893), p. 24.

15. Frederick Greenwood, "1865-1897," *Pall Mall Gazette* (14 April 1897), 2.

16. Noted by H. W. Massingham in "The Great London Dailies: The Penny Evening Papers. – The "Pall Mall Gazette'," *Leisure Hour* XXXXI (1891-1892), 610.

17. O'Connor, "New Journalism," p. 434.

18. Stephen, "Journalism," pp. 57-58.

19. In his suggestion that the press has appropriated the functions of government, Stead echoes another document of the Victorian press in which an attempt was made to mark off the journalism of midcentury from that of its immediate predecessor, Walter Bagehot's "The First Edinburgh Reviewer," which appeared as the first article in the second number of the *National Review* in 1855, a review occasioned by the publication of the collected periodical essays of these reviewers; it was republished in 1878 and again in 1884 in Bagehot's

own collected periodical essays, *Literary Studies*. In that essay Bagehot writes on the instruction by the press of "the mass of influential persons, to the unelected Commons, the unchosen Council, who assist at the deliberations of the nation" (1884 ed., pp. 3-4).

20. Quoted by Raymond Williams, "Radical and/or respectable," R. Boston, ed., in *The Press We Deserve* (London, 1970), p. 18.

21. Frederick Greenwood. "1865-1897," *Pall Mall Gazette* (14 April 1897), p. 2.

22. Scott, *Story of the Pall Mall Gazette*, p. 24.

23. "The 'Pall Mall Gazette'," *Review of Reviews VII* (1893), p. 143.

24. Ibid., p. 146.

25. Ibid., p. 154.

26. Matthew Arnold, "Up to Easter," *Nineteenth Century XXI* (1887), p. 629.

27. Ibid., p. 631.

28. Stead, "Government by Journalism," p. 654.

29. Arnold, "Up to Easter," pp. 638-639. Typical of the *Nineteenth Century* symposium format, this article is followed by one on a related subject — the Coercion Bill — and an article by Gladstone (on Apollo), as well as another, shorter reply to Huxley and an article on "The Fallacies of the French Press," another related subject.

30. *Saturday Review* LXIII (23 April 1887), p. 579.

31. "Pall Mall Gazette," p. 139.

32. *Pall Mall Gazette*, 3 January 1881, p. 11.

33. "The Great London Dailies," p. 608.

34. "After Seven Years," *Review of Reviews* XV (1897), p. 1.

35. "The Great London Dailies," pp. 609-610.

36. "Women and the Study of Contemporary History," *Review of Reviews* I (1890), p. 471.

37. Ibid.

38. "Mr. Cook's Impressions," *Review of Reviews* VII (1893). p. 156.

39. W. T. Stead, "The Future of Journalism," *Contemporary Review* L (1886), p. 663.

40. "How to Become a Journalist," in *A Journalist on Journalism, Being a Series of Articles by W. T. Stead on Journals and Journalism*, ed. with introduction by E. H. Stout (London [1892]), p. 23. Originally in *The Young Man* (January 1891).

2

B. I. Diamond

A Precursor of the New Journalism: Frederick Greenwood of the *Pall Mall Gazette*

A year before his death in 1888, Matthew Arnold, reflecting on the so-called New Journalism, conceded its "ability, novelty, variety, sensation, sympathy, [and] generous instincts" but decried its failure to benefit the readership of the British press.[1] He was equally uneasy with such other elements of the New Journalism as "popular" tone, dramatic reporting, striking typographical devices, and alleged profit seeking.[2]

Arnold's critique was, of course, aimed at William Thomas Stead, editor and perpetrator of the *Pall Mall Gazette's* sensational "Maiden Tribute of Modern Babylon" series in mid-1885.[3] Yet in his criticism of the New Journalism, Arnold failed to take into account several interesting—almost ironic—journalistic sensations initiated almost two decades prior to Stead's "Maiden

Tribute" coup. These were created by Arnold's colleague, Frederick Greenwood, founder and editor of the *Pall Mall Gazette*, when he undertook to publish two powerfully written investigations that shocked a previously indifferent public and as happened with Stead's series, evoked an important legislative reform. Indeed, Greenwood's series on the iniquities of London workhouses and the practice of baby farming and infanticide reflected many of the characteristics that Arnold ascribed to the New Journalism as practiced by Stead and his contemporaries.

Thus two decades before Stead developed a journalism marked by an emphasis on increased circulation and social reform and by the techniques of sensationalism and some striking typographical devices, Frederick Greenwood became in a large sense a precursor of the New Journalism by publishing such investigative exposes as "A Night in A Workhouse" (1866) and infanticide/baby farming (1868-1870). This paper attempts to deal with these sensational investigations and some of the marked similarities and dissimilarities between Greenwood's mid-Victorian form of journalism and that of the New Journalism of the 1880s and 1890s.

Like the New Journalists, who sought to use such devices as large headlines and graphic illustrations to lure advertising and increase the revenues of their journals, Greenwood undertook to secure and publish his series on the workhouse primarily to ensure the financial health of the *Pall Mall Gazette*, which in 1866 was on the verge of insolvency. Thirty years later, recalling the pitifully low circulation of the newspaper in its thousandth issue (April 14, 1897), Greenwood wrote:

The public was slow to descry our galaxy of shinning ones through the universal veil. It soon appeared that the new evening journal was not to achieve an immediate success. Ere many days we were conscious of what actors call a frost. A saying appropriate to February, our natal month, runs "As the days lengthen, then the cold strengthens," and, in the actor's figurative sense, with us it was so beyond all reason. March brought no greater warmth, and April less. The wintry thorn remained with us in May, then June rose and perished and there was no rise. . . . It was on a lovely summer day, all nature beaming, that our circulation figured at little more than half a thousand, and our advertisement receipts totalled only four and six. To within a week or two this is a fathful account of a very miserable time, when to stop or go on became a question daily renewed, but without any question of fighting sturdily and spending handsomely as long as we did go on.[4]

It was clear that a device that would draw attention to the *Pall Mall Gazette* had to be found. Thus in January 1866, eleven months after the appearance of the paper's first issue, an anxious Greenwood told George Murray Smith, publisher of the *Pall Mall Gazette,* and George Henry Lewes, the renowned literary critic and "husband" of George Eliot, "that it [the *Pall Mall*] is like a captive balloon, ready to soar, and restive against the rope that held it down. Could we but cut the rope—." Lewes laughed and said: "And whose business is it to find the knife."[5] The point, having been well taken, caused the usually good-humored Greenwood some remorse. It was with some anguish that Greenwood found a possible solution for his difficulties. That very evening, he later wrote,

. . . I set about looking for the knife (for the seventy and seventh time) in confidence that this time it would be found. And so it was. It came wrapped in the recollection of some dreadful reports of investigation into certain infirmaries, which reports excited no public attention whatever, being printed in a medical journal. This recollection suggested a night in a casual ward of a London workhouse as a sort of knife that might accomplish several beneficent bits of business at one stroke.[6]

Although Greenwood was loathe to call his idea of "A Night in a Workhouse" a sensation, the New Journalists defined sensationalism as something designed to "arrest the eyes of the public" and it is clear that Greenwood had every intention of doing just that with his workhouse series. Stead echoed Greenwood's pointed remarks that "the public was slow to descry our galaxy of shinning ones" by asserting that "the British public is not Laputan, but it often takes a deal of rousing."[7] Moreover, although it is not clear whether Greenwood believed that his series would improve the life of the workhouse lot, his decision to publish reflected Stead's perception of "the immense power and . . . duties which devolve on the editor who undertakes to champion 'the disinherited and outcast' and became the social Gospel of the 'New Journalism.' "[8]

In that series, which began on January 12, 1866,[9] James Greenwood, Frederick's brother, and a young stockbroker named Bittlestone ventured into the Lambeth workhouse for a night. What the New Journalists fifteen years later might have used as a front-page exposé was published on page nine of the *Pall Mall Gazette* under the simple heading, "A Night in a Workhouse." Stead later wrote (from the perspective of the New Journalist), that

Mr. Greenwood did not give his knife a fair chance. . . . One finds in amazement that instead of being displayed or set out in any way calculated to arouse the attention of the reader to the fact that there was anything in it more than ordinary, we find the first article stowed away on the last page of the paper. . . . And yet these articles practically made the *Pall Mall Gazette!* There was nothing about the Amateur Casual, there was no reference to it in either the leader or the "Occasional Notes"; it was simply printed—that was all.[10]

Stead's observation that nothing extraordinary set the workhouse series apart from the *Pall Mall Gazette's* other matter exposes Greenwood's wariness, for inside the workhouse that evening James Greenwood (as the Amateur Casual) and his friend encountered filthy bedding, hardened criminals, and hapless tramps.

In the initial article James Greenwood and his friend described three great baths in which grimy casuals were required to immerse before taking to their cots for the night. "Each one [bath]," wrote James, contained "a liquid disgustingly like weak mutton broth." They were instructed to doff their clothes so that the custodian—called Daddy—could lock them up. "Whatever you

take in of your own will be nailed [stolen], you know," warned
Daddy. The "Amateur Casual" wrote that he then closed his eyes
and "plunged desperately into the mutton broth," adding

I wish from the bottom of my heart my courage had been less hasty; for hearing
the splash, Daddy looked round and said, "Lor, now! there was no occasion for
that; you look a clean and decent sort of man. It's them filthy beggars" (Only he
used a word more specific then "filthy,") "that wan washing."[11]

James recounted an encounter with a lame old man who hobbled
about, seeking a hat that another casual had taken. "He was a
timid man, with a mild voice; and whenever he asked some ruf-
fian 'whether he had seen such a thing as a black hat,' and got his
answer, he invariably said 'thank you,' which was regarded as
very amusing." Continuing his story, James wrote:

At last one sidled up to him with a grin, and showing about three square inches
of some fluffy substance, said – "Is this anything like wot youre lost, guv'ner?"
The cripple inspected it. "That's the rim of it!" he said. "What a shame!" and
hobbled off with tears in his eyes.[12]

The following morning, a haggard James Greenwood, accompanied by his friend, retired to the offices of the *Pall Mall Gazette*
to write the exploit, and Frederick, fearful that the public might
fail to accept the series, "retouched it . . . with the intention to
avoid suspicion of exaggeration."[13]

Greenwood made no editorial comment on the series until
January 16, when, in a front-page leader, he declared ruefully:
"part . . . of the picture . . . was far too disgusting to be
drawn."[14] In fact, Greenwood's care and caution to avoid both exaggeration and especially "disgusting" details were characteristic
of most mid-Victorian journalists. Thus three decades later in
Blackwood's Magazine, Greenwood averred that in daily journalism "there was for many years about as much decency of
language in the responsible columns as at the dinner table."[15] Of

the workhouse series, he remarked that "all that might have been written after this visit to a casual ward [in 1866] was not written: could not be described in a public print [in an] insufficiently advanced period of the century." Yet Greenwood conceded that by 1866 "journalism was at a turning point. . . . Some unaccustomed emulations were not roused; others were stimulated. . . ." Still, almost apologetically, Greenwood asserted that the press "at . . . times . . . discovers too much truth, and makes inconvenient exposure of neglect, error, fraudulent practise and false people."[16]

Indeed, Greenwood's inherent aversion to stark and graphic portrayals and the use of his beloved *Pall Mall Gazette* as a vehicle for "journalistic sensationalism" was well reflected in a letter he wrote to William Blackwood in July 1885, immediately after the publication of Stead's "Maiden Tribute" series:

The Pall Mall won't quit its filth, you see, or its hypocrisies. Both have done the paper a world of harm amongst the decent folk, who will not take that sort of thing in their homes. This we find in the circulations of the *St. James's* wh. has gone up many thousands; our new subscribers, of course, being the best of theirs. . . . It is funny to see how the railroad readers of the *P.M.G.* try to hide that which they are reading; how queerly ashamed they look.[17]

Still Greenwood's inspiration of January 1866, calculated to ensure the life of the *Pall Mall,* had the desired effect. Within weeks the "Night-in-A-Workhouse" series had become a "newspaper sensation, such as has seldom been known."[18] According to the late Victorian historian of the press, James Grant,

This drew a large amount of attention to the journal which at first brought the article before the public, and the consequence was, that from that time for many months afterward the *Pall Mall* rose in circulation with great rapidity, while advertisements, of which it had but very few before that time, flowed in like a stream to its columns.[19]

In his "Character Sketch" of the history of the *Pall Mall Gazette* in 1893, Stead asserted that as a result of the workhouse series, "the circulation of the paper doubled in three days; and although that was comparatively small, seeing that the circulation then was under two thousand a day, an article which doubles even a very small circulation must be placed among the most remarkable of journalistic successes."[20] Commenting on the venture, Stead contrasted the feat of the Amateur Casual with the journalism of the 1890s by declaring that

To us, to-day, after all the immense development of journalism, the exploit of the "Amateur Casual" may seem a little thing; but to the journalists of a quarter of a century ago it seemed something almost superhuman. The *Times* and the *Saturday Review* were simply lost in admiration of the magificent heroism to which these articles bore testimony.[21]

Other journalistic contemporaries of Greenwood had a field day with the series. *The Times,* which reprinted the essence of the stories, remarked archly that "many a Victoria Cross has been bestowed for less daring, as well as for service of vastly less utility and merit.[22] The *Spectator* noted that

all London has been this week admiring the heroism of the gentleman which last week passed a night in a casual ward for the benefit of the *Pall Mall Gazette,* and few incidents of late years have been so shocking as that admiration. So utter is the dislocation of society, so complete the severance between its parts, that for a man of one caste to sleep one night in an official ward occupied by men of another has been pronounced an heroic deed. London this week feels as if it had been sleeping, like the brave author of the narrative which had awakened it, on a bed made endurable only by turning the blood which spotted it downward to the floor.[23]

Later Greenwood wrote that although the series did not have the immense effect ascribed to it, it did have "a very good effect. . . . And from that date the paper rose steadily to a high position of favour and authority."[24]

Undoubtedly Greenwood viewed with ambivalence the *Pall*

Mall Gazette's success with this series. On the one hand, he decried the sensationalism that the series had occasioned, and on the other hand, he enjoyed its fruits. His friend and colleague, T. H. S. Escott, later reminisced that although Greenwood aspired to writing of a higher kind—and was determined that the *Pall Mall Gazette* would feature political and literary contributions by the best writers of the day—he "did not forget the secrets of popular success which he had learned from [Henry] Vizetelly on the *Illustrated Times*" in 1855.[25] Moreover, Greenwood's workhouse gambit reflected Stead's concept of New Journalism that a "newspaper must palpitate . . . [and] . . . that it must be a mirror reflecting all the ever-varying phases of life. . . . "[26]

Besides the increase in circulation and advertising revenue that "A Night in a Workhouse" produced,[27] public reaction to the series soon ranged from the naiveté of a young actress who, after being told that "one of the *Pall Mall* men has been passing a night in a workhouse," exclaimed—"Do they pay them so badly as that?"[28] to a London physician who alleged that vagrancy was the result of "indiscriminate almsgiving."[29] Several letters to the editor of the *Pall Mall Gazette* indicated that generally the public's concern about the casuals was more restrained than that of the press. Thus a "West Londoner" sought to remind his fellow citizens that

In the ninth volume of the Duke of Wellington's "Despatches" there is a short letter to a cavalry officer, warning him, when in the field, against allowing his dragoons to dress their horses skins. . . . "You have no conception," writes his grace, "how much warmth the animals derive from the dust which accumulates in their coats."

I imagine the same rule must apply to half-clad and half-starved tramps, and I wish the Poor Law Board would take the opinion of the gentlemen connected with the hospital for diseases of the chest, as to the effect which the process undergone by your correspondent in Lambeth Workhouse on the night of the 8th of January, 1866, would likely to have on a pauper suffering under incipient phthsis [pulmonary tuberculosis]—a complaint sadly common amongst the class of vagrants who seek refuge in the tramp wards of the London unions.[30]

A letter signed Templar was more direct, exhorting the government to put the tramp to work and urging that "if he chose not to work, and if whipping could not make him work . . . [to] . . . let him die."[31]

Comment on the series continued for some weeks and included the words of a workhouse master who argued that

after the usual fashion of the offended official . . . what trust could they put in the Amateur Casual, seeing that he had admitted that he lied in describing himself as an engraver [upon entering Lambeth). A man who was capable of telling one lie might tell two, and so forth.

It was quite apparent, however, that the Amateur Casual series account was generally accepted and evoked a "storm of indignation." Indeed, with some exaggeration, a contemporary claimed that "from that one night spent in the casual ward of the Lambeth Workhouse may be traced the beginning of the reform of [Britain's] Poor Law."[32]

The series certainly ensured the survival of the *Pall Mall Gazette*. It also enabled Greenwood to increase the twopenny paper from eight to twelve pages and helped facilitate the move of the *Pall Mall Gazette's* offices from Salisbury Street to more commodious quarters in Northumberland Street near the Strand. Although it is possible that had it not published "A Night in a Workhouse" series, the *Pall Mall Gazette* might have ceased publication in 1866 mainly because it appealed to a far more restricted audience than the more widely-circulated *Times,* Greenwood's faith in the eventual success of the *Pall Mall Gazette* never faltered. The result of the Greenwood-inspired sensation was not only a welcome increase in the journal's revenues, but of more importance it enabled Greenwood to attract a more distinguished list of contributors. Whether Greenwood actually had a strong commitment to social reform for the poor is difficult to determine. What is quite clear is that, facing the prospect of the demise of the *Pall Mall,* he concocted a "newspaper sensation" that had become a regular feature of the New Journalism by the 1880s.

Although Greenwood's commitment to workhouse reform is a matter of conjecture, there is no doubt that he was deeply committed to ending the iniquities of "Baby Farming and Infanticide."[33] Like many of the later New Journalists who excited passions about some social evil or issue,[34] in 1868 Greenwood was convinced that he could resolve the "baby farming" problem by shocking London and by attacking those sectors of the press who, he believed, had fostered or abetted the practice. This was consonant with Stead's assertion (in defense of the New Journalism) that "if . . . you do not feel strongly, you will not, as a rule, be able to write powerfully."[35] Although Greenwood had strong feelings about ending infanticide and baby farming, he was determined to use the issue by presenting another sensational series to enhance the welfare of the *Pall Mall Gazette.*

Initially Greenwood began his infanticide investigation by concentrating on two of its major aspects—baby farming and abortion clinics in London. For years the metropolitan penny press had published advertisements for "wet nurses" and for homes where pregnancies could be aborted or infants farmed out, and of these journals Greenwood singled out the *Daily Telegraph* as one of the worst offenders. To Greenwood the *Telegraph* was the most important London daily newspaper whose policy was based upon the practice of taking "money for advertising without a word of inquiry" concerning the nature of the advertisement.[36] One example that Greenwood cited was an advertisement that read: "APARTMENTS, FURNISHED, for a lady in delicate health. Physician or midwife found, *or baby can be left.* −F. T. R., &c. &c." It was well known to Greenwood and other journalists that the women who responded to these advertisements were often condemning their infants to death. For example, as early as July

1865 Greenwood had described a case of infanticide in Exeter as "a story of a murder more terrible in its details, more significant of the depths of human wickedness, than anything we have read in many a year."[37]

The story that aroused Greenwood's particular indignation was the death of Thomas Harris, a four-month old infant who, in 1865, was discovered wrapped in newspaper by the side of a road in Exeter. Miss Mary Harris, the unmarried mother of the child, and Mrs. Charlotte Winsor, a baby-farmer of long experience with whom the mother had contracted to care for the boy, were both charged with murder. Presumably, inferred Greenwood, Miss Harris's initial intention was to pay Mrs. Winsor a fee to take the child with the understanding that the infant would in turn be sold for a profit to a couple seeking to adopt a child. According to Miss Harris's testimony at their trial, however, Mrs. Winsor offered to dispose of the child for five pounds. "I asked her," Miss Harris testified, "how she could do it; she said she could get something at the chemist."[38]

Cases such as this moved Greenwood and George Smith to establish a firm policy for the acceptance of advertisements by the *Pall Mall Gazette.* Thus Greenwood later recalled that he and Smith decided that because

scandalous advertisements . . . were commonly found at that time of day in journals the most respectable . . . [and] . . . quacks made fortunes, money-lenders made victims, [it was clear that] practitioners in actual crime furthered their trade through newspaper advertisements at (in some cases) special rates of payment! But all quacks are not rogues, and some money-lenders deal fairly enough, so that to distinguish among them is difficult . . . a rule was made to exclude the advertisements of them all.[39]

Even by the close of the century, Greenwood argued that the New Journalists could make "improvements" and "advancements" in their craft by deleting scandalous advertisements "by which various kinds of roguery ply their trade."[40]

Yet cases of infanticide and baby farming, when publicized, abated the evil practice only temporarily. Instead of newspaper advertisements, baby-farmers placed their advertisements on placards easily seen in the streets of British towns. As the devoted father of six children, three of whom died in infancy, Greenwood was drawn to the plight of these helpless infants and throughout 1865, 1866, and 1867 published a constant stream of stories and brief reports designed to arouse the conscience of the public on "the heinous crime" of infanticide and baby farming.[41] But judging from readers' reactions to these distressing accounts, the public conscience was hardly stirred by Greenwood's revelation. By mid-1867, only occasional tales and reports of baby farming and infanticide appeared in the London press. In the fall of 1867, however, Greenwood's long-standing campaign was intensified by his publication (in a front page leader) of the story of a notorious baby-farmer, Mrs. Jaggers of Woodlane Grove, Tottenham. This woman, reported Greenwood on September 25th, had in her care eight infants, three of whom had already died, and the "Medical evidence [presented at an inquest into the latest death] showed that the child was not naturally unhealthy, but it had been badly fed. The stomach was nearly empty and there was not a trace of fat on the body." In fact, alleged Greenwood, parents "are not usually sorry to be rid—in a natural way—of the evidence of their shame. Death in such a case is often a 'happy release' indeed."[42]

A month later, the *Pall Mall Gazette* called for government inspection of "baby farms," noting that the mortality rates among the "friendless little creatures" farmed out for care ranged from "sixty to ninety percent and their 'natural protectors' parents are generally only too glad to have heard the last of them."[43] The plea, however, fell on deaf ears and, as Kellow Chesney observed in his account of the *Victorian Underworld,* "in practice it was no one's business to notice how the farmer treated a fosterling unless, or until, she announced its death."[44]

Greenwood's three-year campaign against infanticide and "baby farming" finally succeeded in moving the editor of the *British Medical Journal*, Ernest Hart, to undertake in early 1868 a complete investigation of baby farming. Although pleased with the *British Medical Journal's* commitment, Greenwood was depressed and discouraged by the lack of public interest and the failure of the press to cease publishing advertisements for baby farms. And so he decided to bring his case before the public and the press by launching his own investigation in January 1868 with the assistance of a women (whose anonymity he carefully preserved) and the aid of his very able brother James. Later Greenwood recalled that

The likelihood of enormous mischief carried on by one of these advertising trades led me some years ago to make a pretty close inquiry into it; or rather a courageous, good-hearted, clever woman (long since dead) did so for me. The business was the one that was afterward called baby-farming; but it had various branches, none innocent. . . . Though this is known well enough now, it was not so then; but in a few weeks my ingenious and temerarious investigator had made all that has ever been discovered since. So well did she succeed that she could lodge with me a bundle of letters from various hands which laid the business open more plainly than could have been thought possible.[45]

In the article published on January 31, 1868, Greenwood reported that during his investigation he had made "several interesting acquaintances" and had found that each had some connection with the other.[46] Again, he singled out the *Daily Telegraph* as a major culprit in the publication of baby-farm advertisements by choosing five or six notices from its pages for investigation. With his female accomplice, Greenwood found that

If you put yourself in communication with this person named in the advertisement and at the same time with some similar advertiser who may live three miles off, you will probably find that you have to do, not with separate benevolences, but with a gang. You discover that there is some speedy means of underground communication between the benevolences, for the purpose of inquiry, conference, comparison of notes in your particular case; and you will not be very wrong, perhaps, if you suspect that this system of association, this bond of sisterhood, has been formed more for the protection of the secrets of the business than for security against immoral customers. . . . The business is largely carried on at Camberwell. From 666, Camberwell-road, Mrs. A. offers retirement to ladies in delicate health, guaranteeing that all shall be snug and confidential. From 666, Mrs. B. publishes her readiness to adopt children, which for a consideration may be "entirely given up." From 666, children are transferred for adoption by another lady—or at any rate in another name. The systematic way in which the traffic is carried on appears by this single illustration. . . . At 666 is concealed the cause and the consequence of her illness [pregnancy]—the poor little consequence, who is left to be disposed of on condition that it is never to be heard of again by the delicate lady, its mother.[47]

Greenwood also noted that it was not just the well-to-do woman who used this system, but the servant girl and "sempstress who on the production of say £12 can get rid of her burdensome baby for ever."

As to the disposal of the infants, Greenwood declared:

It wil be a real pleasure to the proprietors of the *Telegraph* to learn that this is done upon [a] system too: and that so neatly, that the prime agent is able to carry on his operations in a back parlour. He—(for gentlemen as well as ladies find themselves adapted for the trade)—is an accoucheur say, duly qualified. He issues two sorts of advertisements, one expressing a desire to adopt children, another offering children for adoption; and so earns an honest crust by trafficking with vicious or unfortunate mothers on one hand (a score of their letters lie before us), and with benevolent old ladies or enterprising persons in the wholesale line, like Mrs. Jaggers. . . . What we have not quite made out to our satisfaction is, whether there is ever any considerable stock on hand; and how that stock is disposed of when the market is dull. Not that the inquiry need be pushed so far to find how pitiful is the lot of the helpless little human creatures who are the subjects of this inhuman trade.

Greenwood cited responses to an adoption advertisement which he and his associate had placed in the *Telegraph* for a "child to be wholly given up," and especially emphasized the following note:

Madam—Seeing the enclosed in the newspaper I have taken the liberty of informing you that I have a male child that would answer the description in every way with the exception of the eyes, which are dark instead of blue; it is ten weeks old, and is a quiet, healthy child. An answer will be expected as soon as possible.

Some of the replies, averred Greenwood in the January 31 article, were from "members of the profession; others . . . from the mothers themselves. They go from their mothers' arms—four-fifths of them—to steady neglect and organized starvation."[48] James Greenwood, who in 1869 published a book based on his and Frederick's investigation of baby farms,[49] described the practitioner's attitude as callous: "I'll take the child and ask no questions of me. That will make matters comfortable for both parties. A simple matter of handing over a bulky parcel and a little one—the child and the money—and all's over, without so much as a 'good night.' "[50]

By March 1868, Frederick Greenwood was able to report, with some satisfaction, that the *Daily Telegraph* had decided no longer to accept advertisements for baby farms.[51] Although the public was somewhat aroused and the *Daily Telegraph* had been constrained to halt these loathsome advertisements, Greenwood continued his vigil. In April 1869 he reported an inquest in London on the death of a two-year-old child, Frederick Wood, who had been farmed out for ten months. The boy's bed, wrote Greenwood, was "an egg-box with a little straw in it—a short box, sixteen inches wide; the child could not turn in it."[52] Worse yet, the baby-farmer, Mrs. Caroline Saville, had fallen on the child (probably in a drunken stupor), broken his thigh, and then put him to bed. In describing this case in his book, James Greenwood remarked that

It would have been a mercy when his unsteady nurse fell on and crushed him on the edge of the stairs, if she had crushed his miserable life out, instead of only breaking a thigh. . . . He must have had a dismal time of it, poor little chap, and glad, indeed, must his spirit have been when its clay tenement was lifted out of his coffin cradle—the egg-box with the bit of straw in it—and consigned to the peaceful little wooden house that the cemetery claimed.[53]

A year later, the public awareness resulting from Greenwood's antibaby-farming campaign led to the arrest, manslaughter conviction, and subsequent execution of a Margaret Waters[54] for the death of an infant from malnutrition and "thrush" in Brixton. Testimony in the case, however, indicated that Mrs. Waters and her sister Sarah Ellis might well have been guilty of "disposing" of other infants in a variety of ways ranging from narcotic overdose to drowning.[55] In fact Mrs. Waters seems to have been the first baby-farmer to be executed, for in similar cases death warrants were issued only to be revoked by the authorities. This inspired Greenwood to declare in a front-page leader in October 1870 that "an act of needful justice has been done . . ." with the execution of Mrs. Waters. Yet he was much irritated by colleagues in the press who persisted in describing his publication of facts in the Brixton case as "revelations." "Properly speaking," argued Greenwood, "[they are] no revelations at all. . . . If a similar experiment [the placing of bogus advertisements in newspapers] had been tried by the police the result of the Brixton case might have been anticipated two years ago."[56]

From Greenwood's "crusade" emerged the seed that two years later (1872) resulted in Parliament's passage of the Infant Life Protection Act. Although the act relieved the infanticide and baby-farming problem, an even more significant development that curbed the "baby-farm" industry was the establishment of the London Society for the Prevention of Cruelty to Children in 1884, reconstituted five years later as the National Society for the Prevention of Cruelty to Children.[57]

Compared to the sensations of later journalistic exposes, Greenwood's crusade seems pale. Indeed, Stead was amazed that the workhouse series was buried deep inside the *Pall Mall Gazette's* pages and that Greenwood's baby-farming campaign hardly merited the front page of the paper. When it did, occasionally, as in the Brixton case in 1870, it was undoubtedly the result of the paper's financial distress.[58] Thus in the baby-farming crusade, as in the workhouse series, Greenwood combined the elements of sensationalism (a term he never used with regard to articles he published in the *Pall Mall Gazette)*, social commitment, and business sense, all characteristics generally ascribed to the New Journalism.

Although Greenwood never considered himself a practitioner of the New Journalism his motives and methods clearly identify him with the New Journalism. Moreover, his contemporaries saw him, at least while at the *Pall Mall Gazette,* as a journalistic innovator. Certainly Sir Henry Lucy was convinced that as editor of the *Pall Mall Gazette,* Greenwood "revolutionized daily journalism."[59] Similarly, Greenwood's successor at the *Pall Mall Gazette,* John Morley, lauded him as representing "a new element and a great change in the spirit of journalism" and as having brought English journalism to a point comparable to the French press where

it is extraordinarily common, that a publicist, an individual writer upon public affairs, impressed his own personality upon the discussion of his country and his time. . . . Greenwood, however, gave a sort of impetus, through his native vigour and originality of mind and character, to that kind of original journalism which it has not since lost.[60]

And W. T. Stead, on the eve of his translation to London as Morley's assistant on the *Pall Mall Gazette* in 1880, declared in the *Northern Echo* that Greenwood had "few rivals and no superiors in the Metropolitan Press, ..." and that although "There is no journalist from whose views we more widely differed . . . there were few whose writings we found more useful."[61]

Toward the end of the nineteenth century, Greenwood reflected on the then current state of British journalism and lamented that it had "dropped into a looseness of speech that does not improve anything" and, worse yet, that its writing had "no charm of its own."[62] To the end of his life and long career in journalism, Greenwood never abated his dislike of the New Journalism and steadfastly refused to acknowledge the fact that he had helped lay the foundation for it.

NOTES

1. Matthew Arnold, "Up to Easter," *Nineteenth Century* CXXIII (1887), 638-639. Arnold wrote that the "New Journalism's" one "great" fault was that it was *"feather-brained"* because "it throws out assertions at a venture because it wishes them true... if they are false; and to get at the state of things as they truly are seems to feel no concern whatever." Ibid., 638.

2. For a brief discussion of the New Journalism, see Raymond L. Schults, *Crusader in Babylon; W.T. Stead and the Pall Mall Gazette* (Lincoln, Nebraska, 1972), pp. 30-33; and, as practiced by Stead, J.O. Baylen, "The 'New Journalism' in Late Victorian Britain," *The Australian Journal of Politics and History* XVIII (1972): 367-385.

3. See W.T. Stead's "The Maiden Tribute of Modern Babylon," *Pall Mall Gazette*, 6, 7, 8, and 10 July 1885; and "The Truth About Our Secret Commission," Ibid., 9 July 1885. See also Baylen, 682-683 and notes, and J.W. Robertson Scott, *The Life and Death of a Newspaper* . . . . (London, 1952), pp. 125-145.

4. Frederick Greenwood, "Birth and Infancy of the *Pall Mall Gazette*," *Pall Mall Gazette*, 14 April 1892, p. 2.

5. Ibid.

6. Ibid.

7. W.T. Stead, "The Future of Journalism," *Contemporary Review* L(1886), pp. 672-673.

8. Quoted in Baylen, "New Journalism," p. 369.

9. See [James Greenwood] "A Night in A Workhouse," *Pall Mall Gazette*, 12-15 January 1866. For a discussion of this series and of James Greenwood's contribution to social reform, see B.I. Diamond and J.O. Baylen, "James Greenwood's London: A Precursor of Charles Booth" *Victorian Periodicals Review* XVII, nos. 1 and 2 (1984): 34-43.

10. W.T. Stead, "Character Sketch: February. The 'Pall Mall Gazette,'" *Review of Reviews* VII (1893), 144.

11. Greenwood, "Night In A Workhouse," *Pall Mall Gazette*, 12 January 1866, p. 10.

12. Greenwood, "Night in a Workhouse," Ibid., 15 January 1866, p. 10.

13. Stead, "Character Sketch," p. 144.

14. Frederick Greenwood, "Casual Wards," *Pall Mall Gazette*, 16 January 1866, p. 1.

15. Frederick Greenwood, "The Newspaper Press; Half a Century's Survey," *Blackwood's Magazine* CLXI (1897), 718.

16. Ibid., 708-709; Frederick Greenwood, "The Press and Government," *Nineteenth Century* XXVIII (1890), p. 108.

17. Frederick Greenwood to William Blackwood, 16 July 1885, Blackwood Archives, National Library of Scotland. Greenwood left the *Pall Mall Gazette* 11 May 1880, following a dispute with its new proprietor, the Liberal Henry Yates Thompson, over the political bent of the paper. By May 31, Greenwood had founded and taken on the editorship of the *St. James's Gazette*.

18. James Grant, *The Newspaper Press; Its Origins, Its Progress and Present Position* (London, 1871-1872), II, 118.

19. Ibid.

20. Stead, "Character Sketch," p. 144. The sale of the *Pall Mall Gazette* - increased so markedly following "A Night in a Workhouse" series that its printer, Richard Lambert, declared that "the machinery was incompetent to produce a sufficient number of copies, extra plates being taken and sent on to Saville and Edwards, in Chandos Street, to help us out of the fix." To obviate such a difficulty in the future, the paper purchased a "four-feeder rotary" press. Ibid., p. 145.

21. Ibid., p. 144.

22. "Summary of the Morning's News," *Pall Mall Gazette,* 18 January 1866, p. 2.

23. "Opinions in the Weekly Reviews; Workhouse Management," *Pall Mall Gazette,* 20 January 1866, p. 3.

25. T.H.S. Escott, *Masters of English Journalism: A Study of Personal Forces* (London, 1911), p. 245.

26. W.T. Stead, "Government by Journalism," *Contemporary Review* XLIX (1866), 655.

27. There are varying reports of the increase in circulation of the *Pall Mall Gazette.* See Grant, *Newspaper Press,* II, 114, 118; Stead, "Character Sketch," pp. 144-145; W. Robertson Nicoll, *A Bookman's Letters* (London, 1913), pp. 276-277; Greenwood, "Birth and Infancy," p. 2.

28. Escott, *Masters of English Journalism,* p. 245.

29. "Summary of the Morning's News," *Pall Mall Gazette,* 23 January 1866, p. 7.

30. "Correspondence; The Ordeal of the Bath," *Pall Mall Gazette,* 18 January 1866, p. 3.

31. "Correspondence; The Ordeal of the Bath," *Pall Mall Gazette,* 23 January 1866, p. 3.

32. Stead, "Character Sketch," p. 145.

33. On Greenwood's strong attachment to children, see his letter to David Hannay, 26 December 1907, David Hannay Papers, D.M.S. Watson Library, University College, London, Add. MS. 203/13.

34. Besides Stead, other journalists who found in the New Journalism a way to express their social concerns were J.A. Spender and H.W. Massingham. According to Stephen Koss, to Spender and Massingham the New Journalism was "distinguished not by its wrappings, but by its social concerns." See Stephen Koss, *The Rise and Fall of the Political Press in Britain: Volume I. The Nineteenth Century* (London, 1981), p. 345.

35. W.T. Stead, "How to Become a Journalist," reprinted from *The Young Man* (January 1891) in Edwin H. Stout, ed., *A Journalist on Journalism. Being a Series of Articles by W.T. Stead on Journals and Journalism* (London, 1891), p. 22.

36. Greenwood, "The Baby Farming Interest," *Pall Mall Gazette* 13 January 1868, p. 5.

37. Greenwood, "Professional Child Murder," *Pall Mall Gazette*, 29 July 1865, p. 4.

38. Ibid.

39. Greenwood, "Birth and Infancy," p. 2.

40. Greenwood, "Newspaper Press," p. 719.

41. For example, see Greenwood, "Infanticide," *Pall Mall Gazette*, 8 October 1866, pp. 1-2, and "Occasional Notes," Ibid., 30 June 1866, p. 11. In his leader on "Infanticide," Greenwood disagreed with the Social Science Congress (which met in London in 1866) on its causes and remedies. One of the suggestions offered at the Congress was that "every woman who has a bastard child shall be able to get as her husband any man who she may choose to describe as its father, or to prosecute for bigamy any married man, or . . . any man married subsequently to the child's conception." His comments in June were in agreement with the Harveian Society that, in a meeting in the summer of 1866, noted that "the main [cause of infant mortality] is . . . that the mother is mostly forced to put her child 'out to nurse.' "

42. Greenwood, "Baby Farming," *Pall Mall Gazette*, 25 September 1867, p. 1.

43. "Occasional Notes," Ibid., 2 October 1867, p. 8.

44. Kellow Chesney, *The Victorian Underworld* (New York, 1972), p. 349.

45. Greenwood, "Newspaper Press," p. 719.

46. "The Baby Farming Interest," *Pall Mall Gazette*, 31 January 1868, p. 5.

47. Ibid.

48. Ibid.

49. James Greenwood, *The Seven Curses of London: Neglected Children, Thieves, Professional Beggars, Fallen Women, Drunkenness, Gamblers, Waste of Charity* (London, 1869). See especially Chapter III, "Baby-Farming." It is most likely that many of the revelations in this book were primarily compilations of Frederick Greenwood's investigations. According to J.W. Robertson Scott, James Greenwood's book was "poorish stuff, probably written when he was hard up, not an uncommon condition." See Scott, *The Story of the Pall Mall Gazette, of Its First Editor, Frederick Greenwood and of Its Founder, George Murray*

Smith (London, 1950), p. 170. Yet James Greenwood's work has recently been reconsidered by historians as quite valuable. See Jeffrey Richard's introduction to a 1982 edition of Greenwood's *Seven Curses of London.*

50. James Greenwood, *The Seven Curses of London: Introduction by Jeffrey Richards* (London, 1982), p. 26.

51. "Occasional Notes," *Pall Mall Gazette,* 2 March 1868, p. 4.

52. "Occasional Notes," *Pall Mall Gazette,* 3 April 1869, p. 3.

53. Greenwood, *Seven Curses* (1982 ed.), p. 37.

54. For an account of the Margaret Waters case, see "The Baby Farming at Brixton; Verdict," *The Times,* 2 July, 1870, p. 11.

55. Ibid.

56. Greenwood, "Child-Murder and Baby-Farming," *Pall Mall Gazette,* 13 October 1870, p. 1.

57. For an examination of Parliamentary and private social efforts to prevent child abuse, see George K. Behlmer, *Child Abuse and Moral Reform in England, 1870-1908* (Standford, California, 1982).

58. Greenwood and George Murray Smith revived, on the basis of the success of the *Pall Mall Gazette* between 1866 and 1870, the morning edition of the journal that the publisher had first begun and then terminated in the early days of 1865. After four months' struggle and the expenditure of £25,000, the morning *Pall Mall Gazette* died a second time. Stead recalled in *The Review of Reviews* that this paper — also edited by Greenwood, with the production attended to by Smith — expired in 1870, only three months short of the outbreak of war between France and Germany, an event "which made the fortune of the *Daily News,* and which might also have made that of the morning *Pall Mall.*" See Stead, "Character Sketch," p. 145.

59. Sir Henry Lucy, *The Diary of A Journalist; Fresh Extracts* (London, 1923), III, 47.

60. C.K. Shorter, *Honouring Frederick Greenwood: Being Speeches Delivered in Praise of Him at a Dinner Held April 8, 1905. With an introduction by C. K. Shorter* (London, 1905), p. 4-5.

61. *Northern Echo,* 4 May 1880, p. 3.

62. Greenwood, "Newspaper Press," pp. 708, 718.

3
Joel H. Wiener
How New Was
the New Journalism?

"We have had opportunities of observing a new journalism which
a clever and energetic man has lately invented . . . its one great
fault is that it is *feather-brained*. It throws out assertions at a venture because it wishes them true; does not correct either them or
itself, if they are false; and to get at the state of things as they truly are seems to feel no concern whatever."[1] Matthew Arnold's
well-known jeremiad on the popular press and on W.T. Stead in
particular, published in May 1887, first articulated the presence
of a New Journalism and gave it a name. It set the tone for the
primarily negative reactions of contemporaries to the changes in
popular journalism at the end of the nineteenth century.[2] Following Arnold's lead, critics of the New Journalism abounded.
Henry D. Traill, a well-known journalist and literary critic who
worked for the *Daily Telegraph* and other newspapers, maintained that the press was becoming inundated with "quaint
Americanisms and (the) knowing slang of the racecourse,"

whereas Edward Dicey, another prominent journalist, concluded that "the newspaper-reading public of today wants to be amused, not instructed. . . . They like to have their mental food given them in minces and snippets, not in chops or joints."[3] In George Gissing's influential novel *New Grub Street,* published in 1891, images of mechanization and decline cohere. Jasper Millvain, one of several Grub Street types who people the novel, offers perhaps the most depressing insight into the changes of the period: "The truth is, I have been collecting ideas, and ideas that are convertible into coin of the realm, my boy; I have the special faculty of an extempore writer. Never in my life shall I do anything of solid literary value; I shall always despise the people I write for. But my path will be that of success. I have always said it, and now I'm sure of it."[4]

If contemporaries of Arnold were critical of the New Journalism, the same has been true of many historians of the press. A few have been judicious in their approach, like Joseph O. Baylen, who makes an important distinction between the salutary contributions of Stead and other early exemplars of the New Journalism, and the sensationalist "Daily Journalism" of proprietors such as Alfred Harmsworth, the future Lord Northcliffe. According to Baylen, Stead's journalism represented a "projection of the Nonconformist conscience." It had "a 'moral thrust,' social conviction, directness of language and political ambition, . . . " whereas Harmsworth and others like him pursued only commercial gain.[5] Although he is more favorable to the New Journalism as a whole, Harold Herd argues along similar lines in his studies of the press. He concedes by implication the existence of two types of New Journalism while conceding that, fortunately, popular newspapers have made the right choice as between the two. They have rejected the "old guard of journalism" with its "rigid conscientiousness" and have substituted for it "the best features of the new journalism without any loss of dignity, and with an immense gain in readableness and breadth of interest."[6] Raymond Williams in *The Long Revolution,* an influential study of popular culture, integrates economic and cultural change into a long-range view of the press. He argues that the strength of popular journalism derived from its economic base; at the same time, he suggests that class biases have created a negative perception of its content.[7]

Still most historians of the British press, including Alan J. Lee and Piers Brendon, whose surveys are the best on the subject, have been critical of the New Journalism. Lee focuses on the economic aspects of popular journalism after 1855. He concedes that many of the typographical and stylistic changes were creative. Yet, he concludes pessimistically: "In the simplest of terms, the press had become (by 1914) . . . a business almost entirely, and a political, civil and social institution hardly at all."[8] Brendon provides an interesting comparative treatment of popular journalism in Britain and the United States. He attacks press barons such as Northcliffe ("Northoleon") and William Randolph Hearst ("God Almighty's ghostwriter"), who introduced "yellow journalism" into the United States in the belief that the editor of a newspaper should have "no objection to facts if they are also novel. But he (should) prefer a novelty that is not a fact to a fact that is not a novelty."[9] In Brendon's opinion, the press barons diminished substantive content at the expense of "mass production . . . standardised, assembled and sold cheaply."[10]

This essay is not concerned with assessing the merits or weaknesses of the New Journalism but with a parallel question whose resolution may shed light on the validity of Arnold's fiercely negative response. Simply expressed, the question is: How new was the New Journalism? Did it represent a dramatic break with a staid journalistic past, which could no more keep pace with an emerging democracy of print than the Victorian three-decker novel could satisfy the demand for cheap fiction?[11]

Or, as Alfred Harmsworth himself suggested, was it but a varia-tion on the history of popular culture, a case of early Victorian "penny dreadfuls" being transformed into late Victorian "penny Steadfuls?"[12] The questions are linked because, in Arnold's case at least, there is a bias against both newness ("revolutionary temper") and popular journalism. If, as it will be argued in this essay, the former part of Arnold's critique is in need of substan-tial revision and that changes in late nineteenth-century jour-nalism were not as new or original as has been assumed, it is perhaps true that the qualitative aspect of his argument is equally open to challenge.

To deal with the question of newness, it is necessary first to show how the New Journalism was conceived by contemporaries and why it excited Arnold and others to indignation. Notwithstan-ding a fluid chronology and shifting nomenclature (phrases such as "Northcliffe Revolution" and "commercial journalism" are sometimes substituted for New Journalism),[13] it is evident that the years 1880 to 1914 witnessed significant changes in British journalism. These fall principally into three categories: typography and makeup, content, and the commercialization of the press. Before attempting a general estimate of the New Jour-nalism, each of these areas will be considered separately in order to place them in their historical context.

The visual appearance of newspapers is a map to their understanding, as was noted by that avid newspaper reader Sherlock Holmes in 1901 while busily engaged in solving the mystery of the Baskerville hound: "There is as much difference to my eyes between the leaded bourgeois type of a *Times* article and the slovenly print of an evening halfpenny paper as there could be between your negro and your Esquimaux."[14] Had Holmes made a similar observation four decades previously, he would have noted an even greater difference between the "negro" and the "Es-quimaux." For mid-Victorian newspapers, by comparison with their post-1800 sucessors, were of a markedly conservative appearance. Articles of opinion generally took precedence over most types of news, and advertisements were frequently given primacy over both in the makeup of the paper. In newspapers such as *The Times* and the *Morning Post*, political and Parliamentary news reports were spread out across six unbroken columns per page, whereas leaders occupied between three and five columns of text. Banner headlines and scare heads of the kind used in today's popular press were never seen. Illustrations were scarce, and there were few traces of the "bright" paraphernalia of modern journalism, designed to attract the eye. In the words of Stanley Morison, the foremost historian of the typography of journalism, "the upper- and middle-class typographical orthodoxy" of the early nineteenth century remained dominant until the final decades of the century.[15]

During the 1880s significant changes in makeup began to occur, which attracted adverse comments from Arnold and many other critics. These changes were particularly evident in the *Pall Mall Gazette*, an influential penny evening newspaper that W.T. Stead edited from 1883 to 1889, and in the halfpenny evening *Star*, edited by T.P. O'Connor from 1888 to 1890. Stead and O'Connor introduced important typographical innovations into their papers, which were influenced by popular American newspapers such as Joseph Pulitzer's New York *World*. They used headlines and crossheads, much in the way that titlepages and chapter headings were employed to increase the appeal of popular fiction. In 1892 the *Morning*, a halfpenny London paper that sported a "cheap look as well as a cheap price,"[16] became the first daily newspaper to place news regularly on its front page in place of advertisements. This adventurous practice had been employed since midcentury only by "nonrespectable" Sunday papers and by weeklies such as the *Illustrated London News*. It was soon adopted by Arthur Pearson's *Daily Express* (which absorbed the

Morning in 1900) and by other newspapers, though, surprisingly, not until 1939 by Harmsworth's halfpenny *Daily Mail*, a pioneer of the New Journalism since its founding in 1896.[17]

A miscellany of visual "looks" began to characterize the press in the 1880s and 1890s as newspapers experimented with different formulas. For example, the *Star* was the first daily newspaper to introduce a "Stop Press" and to use lower case type for its crossheads and lesser headlines.[18] Advertising began to acquire a more attractive look. Display advertising, imported from the United States, was introduced to supplement traditional single-column advertising. Most striking was the increased use of illustrations. Both Stead and O'Connor made frequent use of pictures based on line drawings (the *Star* playing a pioneering, role in cartoons), while in the 1890s the *Daily Graphic*, and in particular the weekly *Sketch*, became the first newspapers to employ half-tone blocks to reproduce the tones of a photograph.[19] As a result of further mechanical advancements it became possible within a few years to use news photographs effectively in daily journalism. The success of Harmsworth's *Daily Illustrated Mirror* in 1904 (which shortly afterward reverted to its original title of *Daily Mirror*), "the first halfpenny daily illustrated publication in the history of journalism," made clear the crucial link between journalism and pictures.[20] By the early twentieth century the textual and visual aspects of the popular press began therefore to complement each other. The way was clear for the increasing dominance of the visual in much of modern popular journalism.[21]

Beginning in the 1880s changes in content paralleled those in makeup. These included a "brighter" method of writing. In the words of Frederick Greenwood, the first editor of the *Pall Mall Gazette* (1865-1880), a "formal," artificial, and hackneyed style of journalism gave way to a "good English of common life" (which by the turn of the century he felt was already becoming too familiar).[22] T. P. O'Connor, whose clear writing style in the

Star exemplified this shift, discussed the change in an essay in which he compared modern newspapers to street pianos. The music of the former, O'Connor maintained, is "not classical, nor very melodious, and perhaps there is a certain absence of soul, but the notes should come out clear, crisp, sharp."[23] "Journalese," a "lifeless, mechanical" style of writing, was, according to Kennedy Jones, who managed the *Evening News* and the *Daily Mail,* replaced by "Telegraphese," a method of writing pioneered in the 1860s by George Augustus Sala and other writers on the *Daily Telegraph.* These journalists emphasized speed and human interest.[24] Even T. Wemyss Reid of the *Leeds Mercury,* a self-described Old Journalist and a bristling critic of the new, acknowledged the latter's "brightness, its alertness, its close grip of actualities...."[25]

In addition to changes in style, many newspapers gave considerably less space to leaders, which were sometimes shortened to a column or a half column ("leaderettes").[26] News coverage was increasingly separated from the expression of political opinion. It became the staple of many newspapers, and large numbers of "descriptive writers" and special correspondents were hired to report—rapidly and efficiently—on domestic and foreign events. A "keen news sense" became a prized requirement in journalism. Harmsworth was very much in harmony with the mood of the New Journalism when he characterized the popular press as a "news recording machine" and asserted that his objective as the proprietor of newspapers was to provide a "quick, accurate presentation of the world's news in the form of a careful digest."[27]

Yet the existence of such mechanical aids as the electric telegraph and the telephone in collecting news ensured that reporting became "bittier" and more standardized. Although throughout the pre-1914 years, dispatches by post continued to supplement those by other means, by the 1890s many newspapers began to publish wire service summaries of the news. Dispatches transmitted to newspapers by agencies such as Reuters and the Press Association followed the more commercial style of the Associated Press in New York and were stripped of their descriptive prose style and the story was concentrated in a "lead." Less justifiably from the perspective of readers, subeditors often boiled dispatches down to precis length to fit the demands of space. The assumption about news seemed to be like that made by Corker, the hard-bitten correspondent in Evelyn Waught's *Scoop*: that it was "what a chap who doesn't care much about anything wants to read."[28]

The content of newspapers was also affected by the New Journalism. There was a shift away from Parliamentary and political news to sport, gossip, crime, and sex. Seemingly this was what the growing numbers of readers of newspapers wanted when they sought rapid "enlightenment" or scanned the papers quickly on the buses and trams that carried them to and from their suburban homes to their places of work. As Frank Harris, who edited the *Evening News* in the early 1880s, before it came under the control of Harmsworth and Kennedy Jones, noted: "Kissing and fighting ... were the only things I cared for at thirteen or fourteen, and those are the themes the English public desires and enjoys today."[29] "Captain Coe" (Edward E. Mitchell), the well-known sports correspondent of the halfpenny *Echo* and the *Star*, advised young John A. Spender to forego leader writing and to concentrate on sports if he wished to be successful in journalism. According to Mitchell, sports reporting represented the wave of the future, a prophecy that seemed to be borne out by the immense success of the *Evening News* in the 1890s when it made effective use of betting results flashed by telegraph and became the first London paper to introduce a Saturday sports edition that later included a football competition. Crime also played a significant part in the transformation of the press. The *Star* first guaranteed its success in the popular evening market in the autumn of 1888 with its sensational coverage of the "Jack the Ripper" murders, which involved it in some questionable journalistic practices.[30]

Other daily newspapers, including even *The Times,* became equally obsessed with the Ripper murders. One veteran crime reporter observed subsequently that "even the palmy days of the late Boer War never saw so many editions on the street as that ghastly time when the terrible Whitechapel maniac was at his grisly work."[31]

By the final decades of the century, newspapers increasingly catered to readers' special tastes. These included gossip columns, women's pages, children's features, and in the first decade of the twentieth century, comic strips. The women's market was a particularly striking feature of the New Journalism. Both of Harmsworth's leading newspapers, the *Evening News* and the *Daily Mail,* featured women's columns, and in 1893, he founded *Woman at Home,* a weekly paper whose successful run of 27 years was based primarily on a famous personal column by Annie Swan titled "Over the Teacups."[32] Readers of newspapers were also regaled with excerpts and summaries from larger works, a journalistic device that reached fruition in the popular *Tit-Bits,* founded by George Newnes in 1881. Newspapers also included notes to correspondents (the best example of this being Harmsworth's *Answers to Correspondents,* founded in 1888, whose entire raison d'être was built around this idea) and heapings of serialized popular fiction. When the monthly *Strand Magazine* was commenced by Newnes in 1891, its stated aim was to make illustrated short fiction available to a mass audience. It was so successful in doing this that it spawned a number of imitators.[33]

Interviews and investigative stories modeled on American examples were also pioneered by Stead, O'Connor, and other New Journalists. The *Pall Mall Gazette* made the biggest impact in these areas with its famous interview with General Gordon in January 1884, prior to his being sent to the Sudan, and with its articles exposing juvenile prostitution titled the "Maiden Tribute of Modern Babylon." It also printed special reports commissioned by Stead on London "fighting gangs," East End housing conditions, and related topics, some of which the paper's previous editor, John Morley, had tried to play down.[34] Similarly, the *Star* sponsored investigations into conditions in sweatshops and the failure to enforce factory legislation,[35] although it did so with less consistent political conviction than the *Pall Mall Gazette*.

The third general way in which the press became transformed after 1880 was by its commercialization. The relationship between business and journalism was redefined during the years from 1880 to 1914 when the number of purchasers of daily newspapers approximately quadrupled.[36] The *Pall Mall Gazette* continued as a relatively small-scale venture in evening journalism, but within a short period of time the *Star* gained a daily circulation of more than 200,000. Among weekly journals both *Tit-Bits* and *Answers to Correspondents* (whose name was shortened to *Answers* in 1889) achieved sales in the hundreds of thousands. More spectacular yet was the expansion of the morning press. The *Daily Mail,* founded in 1896 as the "busy man's daily journal," amassed a circulation of almost one million by 1900, partly stimulated by a rabid jingoism that was a common feature of the New Journalism. In 1911 the *Daily Mirror* (with more and better pictures and less text) went its competitor one better: It became the first newspaper to break through the mythical barrier of one million daily readers.[37] To supply this greatly expanded market, improved technology was brought into use: American Hoe rotary presses that produced 200,000 copies per hour, linotype machines also pioneered in New York, even a machine, developed by the *Daily Mail,* that folded newspapers. The objective of the latter was, presumably, to give servants time to read the newspaper in lieu of their quondam task of folding it!

As a function of increased circulation, "press barons" such as Newnes, Pearson, and, above all, Harmsworth, began to exercise influence and power over important aspects of journalism.

A shift occurred, away from small-scale family businesses and papers run by editor-proprietors to journals owned by large companies. In the late 1890s the *Daily Mail* became the first newspaper to offer its shares for public sale. Substantial profits through sales of copies and particularly advertising became the chief objective of the new proprietors. And to ensure that their goals were met, they introduced prize competitions and insurance schemes. For a time, the luckiest reader of *Pearson's Weekly* was the person who had the longest name, and the most fortunate purchaser of *Tit-Bits* was the man who died with a copy of that paper tucked under his arm because his family would then receive insurance payments.[38] Moberly Bell, the innovative manager of *The Times,* lamented that "the ideal of modern journalism" had become synonymous with the "ideal of modern business."[39] His counterpart on the *Evening News,* Kennedy Jones, more crudely acknowledged the pickings of the system. He and Harmsworth, asserted Jones drily, had "found journalism a profession and left it a branch of commerce."[40] Perhaps the final word on the subject may be left to another influential journalist, T.H.S. Escott, who was fiercely critical of the effects of commerce on the press. Writing in 1917, Escott contended that "journalism has sunk, or at least is in danger of sinking, from a liberal profession to a branch of business."[41]

Paradoxically, working journalists (and even critics such as Arnold) were less concerned with the commercialization of newspapers than with changes in their appearance and content. In part this resulted from the stimulus given by these changes to the ambitions of journalists. Many jobs were created for journalists, who began to earn better incomes and to gain increased professional opportunities, as witnessed particularly by the high salaries paid by Harmsworth to his employees.[42] The gulf between leader writers, who were mostly university educated, and ordinary foot soldiers of the trade, which had seemed unbridgeable several decades earlier, began to break down. Thousands entered the profession of journalism, their existence and ambitions given expression by the formation of organizations such as the Institute of Journalists in 1889.[43]

Yet the debit side of commercialization loomed large, Although differences among journalists diminished, a significant divide opened up between the owners of newspapers and those who worked for them.[44] Writing editors such as John A. Spender and H.W. Massingham became scarcer, and editors, including Ernest Parke of the *Star* and the *Morning Leader,* Edward Levy-Lawson of the *Daily Telegraph* ("the doyen of English journalism"), and Thomas Marlowe, an able pressman who edited the *Daily Mail* successfully for 27 years, who possessed outstanding managerial skills flourished. By 1900 Fleet Street was becoming an abode of specialization and of proprietorial interference. No longer did a single editor control all operations of a newspaper. Instead, there were many subeditors and managers of departments. Frequently this system produced a more efficient product, especially in the new evening newspapers that produced several editions throughout the day. Yet at its worst, it converted both journalists and newspapers into "complete machines," lacking creativity and initiative.[45]

In this brief survey it has been established that popular journalism underwent a considerable measure of change in the years after 1880. Still the basic question remains: How new was this New Journalism? Perhaps surprisingly, the answer is that it was not as new as many writers assumed. For purposes of argument, three general points may be conceded at the outset: First, a large-scale capitalization of the press did not take place prior to the 1880s. Second, some of the most crucial changes in the makeup and content of newspapers took root initially in the final decades of the century. Finally, the contributions of Stead, O'Connor, Newnes, Ernest Parke, Pearson, Harmsworth, and other leading

New Journalists were critical to the formation of the modern popular press and should in no way be belittled. These men experimented with new techniques and drew upon American examples at a time when a considerable expansion of the press was taking place. They were innovators of a new type of journalism and deserve to be remembered as such.

Yet to concede these points is not to diminish the case for a broader view that takes account of half a century of change in the popular press. The danger of focusing too narrowly on the decades after 1880 is that one is left with a schismatic view of history. In an area such as journalism, where incremental transformations occur over long periods of time often within a complicated geographical framework, such a view of historical change may yield insufficient insights. It is preferable to extend the range of discussion and to cast as wide a net as possible. When this is done, new perspectives are uncovered: significant developments in the radical and popular press dating from the 1830s; the importance of mid-Victorian Sunday papers; the contributions of bohemian journalists; the influence of subliterary elements of popular culture and cheap fiction on the press; the work of innovative journalists such as Frederick Greenwood and Edmund Yates; and, in the three decades prior to 1880, a general expansion of the press resulting from the repeal of the taxes on knowledge and the unfolding of educational opportunities. Perhaps increasingly, it is to the years 1850-1880 that one must turn to gain a more balanced view of the phenomenon of the New Journalism than was expressed by Arnold.

Except for certain well-researched segments of the story—the history of the unstamped and Chartist press, the spread of cheap popular fiction, the great success of Sunday papers beginning in the 1840s[46]—relatively little work has been done on popular journalism in the mid-Victorian decades. For instance, G.W.M. Reynolds, who edited several popular weekly newspapers, remains a tantalizing figure as he swims vigorously amid the shoals of political radicalism and sensational fiction.[47] As yet there is no published history of the *Illustrated London News*, one of the key newspapers of the century.[48] Comic journalism has been studied only in segments. The coverage of crime and sex in Victorian newspapers, a significant facet of popular culture, has not been analyzed adequately. Subeditors such as Horace Voules and Thomas Catling remain shadowy figures notwithstanding their important influence on the press.[49]

What is known about the mid-Victorian popular newspapers, however, tends to support the view that they laid the foundation for the New Journalism. As early as the 1830s, the unstamped political press, along with police gazettes and fictional "penny dreadfuls," began to experiment with changes in makeup. Small "headlines" were sometimes introduced as illustrations of poor quality. Radical papers such as the *Poor Man's Guardian* (1831-1835), and others of a less serious political cast gave coverage to popular news, including crime. The aim of these unstamped newspapers was to lessen the gap between a radical political culture and subliterary journalistic forms such as the chapbook and the almanac. In the 1840s these papers were replaced primarily by Sunday newspapers such as *Lloyd's Weekly Newspaper* (1842), the *News of the World* (1843), and *Reynolds's Newspaper* (1850), which gained a substantial readership among the lower middle class and the working class. These newspapers pioneered pictorial journalism, gave increased coverage to crime (which diminished their reputation among "respectable" readers), and mixed cheap fiction with a diluted radicalism. They also made minor breakthroughs in layout, particularly in the coverage of crime stories, which often featured crossheadings like "Execution" or "Confession." It is clear that crucial elements of the New Journalism were prefigured by mid-Victorian changes in popular journalism.[50]

During subsequent decades a further transformation of the press occurred in the provinces as well as in London. The price of newspapers fell rapidly as a result of the repeal of the newspaper tax in 1855, and in September of that year the *Daily Telegraph* became the first London morning paper to sell for a penny. In its initial number the paper proclaimed a "new era of journalism which we this day inaugerate"; its "Young Lions" (Sala, Edwin Arnold, William Beatty-Kingston) helped to define this "era of journalism" by means of a lighter writing style, increased attention to crime and human interest stories, "magazine features" in its Saturday edition, and occasional "sensational" news items, some of them fictionalized, such as a famous account of a "man and dog fight" in Staffordshire.[51] Other pioneering newspapers followed: Samuel Lucas's penny *Morning Star*, founded in 1856, which published Edmund Yates's influential gossip column, "The Flâneur"; the *Echo* (1868), the first halfpenny London evening paper; and the *Referee* (1877), a radical penny Sunday paper specializing in theatrical and sporting coverage and "society journalism," whose leading contributor, George R. Sims ("Dagonet"), was a particular favorite among the new reading classes of the metropolis.

Between 1850 and 1880, many special features of the later New Journalism began to take root: women's articles in papers such as the *Queen;* gossip columns by Yates in the *Illustrated Times* and the *World* and by Henry Labouchere in *Truth;* sports coverage in papers such as *Sporting Life* and the daily *Sporting Times* (from 1876) and in influential provincial newspapers such as Joseph Cowen's *Newcastle Daily Chronicle.*[52] Parliamentary and political sketches by journalists such as Henry W. Lucy ("Under the Clock" in the *World*) and Frank H. Hill ("Political Portraits" in the *Daily News*) began to complement or even replace extensive accounts of Parliamentary speeches.[53] Greater use was made of illustrations, and papers such as the weekly

Graphic were founded (1869) exclusively for that purpose. Although most newspapers continued to be run as personal or family enterprises, the commercial side of journalism became more obvious. The repeal of the newspaper tax stimulated a great upsurge in London and provincial journalism. Before 1855 only *The Times* among daily newspapers had a circulation higher than 60,000. By 1870 both the *Daily News* and the *Daily Telegraph* exceeded sales of 150,000, while in Manchester (where no daily newspaper had existed before 1855) the overall daily circulation surpassed 100,000 copies.[54] Profits were increasing, and it is quite clear that many newspapers were becoming a business rather than a political investment. It has been estimated that by 1882 the penny *Standard* and the *Daily Telegraph* were making annual profits of £60,000 and £120,000 respectively.[55]

In attempting to emphasize the evolutionary development of the popular press, it may be useful to complement a macrocosmic approach by focusing on a narrower aspect of the history of journalism. The example chosen is the *Illustrated Times*, a widely-circulated twopenny newspaper founded by David Bogue in 1855 and edited initially by Henry Vizetelly, who later became a famous publisher. The history of the *Illustrated Times* (which survived for seventeen years) provides valuable insights into the connection between the mid-Victorian popular press and the later New Journalism, for in addition to its innovative use of illustrations to report on events ranging from the Crimean War to the latest poisoning murder in London, three important journalists worked together on the paper during its formative years. They were Frederick Greenwood, George Augustus Sala, and Edmund Yates, and all helped to give form and shape to the New Journalism.[56]

Greenwood has been described as the "creator of New Journalism."[57] As the first editor of the *Pall Mall Gazette*, he introduced several innovations into the paper: its celebrated

"Occasional Notes," leaders containing natural paragraph breaks in place of lengthy artificial essays, and sensational articles by his brother James ("An Amateur Casual") that described his experiences in a Lambeth workhouse. Greenwood continued to play an active role in journalism until the end of the century, notably as the editor of the *St. James's Gazette*. But his most significant work was done in the 1860s and 1870s, when Stead and O'Connor were mere striplings in the trade of journalism. Sala was for many years the best known of the *Daily Telegraph's* "Young Lions." He wrote light leaders and reported exuberantly on overseas and domestic events for the paper. His fluid "pen-pictures" influenced a generation of popular writers, and, perhaps more than any other journalist, he helped to create a style of "bright," human interest writing that was to become so integral a part of the New Journalism.[58] He has been characterized by a well-informed contemporary as "the best all-round journalist of his time."[59] Yates pioneered "keyhold journalism": gossip columns and celebrity interviews in many papers, particularly the *World,* which he founded in 1874. He was a prolific writer, lightweight but experimental, who has been described accurately as "a new journalist before the new journalism was ever heard of."[60]

It is unlikely that the sparks that these three journalists set off in so many directions were unconnected. Perhaps the influence of their mentor, Vizetelly (an undeservedly neglected personality in the history of Victorian journalism), was the catalyst. Possibly it was the presence on the *Illustrated Times* of other young writers such as Robert Brough, James Hannay, and Sutherland Edwards, all of whom had brief if sparkling journalistic careers. Yet there is another explanation, marginal perhaps but suggestive precisely because it lies in that tangled undergrowth of human experience that the historian of the press must uncover if he is to understand transformations in popular journalism. All three men—though particularly Sala and Yates—were strongly influenced by the bohemian atmosphere of London in the 1850s and early 1860s. They helped to define the concept of a journalistic bohemia, which one participant nostalgically recounted as a land of "Goodfellowship, loyalty to one another, a fine sense of chivalry, a constant readiness to help the lame dog over the style, a stern ostracism of the unhappy wight who evinced a congenital inability to play the game."[61] The West End theaters and Covent Garden taverns became places where novels and light verse and satirical paragraphs for comic magazines were hatched. Fame and friendship were equally prized commodities in this venue.

Was there a connection between the bohemianism of Sala, Yates, and young Greenwood, with its sanctification of pleasure and affected unconcern with poverty, and the later New Journalism, which was defined in part by a growing commercial ethic and professionalism?[62] Almost certainly. What Greenwood, Yates, Sala, Brough, Sutherland Edwards, Edward Draper, and other writers on the *Illustrated Times* possessed in common was a quality that contemporaries referred to as "vagabondage of character." They were willing to try anything once, provided it was new, especially in their capacity as struggling newspapermen. And in this experimental, bohemian mood, they made significant breakthroughs that anticipated new journalistic forms and in turn inspired journalists such as Henry Lucy and Henry Labouchere to become central participants in the New Journalism.

They also tried their hand at writing novels and theatrical reviews, qualities that connect parenthetically to the New Journalism. For one of the basic objectives of Stead, O'Connor, and other pressmen of the 1880s and 1890s was to tell a good story clearly and well.[63] O'Connor made it a point for the *Star* to narrate the events of the day in a "story line" fashion to its readers. His aim, as expressed in a ringing defense of popular journalism, was to strike the reader "right between the eyes" by creating a situation in which "everything that can be talked about can also be written about."[64] Stead likewise emphasized the importance of the narrative element in journalism. The press, he wrote, is "at once the eye and the tongue of the people. It is the visible speech if not the voice of the democracy. It is the phonograph of the world."[65] Most revealing in this context is the comment by Kennedy Jones who admitted, somewhat defensively, that "the methods of the detective story or the blood-and-thunder stage" were frequently employed in putting together the *Evening News* and the *Daily Mail.*[66]

What conclusions can be drawn from this discussion of the origins and evolution of popular journalism? It is clear that the New Journalism had a more secure pedigree than Arnold and many of his contemporaries and subsequent writers were prepared to concede. Its roots are to be found in the deep though as yet primarily unexplored soil of Victorian journalism. If Arnold's emphasis on newness requires modification, it may be that the obverse side of the coin—his argument concerning quality—is also in need of amendment. Perhaps the most tenable conclusion is that additional work needs to be done before definitive judgments about Victorian journalism can be made. We are as yet at an early stage in our research.

NOTES

1. Matthew Arnold, "Up to Easter, p. 638, *Nineteenth Century* XXI (1887).
2. Arnold was equally devastating about American journalism: "If one were searching for the best means to efface and kill in a whole nation the discipline of respect, the feeling for what is educated, one could not do better than take the American newspapers." ("Civilisation in the United States" in *The Complete Prose Works of Matthew Arnold* (Ann Arbor, Michigan, 1977), vol. II, p. 361.)
3. H.D. Traill, "The Evening Newspaper, 1872-1897," *Pall Mall Gazette*, 14 April 1897; Edward Dicey, "Journalism, New and Old," *Fortnightly Review*, LXXXIII (1905) p. 917. Evelyn March Phillips complained that readers of the New Journalism were being "carefully trained to a distaste for intellectual

exertion, a dread of being bored, a need for mental relaxation, and a coarse habitual tickling of the senses." ("The New Journalism," *New Review* XIII (1895), p. 187. In a series of articles written for the *Leisure Hour* in 1892, H.W. Massingham was critical of the "haste and love of . . . mere scandal and sensation" that characterized American journalism. He was hopeful that the English, by their longing for "culture, gravity, enthusiasm," might yet resist the New Journalism. (H.W. Massingham, *The London Daily Press* (London, 1892), pp. 183, 192.)

4. George Gissing, *New Grub Street* (London, 1893), p. 65. Perhaps the quirkiest comment on the New Journalism was made by G.K. Chesterton, who attacked it for reflecting a "tired view of life" and not being "sensational or violent enough." (Chesterton, "The Mildness of the Yellow Press" in *Heretics* [New York, 1905], p. 113.)

5. J.O. Baylen, "The 'New Journalism' in Late Victorian Britain," *Australian Journal of Politics and History* XVIII (1972), pp. 369, 375.

6. Harold Herd, *The March of Journalism: The Story of the British Press from 1622 to the Present Day* (London, 1952), pp. 222, 232, and *The Making of Modern Journalism* (London, 1927), pp. 91-92. Edward Raymond Thompson ("E.T. Raymond") makes much the same point when he describes the *Star*, a product of the earlier New Journalism, as "half a joke and half a crusade" while bewailing subsequent changes in the press as "the complete standardisation of things of the spirit." (*Portraits of the Nineties* (London, 1921), pp. 303, 304.)

7. Raymond Williams, *The Long Revolution* (London, 1961), p. 202.

8. Alan J. Lee, *The Origins of the Popular Press in England, 1855-1914* (London, 1976), p. 232.

9. From an unpublished letter by Hearst, cited in Brendon, *The Life and Death of the Press Barons* (London, 1982), p. 134.

10. Ibid., pp. 110, 114. Another critic is Francis Williams, who attacks the "new conception of journalism (in which) power was seen as deriving from mass suggestion, from the slogan repeated over and over again until it produced an instinctive reaction, from the translation of a highly complicated situation into an emotional challenge capable of being expressed in short phrases that could be beaten home day after day after day by every technique of propaganda." (*Dangerous Estate: The Anatomy of Newspapers* [London, 1959], p. 132.)

11. J.A. Spender draws this analogy, as cited in Herd, *March of Journalism*, p. 249. Spender claimed that Harmsworth "put the three-decker journalist out of action." Quoted in Henry Wickham Steed, *The Press* (Harmondsworth, Middlesex, 1938), p. 39.

12. The phrase "Penny Steadfuls" is taken from Nigel Cross, *The Common Writer: Life in Nineteenth-Century Grub Street* (Cambridge, 1985), p. 209. It appears to have been used first by *Punch* in 1897 in a comment on Stead's Masterpiece Library ("Penny Classics for the People"). A.A. Milne wittily turned this insight against Harmsworth when he observed: "It was Lord Northcliffe who killed the penny dreadful; by the simple process of producing a halfpenny dreadfuller." (Tom Clarke, *Northcliffe in History: An Intimate Study of Press Power* (London, 1950), p. 73.)

13. In his important study of the popular press, Ralph Blumenfeld, the editor of the *Daily Express,* uses the phrase "massocratic journalism." (*The Press in My Time* [London, 1933], p. 208.)

14. Arthur Conan Doyle, "The Hound of the Baskervilles" in *The Complete Sherlock Holmes Treasury* (New York, 1976), p. 209.

15. Stanley Morison, *The English Newspaper: Some Account of the Physical Develolpment of Journals Printed in London between 1622 and the Present Day* [London, 1932], p. 271.

16. Kennedy Jones, *Fleet Street and Downing Street* (London, 1919), p. 124.

17. When Northcliffe bought *The Times* in 1908, he refused to move advertisements off the front page. He told a critic: "Advertisements? They are the most important news. And where would you have it if not on the front page?" (Philip Howard, *We Thundered Out: 200 Years of 'The Times', 1785-1985* [London, 1985], p. 86.) *The Times* did not adopt this practice until May 1966.

18. John Goodbody, 'The Star: Its Role in the Rise of Popular Newspapers, 1888-1914," *Journal of Newspaper and Periodical History* I (1985), p. 22.

19. Clement Shorter, the editor of the *Sketch* and a major figure in the history of pictorial journalism, claimed to have discovered the importance of "the greatest possible attraction of the picture as against the best possible writing matter." J.M. Bulloch (ed.), *C.K.S.: A Fragment by Himself* (London, 1927), p. 84.

20. The *Daily Illustrated Mirror* stated in its first number: "The old tradition that pictures were only a makeweight, only a sop to the curiosity of the less serious kind of reader, has altogether passed away. Our pictures do not merely accompany the printed news. They are a valuable help to the understanding of it." (28 January 1904, as cited in Jones, *Fleet Street*, p. 235.) The key breakthrough in daily journalism was the invention of a method for printing photo blocks on a rotary machine.

21. It is interesting to note that the two new morning papers commenced in London in 1986—*Today* and the *Independent*—provide outstanding photographic coverage.

22. Quoted in J.W. Robertson Scott, *The Story of the 'Pall Mall Gazette'', of its First Editor Frederick Greenwood and of its Founder George Murray Smith* (London, 1950), p. 129.

23. T.P. O'Connor, "The New Journalism," *New Review* I (1889), p. 434. In the first number of the *Star*, O'Connor vowed: "In our reporting columns we shall do away with the hackneyed style of obsolete journalism." (17 January 1888, as quoted in Morison, *English Newspaper*, p. 289.)

24. Jones, *Fleet Street*, pp. 27, 84. The *Sun*, a halfpenny daily paper edited by O'Connor after the *Star*, boasted of its determination "to tell the story of each day in the briefest, the most picturesque, the most graphic fashion." (Quoted in Hamilton Fyfe, *Sixty Years of Fleet Street* (London, 1949), pp. 48-49.)

25. Stuart J. Reid (ed.), *Memoirs of Sir Wemyss Reid* (London, 1905), p. 313. Robert Blatchford described the much rougher style of the Manchester *Sunday Chronicle* in the 1880s as "splashy, jolly, colloquial." *My Eighty Years* (London, 1931), p. 184.

26. Frederick Greenwood of the *Pall Mall Gazette* was apparently the first editor to divide the leading article into three natural paragraphs. He did it in the late 1850s. (Henry W. Lucy, *Diary of a Journalist: Fresh Extracts* [London, 1923], p. 47.)

27. "The Daily Newspaper of Today," *Mitchell's Press Directory* (1905), p. 8. One by-product of this focus on news was the gradual separation of function between newspapers and journals of opinion.

28. Moberly Bell, the manager of *The Times* after 1890, told the paper's correspondents: "Remember that telegrams are for facts; appreciation and political comment can come by post." E.H.C. Moberly Bell, *The Life and Letters of C.F. Moberly Bell* (London, 1927), p. 160.

29. Frank Harris, *My Life and Loves* (New York, 1963), p. 630.

30. T.P. O'Connor, *Memoirs of an Old Parliamentarian* (London, 1929), vol. II, p. 257.

31. Chris Healy, *Confessions of a Journalist* (London, 1904), p. 342. H.W. Massingham recollected that at the time of the Ripper murders, the presses of the *Evening News, Star,* and *Echo* kept running virtually around the clock. (*London Daily Press,* p. 182.)

32. Annie Swan observed that readers of "Over the Teacups" wrote some "sex stuff" to her that was "an education to me in the sordid side of life." *My Life: An Autobiography* (London, 1934) p. 82. The *Daily Mirror,* founded by Harmsworth in 1903, was intended to be the first daily journal dedicated to women's interests. It failed, and Harmsworth allegedly concluded that "women don't want a daily paper of their own." Viscount Camrose, *British Newspapers and Their Controllers* (London, 1947), p. 58.

33. Reginald Pound, who later edited the *Strand Magazine,* observed: "Certainly the middle-classes of England never cast a clearer image of themselves in print than they did in the *Strand Magazine.* Confirming their preference for mental as well as physical comfort, for more than half a century it faithfully mirrored their tastes, prejudices, and intellectual limitations." Pound, *The "Strand Magazine", 1891-1950* (London, 1966), p. 7.

34. Aaron Watson's reports were usually printed under the by-line "Our Special Correspondent." While John Morley was editor of the paper, however, he occasionally sought to distance himself from these reports by using the phrase "A Correspondent Writes." Watson, *A Newspaper Man's Memories* (London, 1925), pp. 117-118.

35. Goodbody, *"The Star: Its Role,"* p. 21.

36. Williams, *Long Revolution,* p. 204.

37. Among the popular Sunday papers *Lloyd's Weekly Newspaper* first reached this figure in 1896. (Alan Lee, "The Structure, Ownership and Control of the Press, 1855-1914" in George Boyce, James Curran, and Pauline Wingate (eds.), *Newnspaper History: From the Seventeenth Century to the Present Day* [London, 1978], p. 123.)

38. *Pearson's Weekly,* founded in 1890, also devised a "missing word" competition and, most ingeniously, a competition in which the winning prize for a female reader was the choice of a husband. Sidney Dark, *The Life of Sir Arthur Pearson* (London, 1922), pp. 57-58.

39. Quoted in H. Simonis, *The Street of Ink: An Intimate History of Journalism* (London, 1917), p. 19.

40. Jones, *Fleet Street,* p. 202. This statement is also cited in Reginald Pound and Geoffrey Harmsworth, *Northcliffe* (London, 1959), p. 587.

41. "Old and New in the Daily Press," *Quarterly Review* CCXXVII (1917), p. 368.

42. Fyfe, *Sixty Years,* pp. 51-54.

43. Aaron Watson recollects that in the 1890s many jobs were available in journalism, and "anybody who could write at all might find an opening." (*Newspaper Man's Memories,* p. 203) To counter this trend, the newly-formed Institute of Journalists set itself the hopeless task of establishing an examination for journalists to keep out "the Toms, Dicks and Harrys who answer advertisements." (Cited in Cyril Bainbridge (ed.), *One Hundred Years of Journalism: Social Aspects of the Press* [London, 1984], p. 54.) Another journalist, Raymond Blathwayt, who specialized in interviews, admits that he came "into touch with the journalistic world just exactly at the right moment. . . . The moment I started in new papers began to flood the market." *Through Life and Round the World: Being the Story of My Life* (London, 1917), p. 157.

44. On this point, see Lee, "Structure, Ownership and Control," p. 127.

45. "The Lament of a Leader-Writer," *Westminster Review* CLII (1889), p. 662. A different view is offered by Tom Clarke, a famous journalist who edited the *Daily Chronicle:* ". . . despite all the Jeremiahs, I am not prepared yet to believe that, in the world as it is, commercialization of the Press has been the evil some people think. It can, I think, be argued that it has been good for the public and good for the Press, and has rid us of a lot of humbug." Quoted in Steed, *The Press,* p. 162.

46. On these subjects see, for example, Joel H. Wiener, *The War of the Unstamped: The Movement to Repeal the British Newspaper Tax, 1830-1836* (Ithaca, New York, 1969); Patricia Hollis, *The Pauper Press: A Study in Working-Class Radicalism of the 1830s* (London, 1970); Louis James, *Fiction of the Working Man, 1830-1850: A Study of the Literature Produced for the Working Classes in Early Victorian Urban England* (London, 1963); Margaret Dalziel, *Popular Fiction 100 Years Ago: An Unexplored Tract of Literary History* (London, 1957); Virginia Berridge, "Popular Sunday Papers and Mid-Victorian Society," in Boyce, *Newspaper History,* pp. 247-264.

47. The best account of Reynolds is Anne Humpherys, "G.W.M. Reynolds: Popular Literature and Popular Politics" in Joel H. Wiener (ed.), *Innovators and Preachers: The Role of the Editor in Victorian England* (Westport, Connecticut, 1985), pp. 3-21.

48. Three other popular newspapers have been studied in Virginia Berridge's important unpublished doctoral thesis, "Popular Journalism and Working Class Attitudes, 1854-1886: A Study of *Reynolds's Newspaper, Lloyd's Weekly Newspaper* and the *Weekly Times,*" University of London, 1976.

49. Voules worked on several important newspapers, including the *Echo, Truth,* and the *Pall Mall Gazette.* He has been described by T.H.S. Escott as "a memorable specimen of the new journalism in its most practical and propulsive aspects." (*Masters of English Journalism: A Study of Personal Forces* [London, 1911], p. 268.) Catling was the subeditor of *Lloyd's Weekly Newspaper* for more than fifty years.

50. Morison, *English Newspapers,* p. 279. Berridge concludes that the "mass-circulation Sundays" were "important as a half-way stage in the development of the modern popular press." ("Popular Sunday Papers," p. 247.)

51. *Daily Telegraph,* 29 June 1855, as cited in Henry R. Fox Bourne, *English Newspapers: Chapters in the History of Journalism* (London, 1887), vol. II, p. 236; Scott, *Story of the "Pall Mall Gazette,"* p. 152; Lord Burnham, *Peterborough Court: The Story of the "Daily Telegraph"* (London, 1955), especially chapters 3 and 6.

52. On sport, see Tony Mason, "Sporting News, 1860-1914" in Michael Harris and Alan Lee (eds.), *The Press in English Society from the Seventeenth to Nineteenth Centuries* (London, 1986), pp. 168-186. Interestingly, Edward Baines, who had no sports coverage in his *Leeds Mercury,* attempted unsuccessfully to get Cowen to terminate his coverage. (Watson, *Newspaper Man's Memories,* pp. 36-37)

53. Lucy, who also wrote political sketches for *Punch* and the *London Charivari,* has been described as "a fresh after-Dickens example of how a reportership in the House of Commons can stimulate native humour." Walter Sichel, *The Sands of Time: Recollections and Reflections* (London, 1923), p. 232.

54. Richard D. Altick, *The English Common Reader: A Social History of the Mass Reading Public, 1800-1900* (Chicago, 1963), pp. 356, 395; Williams, *Dangerous Estate,* p. 101; Williams, *Long Revolution,* pp. 192-199.

55. Donald Read, *England, 1868-1914* (London, 1979), pp. 91-92. On the profitability of the press before the New Journalism, see Lee, *Origins,* pp. 79-93, and "Structure, Ownership and Control," pp. 117-129.

56. T.H.S. Escott has observed perceptively that the *Illustrated Times* "sowed in the journalistic soil of the middle Victorian Age the seeds of ideas that were to become powerful growths a little later and whose fruit is still being gathered in the twentieth century's present years." (*Masters of English Journalism,* p. 225.)

57. Henry W. Lucy, "New Journalism" in *Lords and Commoners* (London, 1921), p. 190.

58. Sala's prose, though immensely witty, was discursive, and he has been criticized, even mocked, for an "elaborate, rounded, allusive style." (Massingham, *London Daily Press*, p. 93.)

59. William Mackay, *Bohemian Days in Fleet Street by a Journalist* (London, 1913), p. 54. Sala was prepared to write about anything, "from the price of beef to a coronation," as he told a colleague. J. Hall Richardson, *From the City to Fleet Street: Some Journalistic Experiences* (London, 1927), p. 112.

60. Frederick Moy Thomas (ed.), *Fifty Years of Fleet Street: Being the Life and Recollections of Sir John R. Robinson* (London, 1904), p. 205. One of the popular features of the *Daily Mail* was a column titled "In Society" that was modeled on Yates's column "What the World Knows" in the *World*.

61. Mackay, *Bohemian Days*, p. 67. Sala described two of his journalistic bohemian companions affectionately as "droll dogs, merry men, mad wags." *The Life and Adventures of George Augustus Sala Written by Himself* (London, 1895), vol. I, p. 326.

62. A recent book that is critical of bohemianism describes it as "the perfect alibi for indigence." Cross, *Common Writer*, p. 92. Edward Raymond Thompson observes that the New Journalism "set out to industrialise Bohemia and succeeded." (*Portraits of the Nineties*, p. 303.)

63. Sala, in his bohemian phase, described the Crimean War as a "disastrously bad novel." (*Life and Adventure*, vol. II, p. 402.)

64. O'Connor, "New Journalism," pp. 430, 434.

65. W.T. Stead, "Government by Journalism," *Contemporary Review* XLIX (1886), p. 656.

66. Jones, *Fleet Street*, p. 311. Ralph Blumenfeld observed that the "journalism of the twentieth century differs fundamentally from that of the nineteenth century in that it recognises that all the episodes of life worthy of being reported in print are stories about human beings, dramas or comedies, the pathos or humour of which is intensified by the fact of their being true." (*Press in My Time*, p. 91.)

4

Harry Schalck
Fleet Street in the 1880s: The New Journalism

Although John Buchan, among others, looked back nostalgically to the 1880s as a time "unbelievably secure and self-satisfied," with London "a true city of pleasure, every windowbox gay with flowers, her streets full of splendid equipages,"[1] the perspective of a century reveals to us a time less serene, one pushed by conflicting currents, an era of movement and social ferment. Indeed, the only common thread in the puzzling "pattern" of the 1880s would seem to be change. And in one area, at least, contemporaries became acutely aware of changes before the end of the decade: the London newspaper press.

"Fleet Street" in the 1880s, as now, covered a great deal more land than the crowded strip between St. Clement Danes and Ludgate Circus and quite wide areas of interest. There were journals devoted to every sort of concern, from the dreams of missionaries to those of licensed victualers. Their subscribers did not forget the specialized periodicals nor did the peddlers of Beecham's Pills or Pears's Soap, but for the serious late Victorian

*Reprinted by permission of the Association for Education in Journalism and Mass Communication, publishers of *Journalism Quarterly,* vol. 41, No. 3.

reader the list of papers was limited to less than a dozen—those influential dailies whose image held the confidence of right-thinking people.

At the head of the list was the venerable *Times*, watched by the great everywhere in the world and read at home by the solid governing class. It was an influential journal indeed, independent in view, and until the 1887 Pigott forgeries, considered infallible. In the eighties, however, its conservative editorial methods made the initiated suspect that with its long editorials and learned, sometimes esoteric articles, the "Thunderer" was becoming dull reading. Somewhat livelier was its coeval rival, the *Morning Post.* The darling of a confident aristocracy and the Primrose League, this sheet quite naturally espoused Tory Democracy at home and jingoism abroad. The *Standard,* on the other hand, although politically to the right, represented the opinions of businesslike Conservatives, in short, the City.

Most widely read of all was the curiously-managed *Daily Telegraph,* the first of the great penny papers. It had a Liberal tone in domestic politics and an imperialistic one in foreign affairs. Almost alone of the large morning papers it concerned itself with both lively writing—"Telegraphese"—and some non-political subjects. Further to the left were the *Daily Chronicle,* read by radical labor in England and by the builders of the Empire abroad, and the *Daily News,* which scarcely ever deviated from its traditional doctrinaire Liberal course. But this kind of Liberalism was going out of style, and the fortunes of the paper increasingly reflected the change. And then there were two evening journals, the independent *Pall Mall Gazette* and the radical *Star,* whose special importance in this period we must note later.

Because these papers had a combined circulation of less than a million, it is obvious that most ordinary Englishmen did not read them. Herein lies a striking incongruity of the time: the working classes were becoming increasingly vocal in mass meetings and at the polls, but politics and important organs of opinion were still controlled by men of upper- and middle-class habits. And when one segment of Fleet Street journalists began to practice a kind of sensationalism likely to appeal to the lower classes, their goals remained serious in intent. But transitions were under way.

The changes were of two kinds. We need mention only in passing the first, those evolutionary technological advances: refinement of the Hoe and Walter rotary presses, the printing of illustrations from a reel, the widespread acceptance of wood pulp newsprint, to name a few. Much more striking were the editorial novelties, which, taken together, were shortly to be labeled the New Journalism, for this movement was a significant, if short-lived transition between the stolid, respectable Victorian press and the sensationalism and commercialism of Harmsworth's and our own time.

Both the New Journalism and the Old, it is true, had several important features in common. Unlike turn-of-the-century papers of mass circulation and little intellectual content, both assumed that their literate audience was primarily interested in politics.

Two methods were used to call attention to political phenomena. By means of the first—the reporting of political activities in Parliament and out-of-doors—the papers attempted to provide unbiased raw materials for readers; by means of the second—the leading article—editors stated their own opinions and attempted to guide their readers.

Newspaper editors scheduled their working day—beginning at 10:00 A.M.—around political news. Reports, as distinguished from columns of comment, were handled by subeditors, who not only had to decide which to accept from outside London but also had to think about how to copy-fit the columns just written by the paper's reporter in the House of Commons. *The Times,* which gave the priority to the latter reports and often had three or four pages of them, not only had several choice seats in the cramped

Reporters' Gallery but even received advance copies of questions and answers directly from ministers. [2]

Among these journalists there was a fine esprit de corps, for their position was viewed as quite desirable, and, as one of them said, both reporters and members of Parliament dreaded leaving the House of Commons. [3] Countless anecdotes and legends have their origins in the Reporters' Gallery; we may accept as truthful accounts of the rapidity with which a good Gallery journalist could write an able report and the skill with which several could fit together their individual reports. H. W. Massingham claimed that in reporting the debates on the Parnell Commission, T. P. O'Connor had four or five columns completely written within a minute after the court rose. [4] Justin McCarthy, who recalled that George Bussey won a ten shillings and sixpence wager by writing within an hour a complete Parliamentary column for *The Times*, also noted that such columns usually brought the writers several guineas from various clients. [5] The reports of these men, some later published in book form, are not without interest and humor even now, though after the popular press became widespread, this kind of writing appeared to be caviar to the general.

A closely-related practice of the time bothered a later generation for which oratory had gone out of style: the verbatim reporting of political speeches. Looking back, the critics were fond of quoting Lord Rosebery, who had once let slip: "I can conscientiously say, having been a speaker myself, that I could never find anybody who read any speeches." [6] For years, however, the habit was prevalent not only in the biggest London papers but in provincial journals such as Hull's *Eastern Morning News*, in which the speeches of Gladstone, Lord Salisbury, and Joseph Chamberlain never got "less than the full honours of a verbatim report." [7] To bring such reports to the public at the earliest possible moment all sorts of ingenious methods were used — carrier pigeons, corps of bicyclists, special trains, pneumatic tubes, and telephones. One practicing journalist, telling how the Edinburgh *Evening Dispatch* reported Gladstone's 1890 speech at Midlothian, revealed that the paper employed nine reporters, working in one-minute shifts, along with two other men who collected copy and kept time. In this way it was able to have an edition with a complete report of the speech on the streets by the time most people who had heard it were coming out of the meeting.

Although the news columns provided raw material, it was the leading article – the "editorial" of our own day – that editors and managers considered their most potent weapon. This traditional Victorian device had long exerted a fascinating spell over readers, particularly readers of *The Times* whose leader-writers were always kept anonymous. Anonymity had the advantage of allowing the reader to feel a sense of continuity in his favorite paper regardless of who was writing and also, incidentally, of giving unknowns a chance to enter daily journalism.

With exceptions we shall note later, leading articles did not change during the eighties. They continued to receive much attention from the best writers, many of whom – John Morley, Justin McCarthy, and Lord Salisbury, to name three varied types – went on to political careers. Often, as in the case of the *Pall Mall Gazette,* where it was a tradition, editors continued to write leaders themselves. At many papers, too, leaders were written by several persons. "The editorial 'we,' " said one journalist, "is not a fiction."[8] On the best papers one could be sure that editorial ideas were often inspired by men close to the ministry or even in it. Thus journalist Abraham Hayward wrote to his sister how, after Gladstone, Granville, and Hartington had explained to him the complexities involved in the queen's choosing a prime minister in 1880, "I went off in the middle of the night to *The Times* office . . . and the first leading article of today was the result."[9] John Morley told Edward T. Cook about how he had gone to Gladstone in 1886 and suggested that if the latter would tell him the line he wished taken, Morley would write leaders "turning the *Daily News"* on the Home Rule question. "He told me," Morley said, "and I wrote three."[10] Between 1886 and 1895 foreign diplomatic circles watched particularly the leading articles of the *Standard* because its chief foreign affairs writer, Alfred Austin, was known to be in very close touch with Lord Salisbury.[11] In 1891 the prime minister pointedly directed Count Hatzfeldt's attention to a *Standard* editorial on England and the Triple Alliance, from which one historian infers that the peer himself had inspired it.[12]

Interest in politcs excepted, the two evening newspapers that originated the New Journalism, the *Pall Mall Gazette* and the *Star,* did not behave much like their contemporaries. The former, a kind of spoiled child throughout its whole existence, was for most of this period under the editorship of W. T. Stead, and its influence on the newspaper world and on politics was quite out of proportion to its size and circulation. The *Star,* which burst upon Fleet Street in 1888, had some equally significant effects upon the newspaper press, though its genial and testy editor, T. P. O'Connor, stayed with it only a few years. Disappointingly for its owners, the *Star* turned out to have almost no political influence, for although its editorial methods were fresh, it was, paradoxically, behind the time in appealing to the cream of the labor leadership rather than to the masses. In days of change "new" movements soon become outmoded; this was the case with both the *Pall Mall Gazette* and the *Star.*

In any chronicle of the late Victorian press, W. T. Stead is very like an engaging ingénue who upstages the long-established actors who have greater resources and more experience. His career included deep involvement in half a dozen sensational press campaigns, a term in Holloway Goal, which resulted from one of them, conversations with the great and near-great in Great Britain and on the Continent, wide acclaim in America for his authorship of *If Christ Came to Chicago,* and finally death as a passenger on the *Titanic.* "Stead's personality," wrote one journalist, "became one of the controlling forces in English Life,"[13] but the personality was so enmeshed in the paper itself that between 1883 and 1890 the *Pall Mall Gazette* and Stead were virtually one and the same.[14]

Long before he was called out of the North to assist *Pall Mall Gazette* editor John Morley (at the suggestion, some claimed, of Gladstone himself[15]) the paper had exhibited strong signs of individuality under Tory editorship. The Liberal victory in 1880, however, brought a change in proprietorship and, incidentally, an unheard of, acrimonious wrangle between the new proprietor, Yates Thompson, and the erstwhile editor, Frederick Greenwood, pursued in the Letters Column of the *Morning Post.* As the shocked *Post* itself noted: "It is not often that the anonymous veil of journalism is raised and that the public are instructed as to the voices and powers which were their favorite oracles."[16] In 1883 came a larger, if nonpolitical change, for in that year Stead, who had thought Morley's mind "not very agile,"[17] assumed the editor's chair. His lively journalistic practices led wags to say that "if a new *Pall Mall* and an old *Pall Mall* met in the street they would assuredly cut one another."[18] Stead slowly changed the appearance of the paper. He introduced illustrations (though not half-tones), crossheads, and political cartoons. He developed the signed leading article. And he brought the interview to prominence in daily journalism.

This last innovation was foreshadowed by some practices of the so-called society journals, especially Edmund Yates's *World,* which ran a "Celebrities at Home" column, printing the results of informal conversations with all sorts of people, ranging from the prince of Wales to "low comedians."[19] Stead's most famous interview was that of January 8, 1884, a fateful conversation with

"Chinese" Gordon at Southampton, which the editor dictated to his secretary in London at night and then published in the *Pall Mall Gazette*. This story perhaps gave the decisive impetus to the movement to send the general to the Sudan. "The interview with General Gordon," Stead wrote later to his father, "and subsequent appointment of that brave and pious man were great achievements for your harum-scarum son to be instrumental in bringing about."[20] Stead's other interviews could hardly be expected to bring such sensational if disastrous results, but some of them stir the imagination. "No one is too exalted to be interviewed and no one is too humble," he once wrote,[21] and to prove it he printed reports of conversations he or his staff had with a wide range of people, from the tsar of All the Russias to poor children in the East End.

The *Pall Mall Gazette* did not keep a monopoly of the interview for long; other journalists, including, by 1891, *The Times* itself, soon adopted it. Yet during the eighties it remained a practice less widespread in England than in the United States, for as old stagers said, "The last thing that a newspaperman of those days [the 1860s and 70s] . . . desired to obtrude was his personal acquaintance with politicians whose speeches he reported and criticised."[22]

Stead's literary style was light, and it could be observed in many nonpolitical leading articles, some of which appeared even on the front pages. Whole series of signed articles on "Centres of Spiritual Activity" (Cardinal Newman at Birmingham, the Y.M.C.A., the Theosophists), on "Great Advertisers of the World" (Pears's Soap, Bryant and May's Matches), and on new ways of dressing (Mr. Oscar Wilde's ideas) relected the personal interests of the editor. The deadly serious political crusades were another matter. When we reflect that "as a little boy [Stead] had wished that God would give him a whip so that he might whip all the wicked people up and down the world,"[23] we gain some idea of the shock with which the late Victorians greeted these endeavors. Moreover, Stead kept the campaigns in the public eye by reprinting certain series as *Pall Mall Gazette* "Extras," "without which," H. W. Massingham wrote, "no politician's library is complete."[24]

The newspaper world itself was shocked by the way this enfant terrible broke precedents of the trade. Wrote one journalist: "The idea in every British newspaper office, small or large, is that the sheet it turns out is, if not literally the only one printed that morning, the only one worthy of notice."[25] This was not true at the new *Pall Mall Gazette*, which, as an evening paper, had the advantage of being able to comment on the foibles of its morning rivals. "*The Times* this morning fell into another of those extraordinary blunders by which it has from time to time bewildered Europe," began a leader of October 3, 1884. Or again, "Our morning contemporaries are becoming too silly for anything" in failing to publish and comment upon the *Standard's* suggestions on redistribution.[26] Nor did the paper draw the line at individuals. "Lord Randolph Churchill," it once said, "always makes a fool of [his cause] . . . by his perversity, his exaggeration, and his slang."[27]

Some of Stead's reviews and articles were even too strong for his staff. Young Alfred Milner frequently toned down his chief's articles when they were in proof. By 1887 he said that he and Stead were in disagreement on seventy-five percent of the *Pall Mall Gazette's* issues. Thus E. T. Cook wrote in that year that the paper was, indeed, "a strange mixture of good and bad. You never know whether you will hear the voice of culture (that's me, you know, and Milner), or the blatantest vulgarity."[28] Objective observers concurred. Wrote one American: "In some respects [the *Pall Mall*] was . . . the best thing England had seen—and then in some others it was far and away the worst. But it was rarely commonplace."[29] Arnold Morley, who had been on its staff wrote: "We were always in hot water with one or other large portions of the public. . . . The *P.M.G.* excited no little animosity."[30] This lack of balance was Stead's Achilles's heel. Lord Crewe spoke of him as one "who was so nearly a great man and yet so definitely failed to be one." [31]

By the end of the 1880s proprietor Yates Thompson seemed to tire of the paper and of its editor. Although the *Pall Mall Gazette* had a certain prestige, it had not enough readers, for, like others of its kind, it could not make ends meet.[32] Stead was not unmindful of circulation figures, but he often forgot profits in the heat of whatever cause he was currently pushing. In 1890 he was replaced by E. T. Cook, whom Milner had brought to the *Pall Mall Gazette* in 1883. It was Cook who worked with moderate success to win back "many an alienated friend" of the paper. He dropped "the imperial tone . . . which often made Liberals think the *P.M.G.* was only a shade less wicked than *The Times.*"[33] After 1890 the paper was, as one critic said, "a trifle steadier than in the days of Mr. Stead."[34] But the staff, said journalist Edmund Garrett, was still working with "high falutin' ideas of prestige and policies."[35] By 1892 Thompson gave it up entirely; it became Conservative in politics and made no further contributions to the New Journalism.

At half the price of the *Pall Mall Gazette* T. P. O'Connor's halfpenny *Star* was a different paper. Mrs. O'Connor and some radical politicians, including Henry Labouchere, discussed the concept of such a paper before presenting it to "T. P.," who had already launched a promising career in Parliament. Indeed, the paper almost missed being started, for John Morley had also been planning a Liberal evening journal that would have brought ruinous competition.[36]

The *Star's* "Confession of Faith," printed in its first issue, gave further impetus to the New Journalism:

In our editorial department we shall find no place for the verbose and prolix articles to which most of our contemporaries still adhere. We shall have daily but one article of any length, and it will usually be confined within half-a-column. The other items of the day will be dealt with in notes, terse, pointed and plain-spoken. We believe the reader wants more than just politics.[37]

Nor was O'Connor's "reader" to be limited to twelve or thirteen thousand men of influence. The initial issues of the *Star* sold about 140,000 copies, and by 1893 (after O'Connor had left it) this number was up to 300,000.[38] No doubt many of these readers came from farther down the social and economic scale than Stead's. For these the editor wrote: "We hope to help in bringing in the day when, as in the United States and in France and in Switzerland, every citizen stands exactly equal before the nation in so far as he has been elevated to a higher position by the confidence of his fellow-citizens.[39]

As with the *Pall Mall Gazette,* however, the *Star* was made unique by being closely identified with its editor. The staff was brilliant. In later years a journalist claimed that "you could hardly open an editorial door on Fleet Street without seeing a former *Star* man."[40] One of them [Lincoln Springfield] said that "no impressionable youngster could work with him [O'Connor] without gaining a capacity, not of course for his glowing, vivid splashes of colour, but for some faint echoes of the cunning of his style. . . . "[41] It was as "T. P." who called his potential enemies, Joseph Chamberlain and A. J. Balfour, "a glass-eyed Kaffir" and "Caligula" respectively. It was he who dared to lecture the prince of Wales on talking too loudly at the theater and on his unnecessary borrowing from Baron Hirsch.[42]

Taking their cue from the editor, the staff—H. W. Massingham, George Bernard Shaw, Gordon Howard, Richard LeGallienne, Sidney Webb—composed lively reviews with piquant headings, sometimes referred to as "talking headlines."[43] When the Progressives won the London County Council elections, one *Star* man reproduced the jubilant "Ta-Ra-Ra-Boom-De-Ay!" a line then popular in the music halls.[44] Shaw called the London Liberal and Radical Union an "idiotic body" and got away with it partly because Massingham, who was supposed to revise the Shavian lines, was entirely in agreement with them. Nor was the *Star's* activity limited to words. More than Stead, O'Connor introduced to the paper the idea of stirring up agitations as protest. In 1889, for example, the *Star* circulated a petition on Irish political prisoners and followed it with a public meeting at which Parnell and Morley spoke.

Unfortunately, this loose manner of editing a newspaper was not pleasing to the owners' syndicate. That precious prima donna, Wilfred Blunt, resigned early because, he wrote, "I cannot go on pretending to believe in the Liberal Party, with which I have not an idea in common beyond Irish Home Rule.[45] Other board members became increasingly dissatisfied. Mr. Colman, the mustard processor, said that his section of the Liberals deplored some of the paper's articles; he might have correctly suspected that some of the members of the staff were Socialists.[46] Many thought that the paper's tone was "vulgar." Perhaps equally exasperating to those men was O'Connor's unbusinesslike way of handling finances. Certainly by 1890 the board, as the editor understated it, "could not be relied upon to deal in a friendly spirit with me."[47] In that year O'Connor resigned of his own accord but not without bitterness. He went on to write and edit at other places but never with any consistent success. The *Star* continued for another eighteen years, less "brilliant" and with several editorial changes.

By 1890 friendly and unfriendly critics alike accepted the arrival of the New Journalism, a label first used by Matthew Arnold in this unfriendly 1887 description:

We have had opportunities of observing a new journalism which a clever and energetic man has lately invented. It has much to recommend it: it is full of ability, novelty, variety, sensation, sympathy, generous instincts; its one great fault is that it is feather-brained. It throws out assertions at a venture because it wishes them true; does not corrent either them or itself, if they are false, and to get at the state of things as they truly are seems to feel no concern whatever.[48]

The "clever and energetic man" himself, who spoke of editors as "uncrowned king[s] of an educated democracy,"[49] insisted that "a chief feature of the New Journalism [is] the conscientiousness with which it tries to get to the bottom of things before pronouncing on them. . . . If there is *one* thing I am always preaching it is 'Get to know your facts.' "[50]

These different views, it now seems, were philosophical and from our perspective, perhaps academic. Soon the turn-of-the-century commercial press, full of trivia, would appeal to masses of new readers and nonthinkers. Some historians would even forget how novel the practices of the eighties had once seemed. But this is understandable, for both the Old and the New Journalists of that decade were at bottom concerned with affairs of the mind and heart; both felt a responsibility toward enlightening the public.

NOTES

1. Quoted in G. M. Trevelyan, *Illustrated English Social History* (London, 1952), vol. IV, p. 102.

2. H. Donaldson Jordan, "The Reports of Parliamentary Debates, 1803-1908," *Economica*, XX (1931), 446.

3. Philip Gibbs, *Adventures in Journalism* (New York, 1923), p. 36.

4. H. W. Massingham, *The London Daily Press* (London, 1892), p. 181.

5. Justin McCarthy, *A Newspaper Man's Memories* (New York, 1899), vol. I, p. 68.

6. Quoted in Harold Herd, *The March of Journalism: The Story of the British Press from 1622 to the Present Day* (London, 1952), p. 223.

7. J. A. Spender, *Life, Journalism and Politics* (New York, n.d.), vol. I, p. 40.

8. James Macintyre, "Theophraste Renaudot: Old Journalism and New," *Nineteenth Century* XXXIV (1893), 604.

9. *The History of the Times, Volume III: The Twentieth Century Test, 1884-1912* (New York, 1947), p. 521.

10. John Saxon Mills, *Sir Edward Cook, K.B.E.: A Biography* (London, 1921), p. 50.

11. Herd, *March of Journalism*, p. 27.

12. Oron James Hale, *Publicity and Diplomacy with Special Reference to England and Germany, 1890-1914* (New York, 1940), p. 90.

13. Harold Frederic in the New York *Sun*, January 1890. See Frederic Whyte, *The Life of W. T. Stead* (New York, n.d.), vol. I, p. 114.

14. Stead rarely dined out and never joined a club. Raymond L. Schults, *Crusader in Babylon: W. T. Stead and the Pall Mall Gazette* (Lincoln, Nebraska, 1972), p. 34.

15. J. W. Robertson Scott, *The Life and Death of a Newspaper* (London, 1952), p. 72.

16. *Morning Post*, 6 May 1880.

17. Schults, *Crusader in Babylon*, p. 18.

18. Scott, *Life and Death*, p. 67.

19. Edmund H. Yates, *Edmund Yates: His Recollections and Experiences* (London, 1884), vol. II, p. 332.

20. Scott, *Life and Death*, p. 97.

21. *History of the Times, III*, p. 781, quoting Stead's own *A Journalist on Journalism*, which he published in 1891. Not all of Stead's targets agreed to be interviewed. In 1888 he was turned down by French President Sadi-Carnot. (Schults, *Crusader in Babylon*, p. 240.) Earlier Matthew Arnold also refused. J. O. Baylen, "Matthew Arnold and the *Pall Mall Gazette:* Some Unpublished Letters, 1884-1887," *South Atlantic Quarterly* LXVIII (1969), 546.

22. Wemyss Reid, "Some Reminiscences of English Journalism," *Nineteenth Century* XLII (1897), 63.

23. A. P. Ryan, *Lord Northcliffe* (London, 1953), p. 38.

24. Massingham, *London Daily Press*, p. 155

25. Henry W. Lucy, "The Power of the British Press," *North American Review* CLXIII (1896), 173.

26. *Pall Mall Gazette*, 10 October 1884.

27. Ibid., 4 October 1884.

28. Milner called Stead "a compound of Don Quixote and P. T. Barnum." Mills, *Cook*, p. 60.

29. Whyte, *Stead*, vol. I, p. 114.

30. Ibid., Vol. I, p. 100.

31. Lord Crewe, *Lord Rosebery* (New York, 1931), p. 175.

32. The other "class" papers of opinion all found themselves in similar circumstances by the end of the nineteenth century. By 1880, when he sold the *Pall Mall Gazette*, proprietor George Smith had lost £25,000 on it. A turn-of-the-

century music hall song ran: "I spend a sum internal/To support an evening journal/But it's nothing to a mighty millionaire. . . ." J. W. R. Scott said of the *Pall Mall Gazette* of that period that "on the business side our journal was below what would nowadays be reckoned efficiency. . . ." See his *Life and Death*, p. 271.

33. Mills, *Cook*, p. 68.

34. Massingham, *London Daily Press*, p. 159.

35. Sir Edward Cook, *Edmund Garrett: A Memoir* (London, 1909), p. 71.

36. Elizabeth O'Connor, *I Myself* (New York, 1914), pp. 210-211.

37. Quoted in Stanley Morison, *The English Newspaper, 1622-1932* (Cambridge, 1932), p. 289.

38. Hamilton Fyfe, *T. P. O'Connor* (London, 1934), pp. 172-173.

39. Ibid., p. 39.

40. Francis Williams, *Dangerous Estate: The Anatomy of Newspapers* (London, 1957), p. 134.

41. Quoted in Fyfe, *O'Connor*, p. 150.

42. Ibid., p. 173. When O'Connor was editing the Sunday *Sun* in the 1890s, the subeditor Kennedy Jones often blue-penciled his articles to save the paper from libel action.

43. Schults, *Crusader in Babylon*, p. 238.

44. T. P. O'Connor, *Memoirs of an Old Parliamentarian* (London, 1929), vol. II, p. 259.

45. W. S. Blunt, *My Diaries* (London, 1922), vol. I, p. 25.

46. Fyfe, *O'Connor*, p. 152.

47. O'Connor, *Memoirs*, vol. II, p. 255.

48. Matthew Arnold, "Up to Easter," *Nineteenth Century*, XXI (1887), 638.

49. Baylen, "Arnold and the *Pall Mall Gazette*," p. 549.

50. Scott, *Life and Death*, p. 274.

PART TWO

THE FLOWERING OF
THE NEW JOURNALISM

5

Ray Boston

W. T. Stead and Democracy by Journalism

The New Journalism debate that raged for months in the heart of London's clubland a century ago was not really about journalism at all. It was about democracy and the disturbing political ideas of a messianic newspaper editor called William Thomas Stead. It might have started with Stead's "Maiden Tribute of Modern Babylon," in July 1885, an exposé of juvenile prostitution proclaiming that "the hour of Democracy has struck," which offended many clubmen.[1] But it only became a white-hot row after several other political writings had also fallen from the magisterial pen of Stead — whom God had called to "the only true throne in England,"[2] namely, the *Pall Mall Gazette* editor's chair.

In May 1886 Stead's bold article, "Government by Journalism," appeared in the *Contemporary Review.* In November an even bolder sequel appeared entitled, "The Future of Journalism." Both articles made large claims regarding the public service duties of an editor, and a brisk national debate ensued over "one of the most audacious assertions of press power ever made in Britain. . . ."[3] Gentlemanly discussion turned into a slanging match, however, when that scholar-poet Matthew Arnold chose to attack Stead and his New Journalism in the *Nineteenth Century* magazine a year later in May 1887. Arnold declared himself "deeply disturbed" by the verbal and visual crudities of the New Journalism. He argued that they were not merely culturally offensive to all right-thinking members of society; they were actually misleading the untutored minds of Britain's emerging democracy. Stead's newspaper, he insisted, "throws out assertions at a venture, simply because it wishes them to be true." It also, he said, gives them (i.e., the masses) "a disposition to be feather-brained"—presumably about matters that did not properly concern them—"just as the upper class is disposed to be selfish in its politics and the middle class narrow."[4]

Arnold was right, of course. Stead's campaigns, or escapades, as he called them, were misleading. They were also disturbing the balance of Victorian society. It can be argued that he was "up to no good but the beat of his inky blood."[5] It can also be argued that his rabble-rousing campaigns were giving simple folk the idea that more things could be achieved by "a newspaper with a conscience"[6] than was constitutionally possible or even politically permissible. But if Arnold was partly right, he was more generally wrong. He was completely wrong about his motives, which were humanitarian rather than commercial. He was also wrong about his effect on ordinary working people, which was uplifting rather than injurious. Stead's highly readable journalism was popular not because it was sensationally vulgar and morally offensive but because it was "radiant, radical and rebellious."[7] It was capable of ennobling as well as entertaining. It was also managing to talk about democracy—democratically—like nobody since William Cobbett or Tom Paine; and it was this aspect of his writing that was having the unbalancing effect.

Stead was no mere "sentimental radical" like the late Mr. Charles Dickens.[8] Stead was a campaigner to be feared. He didn't mind breaking the law if it was necessary, and he positively reveled in going to prison if only because it proved his point about there being a political cover-up.[9] He was not afraid of any bureaucrat who tried to block his inquiries. He had a powerful friend, Lord Esher, who had access to the primary sources and the secret Treasury accounts.[10] He was simply asking for some old-fashioned Christian justice and found talking about the equality of Christians in the eyes of God a most fearsome combination in a society that prided itself on its religiosity! He declared himself to be God's weapon on earth, a man with a mission. He had come down from the north of England to offer the world much more than "a peep-show" and an opposition argument to Mr. Disraeli's "progressive Toryism."[11]

Stead had gone to London to expose corruption and criminal neglect or "private wealth and public squalor" as we would say today. He wanted "to use the press to remove the injustices which exist beneath the fair foundations of . . . wealth and commerce in Britain."[12] In other words, his only business was the business of investigative journalism. He was in one of the most influential seats in the country, and it was his job to supply his readers with some worthwhile, functional information, not with mere candy-floss. He was not prepared to play the role of the traditional London editor, offering petty official secrets and society gossip as inducements to those reluctant to pay good money for more and more advertisements. "The editor," he proclaimed," is the uncrowned king of an educated democracy." Traditional, deferential journalism was no longer enough. The people had a right to know what was being done in their name by their so-called representatives.[13] Stead was proud of himself as a muckraker for God. But he refused absolutely to be a journalistic moonraker for the *Police News.*[14]

At the age of fifteen, Stead was inspired by his reading of James Russell Lowell's preface to the "Pious Editor's Creed": "What a pulpit the editor mounts daily, sometimes with a congregation of fifty thousand. And from what a Bible he can choose his text, the open volume of the world! Methinks the editor who should understand his calling and be equal thereto, would be the very Moses of our nineteenth century . . . the Captain of our Exodus into the Canaan of a truer social order."[15] A few years later, aged twenty-two, never having seen the inside of a newspaper office, Stead was appointed editor of the *Northern Echo,* published at Darlington and having a circulation of 13,000. And from that moment he became the noisiest journalistic evangelist in the whole of England. He was determined (as he told Mme. Novikov) "to secure the final overthrow of the Powers of Darkness in high places."[16] In his diary he congratulated himself on the success of his first editorial campaign to prevent Great Britain from becoming embroiled in a war with Russia. He would not, he said, expend many words on "such immodesty and such self-regard." But he concluded his entry as follows: "I have received the highest compliments from Mr. Gladstone." Thus did the young W. T. Stead record his first major step along the road to future notoriety as a campaigning journalist.[17]

Today it seems incredible that a daily paper that had such a tiny circulation could even pay its way. That its young editor could also think of himself as a partner with the leader of the opposition in shaping Britain's foreign policy is still less easy to credit. There were, of course, no national newspapers in 1877, in the sense in which we define them today. Indeed, according to Gladstone himself, there was more political power in the provincial press in "this year of crisis for *The Times*" than in the whole of the London press.[18] As late as 1882, Joseph Hatton, the Conserative editor of the *People,* remarked that "it is provincial England, not journalistic London, that makes and unmakes Parliament."[19] But

Gladstone's remark was made after he had already invited the young fire-eater to assist John Morley at the *Pall Mall Gazette*. There was as yet no recognition of the news function as the primary purpose of the newspaper. A "viewspaper" was all that was required. But there was belated recognition of young Stead's point that the Liberal party press in Fleet Street as well as in the provinces should become "the engine of social reform."[20] It is therefore no exaggeration to say that Stead's journalistic efforts were motivated as much by what he passionately believed were urgent political needs as they were by his religious and social obsessions. Perhaps one of the best illustrations of this powerful mixture occurs in a sad little tale told by Annie Besant just after his death in 1912: "If Stead's championship of the unemployed alienated the clubmen of Pall Mall, that only made it the more reason why he and I should trudge on foot together, from Soho to Mile End, beside the body of the workless man struck down in Trafalgar Square on Bloody Sunday."[21]

Stead's greatest personal theme, however, was the illimitable range of a free journalist's powers and responsibilities. The divine right of Kings had gone, Stead argued; so too had the divine right of the gentry entrenched in Parliament, the Church, the universities, and the land. It was now being challenged by the divine right of demagogues to speak for the people in the language of the people. The free press was impatiently taking over the function of the Commons. (Stead informed the prince of Wales during an extended and exclusive press interview that he would on no account exchange places with him!) A newspaper, he declared, must "palpitate with actuality"; it must be a mirror reflecting all the currents and phases of life in the locality. The press, he affirmed, "has become to the Commons what the Commons once were to the Lords. The Press has become the Chamber of Initiative and this new power of initiation it has secured by natural right."[22]

All this of course, could have been dismissed as windy rhetoric except for three facts. First, Stead always practiced what he preached. He went always for the primary sources of information and treated official news sources with great suspicion. Second, he was remarkably successful at raising money for good causes and arranging practical help for people in trouble – especially legal trouble. Third, his plan to enable the press to exercise legitimate civil power through a national network of unpaid volunteers, similar to the unpaid J.P. system, which had networked the country for two centuries outside London was not merely radically democratic; it was also perfectly feasible given the sort of official cooperation that he had in mind. He proposed that each newspaper should have its own whip in Parliament, should be invested with the right to inspect all official institutions, and should be assisted by press agents in each government department. "The duty of an editor," he declared, is absolute. He ought to be able to get at, or know someone who can get at, everyone from the Queen downwards, in order to be able to ascertain what they are thinking about the topic of the day." He should be "universally accessible," know everyone and hear everything. According to Stead, "the old-fashioned idea of a jealously shrouded impersonality has given way to its exact antithesis. There is something inexpressibly pathetic in the dumbness of the masses of the people. Touch but a hair on the head of the well-to-do and forthwith, you will hear his protest in the august columns of *The Times*. But the millions who have to suffer the rudest buffets of ill-fortune, those victims of official insolence and the brutality of the better-off, they are as dumb as the HORSE, which you may scourge to death without its uttering a sound. . . . To give utterance to the inarticulate moan of the voiceless, is to let some light into a dark place; it is almost equivalent to the enfranchisement of a class. . . . To be both eye and ear for the community is a great privilege. However, power no less than noblesse, obliges – and much may be done to realize it if we but recognize that the discharge of such responsibility lies in the day's work of every journalist."[23]

Yes, it was a fine piece of oratorical writing. It was also an innovative idea—one that could easily have turned the British press into a fourth branch of government. But it got him into immediate trouble with the establishment. It was too radical by half. And not even Harold Evans, his twentieth-century counterpart in both Darlington and London,[24] would be able to turn it into a practical reality seventy years later. Both men eventually had to take themselves off to America where they spiritually and mentally belonged. And both men eventually were sacked by ungrateful, profitseeking employers for spending their money "like drunken sailors" on profitless crusades![25]

But, to return to Stead's emotional cadenza, it may have brought him trouble with his political bosses, but it also brought him to the brink of his most creative journalistic idea—the *endowed* newspaper. This is how Stead, writing in 1886, introduced the concept: "If some great newspaper proprietor will not content himself with only a reasonable fortune—and will not agree to devote the surplus of his gigantic profits to turning his newspaper into an engine of social reform and a means of government—well then, perhaps some man or woman of fortune will be prepared to devote a mere half-million to *endow* a newspaper, free of all advertising, for the service, for the education and for the guidance of the people?"

He then outlined the steps necessary to "gauge, and at the same time influence," the opinion of the nation. Mere circulation, he insisted, would not avail. Influence depends not half so much on quantity as upon the quality of the subscribers. How then? "There are two methods: the first is by a system of major-generals, and the second by a system of journalistic travellers."

He began with the system of major-generals. "When Cromwell was driven to undertake the governing of England, he mapped out the towns into districts, and over each district he placed a man after his own heart, responsible to him for the peace and good government of the district under his care." That system, Stead declared, could be adopted with advantage by any newspaper that wished to keep in hand the affairs of the whole country. "A competent, intelligent, sympathetic man or woman, as nearly as possible the *alter ego* of the editor, should be planted in each district and held responsible for keeping the editor informed of all that is going on within the area that needs attending to, either for encouragement or repression, or merely for observation and report. . . . It would also be the duty of the major-general to select one associate who would undertake to co-operate with the central office in ascertaining facts, in focussing opinion, and in generally assisting the editor to ascertain the direct views of his countrymen. . . .It might be a squire or it might be a cobbler; it might be the clergyman's daughter, or a secularist newsagent, or a Methodist reporter. . . . And to each there will be posted copies of the paper, in recognition of their position and services, and in order to keep them in touch with the editorial mind." Each of the major-generals would exercise general oversight over all the associates in his division, but the whole organization would be kept together and the personal sense of a common interest kept up "by the periodical visits of the journalistic traveller. . . ." These "peripatetic apostles of the New Journalism," would, he thought, bring the whole organization alive and instill a common interest and a common enthusiasm. If all this was done, the newspaper would become the most powerful and one of the most useful institutions in the country. "Such a newspaper would indeed be a great secular or civic church and democratic university, and if wisely directed and energetically worked, it would come to be the very soul of our national unity; and its great central idea would be that of the self-sacrifice of the individual for the salvation of the community, the practical realization of the religious idea in national politics and social reform."

Parliament, he concluded, has reached its utmost development. "There is now need of a new representative method, not to supercede but to supplement that which exists – a system which will be more elastic, more simple, more direct and more closely in touch with the mind of the people. . . . And when the time does arrive, and the man and the money are both forthcoming, government by journalism will no longer be a somewhat hyperbolical phrase, but a solid fact."[26]

Well, as we know, nothing happened along these lines – at least not during Stead's lifetime – apart from an abortive effort by Stead to produce a newspaper called the *Daily Paper,* which started in 1904 and lasted only three weeks. The world premiere of the endowed newspaper was delayed until 1940 when Marshall Field launched an adless newspaper in New York, the *PM,* which lasted in various forms until 1948.[27] What a pity it now seems that Stead did not find it in himself to accept Cecil Rhodes's offer to buy him the *Pall Mall Gazette* or "some other paper to experiment with."[28] If he had, it might have given Great Britain a much more businesslike precedent than *PM* for the totally adless, endowed newspaper.

We know that throughout the years 1890-1893, Stead was daydreaming continually of the wonderful and unique daily paper that he would presently produce. Unfortunately, not even his well-publicized trip to Chicago in 1893 brought him any closer to his elusive, "millionaire with vision." Part of the trouble was self-doubt. "I do not think that money is the difficulty at all," he is quoted as saying just before he left for Chicago, "the difficulty lies not in the Capitalist but in the Editor. I am a bad manager. I am a very good Master when I have a very good Servant, but I am a very bad Master, indeed the worst, when I have a bad

Servant because I am not hard enough to keep him up to his work."[29] In other words, like most egomaniacs, he was quite unable to delegate responsibility, preferring to do everything himself even when he was clearly not up to it! All his doubts about himself, however, had gone, and he was back to his usual, ebullient self by the time of his interview with the Chicago *Sunday Tribune* on November 10, 1893. The interview begins abruptly: " 'If ever there was a demagogue, said William T. Stead, the London editor, as he slipped further down into his chair and propped his feet up on the railing, if every there was a demagogue in the world, I am one. I'd rather be a demagogue any day, then a Brahmin! It is only necessary that the demagogue should be moved by right ideas.' "

This is only the opening paragrah of a hilarious interview. Stead continued: "One of the things I looked forward to in coming to Chicago was meeting your late Mayor, Carter Harrison. He has been called a demagogue. He had, I am told, a premonition of his violent taking off. I have had a similar warning. I am to die a violent death also, but, before death comes to me, I am to be twice more locked up in prison for my journalism." The interviewer then asked him whether there was anything about the American newspaper he particularly disliked. " 'Yes, there are,' " Stead replied, " 'Many. Above all, the way in which American proprietors of newspapers sell their souls to the advertiser, showing no other ambition than to heap up an immense fortune and fatten on their gains. They have not even as much public spirit as the medieval robber barons.' "

What did he mean by that, asked the man from the *Tribune:* " 'Well, what I mean is this: in the old days when a man had made his pile, he used it to govern and civilize and educate the people in the midst of whom he had established his castle. But there is no such recognition of responsibility on the part of most newspaper proprietors nowadays.

" 'Instead of regarding the wealth they have acquired, as merely the starting point for humanizing the conditions of life among those whose support has provided their wealth, they live self-indulgent, self-centered lives. As individuals they may be excellent persons, but from the point of view of the social organization they are but the fatted swine of civilization.' "

Stead was then asked whether it was possible to change the system. His reply was " 'Yes. But it can be changed only by bringing back into existence the real live Church. . . . We need to use the newspaper as a social pillory in which those who have received much and returned nothing to the community will be stigmatized as they deserve. . . .' " The *Tribune* man asked. "Was it business?" " 'Yes, of course—the very best business,' " Stead replied warmly " 'Read all about THE MIRACLE WORKER OF NAZARETH in this Sunday's paper—That's good business too! So let's have no more of this cheap cynicism!"[30]

Thus spoke "God's Englishman"—managing to sound more like Jehovah than even his model, Oliver Cromwell, was wont to do! He then launched into further morals of thunder against another of his journalistic *betes noires*, the night editor! Stead's main conception of an editor's duty, without a doubt was to be like himself. He had come to the realization, as no editor before him had done, not even Barnes or Delane of *The Times,* what power a newspaper could give him to record himself with headlines and bold type, with recitative and chorus, on a pedestal of fact and news once in every twenty-four hours. Stead's mercurial, hellfire temperament was that of the great pamphleteers. In his boldness and versatility, in his passionate belief in the constructive power of the pen, in so many of his opinions, even in his championship of women, he resembled Daniel Defoe and Jonathan Swift.

He was also a great popularizer, a great translator of the deliberately obscure language of the specialist in terms that most busy generalists could enjoy as well as understand. But his great, almost mesmeric, power over men's minds had its deepest root in the Christian sincerity that every page of his writing confessed. Even by Victorian standards, he was outstanding here. Mr. Gladstone, his most famous guide and mentor, sounded worldly by comparison, and the range of his devotees extended from Cardinal Manning to Annie Besant.

John Ruskin was by no means the only master of letters ready to overlook Stead's journalese in appreciation of his flair for drawing public attention to great moral and political purposes. George Bernard Shaw, a great destroyer of false idols, also felt that way. Here are a few sentences from the very long letters they both wrote to the *Pall Mall Gazette* in June 1887. First, Ruskin: "Permit me to advise you that the function of the P.M.G. is neither to teach theology nor to criticize art. You have taken an honest and powerful position in modern politics and ethics, and you have nothing whatever to do with traditions of eternal punishment, but only to bring, so far as you may, immediate malefactors to immediate punishment." Now, Shaw: "Sir, your paper enjoys a peculiar opportunity—that of leader of the Press in the march to meet the coming twentieth century. Your rivals are too blind, too deaf, too dumb and too full of notions of literary propriety—which are misplaced frivolities. The P.M.G. owes its unique position wholly to its memorable resolution to attack social abuses with the terrible weapon of truth-telling. If you sheathe that weapon, what will maintain that paper in its present place when the Afghan frontier and Home Rule are forgotten? I venture to predict that the future is with journals like the Gazette, which will dare to tell polite society that it lives by the robbery and murder of the poor, and will ask pardon of the poor for its tacit approval of such robbery and murder in the past."[31]

Ruskin and Shaw were hard-headed men who had been around London's clubland, where the establishment resided, much longer than Stead. Their praise was not given lightly. They plainly wanted him to succeed and to persist, despite all the forces ranged against him. They recognised that although no contemporary editor had worked harder at self-education or knew more persons of mark in high society, Stead's upbringing and adult life were, in some respects, narrow. For example, as Robertson Scott, Stead's biographer, tells us, it was not until some years after Stead left the *Pall Mall Gazette* that he paid his first visit to the theatre! They also saw that Stead was emotionally immature, like so many self-made intellectuals. He was frequently referred to in public as childlike. Nevertheless, he was able to secure professional interviews with the tsar of all the Russians as well as with the prince of Wales, and his "Letters from the Vatican," published serially in October and November 1889, added considerably to his world reputation at the time.[32]

His political radicalism seemed to reach back to Cromwell and Lilburne and the Puritan Revolution. It was right out of its time, being almost pure "Mayflower" and mid-Atlantic in spirit. Stead's ideological focus helped to remove academic doubts about the continuing existence of an Anglo-American journalistic tradition of dissent.[33] Stead, in his buttoned-up English way, was consciously trying to imitate Horace Greeley of the *New York Tribune*.[34] He was not at all concerned with emulating that arch exploiter of the American public, James Gordon Bennett of the *New York Herald*. But then he was not desirous of emigrating and becoming an American either—which is why I have suggested that he is somewhat mid-Atlantic in spirit and therefore alienated from both worlds. It is frustrating, for us as well as for him, that he never became an adequately financed newspaper owner in either country. He could have shown the world what he would have done with an endowed newspaper if he had been in sole charge of one.

He managed one thing very well indeed, while still at the height of his powers in the 1880s before he became involved with his "spooks" and "that dreadful craze of his about departed spirits."[35] He provided a salutary reminder to all governments that, in the words of a seventeenth-century poet, "There is on earth a yet Auguster thing, Veiled though it be than Parliament and King"— namely, democracy or government by journalism. This reminder was noted carefully at the time on both sides of the Atlantic though more especially on the New York side, where his political views seemed more naturally to belong. When Stead died in 1912, the *New York Sun* expressed the view, in all seriousness, that "in the years between 1884 and 1888, Stead came nearer to governing Great Britain than any other man in the kingdom."[36] Stead's "Shade" would have liked that! Mr. Gladstone and, of course, Lord Esher would have demurred. But not many others among his contemporaries, even in Great Britain, would have wanted to do likewise.

NOTES

1. Launched on the front page of the *Pall Mall Gazette* on Monday afternoon, 6 July 1885 (following an introductory leader by Stead), these sensational investigative reports and commentaries continued daily until 10 July when Part IV concluded the series.

2. In an article in the *Washington Evening Star* for 24 December 1892, an American journalist, Frank Carpenter, quotes Stead, speaking to him in his editorial office at Mowbray House, as follows: "The fact that we have a Queen and a royal family does not affect the matter (of approaching republicanism in England). They are of no special influence. They have their place. They are ornamental figures on our governmental tables. . . .But this seat here is the only true throne in England." For the first use of this phrase, see also *Journal of W. T. Stead*, 16 April 1871, Stead Papers. The Stead Papers are in the process of being deposited at Churchill College, Cambridge, by Professor J. O. Baylen.

3. Piers Brendon, *The Life and Death of the Press Barons* (London, 1982), p. 78.

4. Matthew Arnold, "Up to Easter," *Nineteenth Century* CXXIII (1887), 638-639.

5. Hugh Kingsmill *After Puritanism: 1850-1900* (Londin, 1929), p. 171. In his psychoanalytical chapter on Stead, the focus is on the self-delusions of a Puritan born too late to simplify the modern world.

6. The phrase is used by A. G. Gardiner in *Review of Reviews,* October 1913, to explain why Stead seemed to him "to challenge the judgment of his fellows in so many ways. But to all of us, whatever our opinion of his opinions, he was the prince of our craft." The phrase was also used by John Ruskin in describing the *Pall Mall Gazette* under Stead, according to John Gross, *The Rise and Fall of the Man of Letters* (London, 1969), p. 26.

7. Ben Tillet, *Memories and Reflections* (London, 1931), p. 92.

8. Dickens shared with men such as Carlyle and Arnold an overwhelming fear of the undisciplined mob. See *Charles Dickens, A December Vision: His Social Journalism,* ed. N. Philip and V. Neuburg (London, 1986), p. 18, in which *Household Words* is described as a vehicle for what George Bagehot called Dickens' sentimental radicalism.

9. See John Morley *Recollections* (New York, 1917) vol. I, pp. 209-210, for Stead's self-delusions. It is also worth noting that the infamous abduction case against Stead, brought by the Attorney-General on 7 September 1885, would have failed had Stead been prepared to produce the evidence (which he possessed) that the Armstrong child was illegitimate.

10. On the confidential Cabinet information passed to Stead by Reginald Brett (Lord Esher), see Brett's letters to Stead, 29 January 1884 – 10 February 1885, in Stead Papers, and in the second Viscount Esher Papers, Churchill College, Cambridge (courtesy 3rd Viscount Esher).

11. Stead's Journal, 31 December 1882, Stead Papers. See also Frederick Whyte, *The Life of W. T. Stead* (London, 1925), vol. I, p. 254.

12. Whyte, *Stead* Vol. I, p. 27, cites this statement by Stead in his reported talks with John Copleston, the first editor of the *Northern Echo,* who became Stead's chief instructor in the art of editing.

13. W. T. Stead, "Government by Journalism," *Contemporary Review* XLIX (1886), 667-668. He condemned "subservient journalism" because it deprived the government of "the advantage of friendly and independent criticism." (Stead wrote this essay while in Holloway Gaol.)

14. A contest, run by the *Pall Mall Gazette* on 3 November 1886, for "the worst of all newspapers," was won outright by the *Police News,* a scurrilous rag owned by George Purkess. Stead's editorial comments regarding his readers' near-unanimity, makes his personal distaste of "so many square leagues of dirtily printed falsehood" almost palpable!

15. See Estelle W. Stead, *My Father* (London, 1913), pp. 4, 21, and 50. See also W. T. S., *James Russell Lowell: His Message and How It Helped Me* (London, 1891), pp. 9-11.

16. *Stead's Journal,* 8 August 1880, Stead Papers; Stead to Mme. Novikov, 25 August 1880, Novikov Collection, Bodleion Library, Oxford. See also Stead's claim to be "a revivalist preacher and not a journalist by nature," as reported in *Review of the Churches,* 15 August 1894, VI, 298.

17. *Stead's Journal,* 23 June 1877, Stead Papers.

18. 'B,' "English Journalism," *Nation* (New York), 22 July 1880, p. 59.

19. J. Hatton, *Journalistic London* (London, 1882), p. 40.

20. On the role of Edward A. Freeman, Joseph Chamberlain, W. E. Forster, and Gladstone in influencing Morley's choice of Stead as assistant editor of the *Pall Mall Gazette,* see W. R. W. Stephens, *Life and Letters of Edward A. Freeman* (London, 1895), vol. II, pp. 35, 97, 127. Also see Gladstone Papers, B.M., Add. MSS 44303, Vol. CCXVIII.

21. Whyte, *Stead,* I, p. 254. See also Arthur H. Nethercot, *The First Five Lives of Annie Besant* (London, 1961), p. 257.

22. *Contemporary Review* XLIX, 671, 673, and L, 678-679.

23. "The Future of Journalism," *Contemporary Review* L, 671.

24. See Harold Evans, *Good Times, Bad Times* (London, 1983), p. 95 ff.

25. See Louis Heren, "Declining with The Times," *Journalism Studies Review,* no. 7 (1982), 4.

26. See Roy Hoopes, *Ralph Ingersoll: A Biography* (New York, 1985), p. 226 ff.

27. "Future of Journalism," pp. 671, 673, 678-679.

28. Whyte, *Stead,* vol. II, p. 33.

29. Ibid.

30. Ibid., vol. II, Appendix II: "Stead's Hopes for a . . . unique daily paper."

31. Ibid., vol. I, pp. 235-242. Only Ruskin's letter was actually used by the *Pall Mall Gazette* on 8 June 1887. Shaw's letter was received and acknowledged but, surprisingly, was not published.

32. Ibid. vol. II, pp. 292-297.

33. See Max Beloff, "Is there an Anglo-American Political Tradition?" *History* XXXVI (1951), 73-91.

34. Brendon, *Life and Death,* p. 75. See also Whyte, *Stead,* vol. II, p. 75. See also Stead's obituary notice for Horace Greeley, which was published in the *Northern Echo,* 5 December 1872.

35. Harold Begbie, *Albert, 4th Earl Grey: A Last Word* (London, 1925?), p. 82 ff.

36. Both quotes are from Whyte, *Stead,* vol. II, p. 238.

6

J. O. Baylen

Politics and the New Journalism: Lord Esher's Use of the *Pall Mall Gazette*

A recent biographer of Reginald Baliol Brett (1852-1930), after 1899 2nd Viscount Esher, described him as "an emigma to his contemporaries and . . . a puzzle to historians. . . ."[1] To such contemporaries as Wilfred Scawen Blunt, Brett was "clever, but unprincipled"; to the Edwardian editor, J. A. Spender, who knew him well, Brett was independent in thought, "no "apple-polisher," and incapable of being shocked by anything—a person who successfully availed himself of every opportunity to cultivate friendships with important people because "he was extremely acceptable and well-informed. . . ."[2] To Gladstone's private secretary, Edward Hamilton, "Regy" Brett was "a very clever shrewd fellow . . . [who] . . . wormed himself into the confidence" of prominent figures in all political and social circles.[3] To Sir Charles Dilke, who first met Brett in 1878, Brett was "an extremely pleasant fellow" and "a most able man" who was far "too clever for his own good" even though "in all he did, he had public ends in view. . . ."[4] Richard Hough, the naval historian and biographer of Admiral "Jackie" Fisher, described Brett as an "early Italian type of mind" and "a brilliant withdrawn figure, a plotter and schemer, a Machiavellian figure who preferred to work behind the scenes but numbered the highest in the land among his closest friends. . . ." Yet Hough accepts the verdict of the royal courtier, Sir Frederick Ponsonby, that Brett's strong point was that "he never minded who got credit for any measure he devised so long as it was adopted by the authorities. . . ."[5] In the view of other historians, Brett was "a mysterious or anomalous figure" but, more accurately, "an intermediary in cross-party intrigue" who, after the mid-1880s, became "an *éminence grise* of the monarchy" for Victoria and her immediate successors.[6] Almost all who knew Brett acknowledged his ability to charm and persuade and to achieve the trust of leading politicians in both parties. Thus he was *persona grata* with the Liberals, Tories, and Liberal Unionists and moved easily as a political intermediary—as a "fixer" and confidant between them. Much of this affinity was the result of the friendships that Brett established at Eton (Lord Rosebery and Lord Curzon) and Cambridge (Arthur Balfour and his brothers, Albert Grey, the Lyttleton brothers, and Sir William Harcourt).

Brett was the son of a renowned judge who served as solicitor-general in the Derby-Disraeli ministry and as a lord justice during Disraeli's second government and was made a viscount in 1897 by Lord Salisbury. In addition to the high politics that Brett absorbed in his establishment family and Tory society, he imbibed the imperialist outlook of his tutor at Eton, William Johnson. At Cambridge, he was admitted to the "Apostles" circle and, through Albert Grey, established "an unusually wide range of social acquaintance which included the social citadels of both political parties." After Cambridge, Brett became associated with the anti-Gladstone Harcourt faction of the Liberal party and in early 1878 became Lord Hartington's private secretary. He was already a Liberal Imperialist when elected to Parliament for Penryn and Falmouth in 1880—hoping that the Gladstone government might soon give way to a Rosebery-Chamberlain ministry that would accomplish economic and social reform at home and imperial expansion abroad. With his personal connections and extensive friendships on both sides of the Commons and the advantage of continuing as private secretary to Hartington, now secretary of state for war, Brett quickly aspired to become "the ideal political mediator."[7]

As the indolent Hartington's chief assistant who had access to Cabinet and War Office discussions and secrets, Brett also acquired "a taste for surreptitious journalism" that involved the use of the press and public opinion to force on the Gladstone government the domestic reform and imperialist policies that he and his Radical and Imperialist friends espoused. Brett's chosen instrument in the daily press was the *Pall Mall Gazette,* primarily because under the editorial direction of John Morley and especially his successor after 1883, W. T. Stead, the paper was widely read among the ruling classes and under Stead advocated both social reform and imperial expansion.[8] This was the beginning of a long-time collaboration and friendship between Brett and Stead that endured until Stead's death on the *Titanic* in 1912[9] and, during Stead's direction of the *PMG* (1883-1890), encompassed the "Chinese" Gordon tragedy in the Sudan, the "Truth about the Navy" agitation, the Anglo-Russian Penjdeh crisis, the Dilke-Crawford scandal, and the Parnell-Pigott affair. Not only did Brett use Stead and the *PMG* to put pressure on the ill-starred Gladstone government whenever (as Dilke later remarked) Brett thought the government was not doing what he believed was right but, as some contemporaries charged, to discredit certain persons and causes.[10]

Yet despite their markedly disparate social and cultural backgrounds (Stead, three years older than Brett, the almost self-educated son of a North Country Nonconformist parson and strongly attracted to women; Brett, sophisticated and bisexual), they developed a very firm respect and affection for each other.[11] Stead greatly admired Brett's "singularly well-balanced mind. . . ." and very often solicited Brett's advice before embarking on one of his many projects.[12] For his part, Brett always regarded Stead as "the most help-giving man" he had ever known." Sometimes they had strong differences of opinion, and there was much truth in Brett's oft-repeated admonishment to Stead that his "childlike faith . . . in the veracity of the average man . . . made him an easy dupe. . . ."[13] There was certainly something of this credulity in Stead's first involvement with Brett in the Gordon affair.

The dispatch of "Chinese" Gordon to the Sudan in January 1884 was quite the result of a conspiracy in the War Office, and Brett, "even to the extent of acting counter" to his chief, Hartington, was implicated in the intrigue and what occurred after Gordon's arrival in Khartoum.[14] Since first meeting Brett in 1880, Gordon had been greatly attracted to the young "Regy" and regularly visited him whenever he was in London.[15] Indeed, Brett was one of the first persons Gordon visited when, on his return from Palestine in late 1883, he was preparing to leave the army for employment as the Belgian king's proconsul in the Congo. It was a fortuitous moment, for the Gladstone government was beset by a crisis in the Sudan where Gordon had served as the Egyptian governor-general in the period 1876-1880. Thus, as the government prepared in September 1883 to abandon the Sudan following the Mahdist revolt and the defeat of an Anglo-Egyptian force, Brett and a War Office cabal, who opposed the abandonment of the Sudan, moved to use Gordon and a press agitation to compel Gladstone and the Foreign Office to do otherwise.[16] On the advice of Brett, Stead and the *PMG,* which had recently used "The Bitter Cry of Outcast London" exposé to move the Gladstone ministry to acknowledge at least the problem of working-class housing and had already called for the succor of the Sudan, became the chosen instruments for achieving the cabal's objectives.[17] Hence on January 8, 1884 Captain John H. Brocklehurst accompanied Stead to Southampton to interview Gordon.[18]

In the ensuing interview with Stead, Gordon (himself not averse to using the press to promote himself and his views) said exactly what Brett and his collaborators wanted to hear—that the abandonment of the Sudan to the Mahdi was unnecessary because the eastern Sudan could be held by the appointment of a governor-general with full power to relieve the Egyptian garrisons in the Sudan and to crush the Mahdist revolt. Stead's publication of the interview on January 9 with a special leader ("Gordon for the Sudan") urging the prompt dispatch of Gordon with power to implement what he proposed was a journalistic scoop quickly taken up by the metropolitan press with the desired result for Brett and his friends.[19] In spite of their misgivings, Gladstone and his foreign secretary, Lord Granville, bowed to the clamor and reluctantly agreed to send Gordon to the Sudan with vague instructions to give advice about the evacuation of Egyptian garrisons from the territory.[20] This was, of course, not what Brett and Stead had in mind.

Yet it was not until a week after Gordon left Cairo for Khartoum on January 26, 1884, that Brett first met Stead.[21] Until that time, his communications with Stead were through such intermediaries as Captain Brocklehurst. Several years later, Stead recalled that he had never received anything directly from Brett until a fortnight after his interview with Gordon, although "There would have been nothing dishonourable in receiving a hint from Brett, since every editor must seek information from all reliable sources. . . ."[22] In his first direct "Private and Confidential" communication to Stead on January 29, Brett conveyed the information that the War Office was demanding the removal of the Egyptian commandant in Khartoum and that *The Times* erred on the source of a new loan to Egypt.[23] On February 6 he approved of the *PMG*'s line on Egypt and the Sudan but urged that the public should be prepared for the possibility of Gordon's capture and the fall of Khartoum even before he reached the town.[24] Ten days later Brett reported (following a parley with Stead) that Gordon's messages were optimistic and that he promised to liberate the Sudan from the corrupt Egyptians by June 1 and urged that the *PMG* stress Egypt's financial difficulties.[25] Between February 19 and 29, in almost daily letters, Brett not only passed on the latest news from Egypt and the Sudan—including Gordon's reports to the War Office—but news of what was occurring in inner government circles and hints about what to emphasize in the *PMG*. He had some papers on Central Asia, Brett told Stead on February 23, which Stead might like to comment on more than he did in the previous issue of the *PMG*. On February 28 he advised that "a little genuine lauding of the P.M. at the expense of his nerveless colleagues will be useful to that scheme . . . we talked of the other day."[26] On March 1 Stead informed Brett that in accord with what they both believed would be best for Britain and the Sudan, he was "going strongly for Sarawaking . . . the Sudan" in the *PMG*. This meant urging the government to permit Gordon to establish himself as a quasi-independent ruler in the Sudan, with the view of using the Sudan to secure the southern frontier of a British-controlled Egypt, and to commit military support for the project.[27] These were the very things that the Gladstone government sought to avoid.

In March and most of April Stead, on the basis of a stream of information from Brett relative to what was occurring in Cabinet meetings,[28] continued (1) to press the government to authorize

Gordon to use the Egyptian garrisons to establish his authority in the Sudan and (2) to declare that the nation is obligated to rescue Gordon should he be trapped in Khartoum by Mahdist forces.[29] Inspired by Brett, Stead insisted that Gordon be empowered to organize a government in Khartoum and accused the government of pursuing a policy that Gordon deemed impossible, of refusing to permit Gordon to negotiate with the Mahdi and to protect his lines of communication, and of compelling Gordon to make use of the notorious slave dealer, Zebehr Pasha.[30] Nor were Gladstone and Granville the only targets of Brett, his friends, and Stead. When Brett took issue with his former patron, Sir William Harcourt, for declaring that Great Britain should withdraw from Egypt as well as the Sudan, Stead assailed Harcourt in the *PMG* with details provided by Brett. But most important to Brett was Gordon's situation (now besieged in Khartoum) and what the Gladstone government intended to do to rescue him. The position of Brett and General Sir Garnet Wolseley and his circle in the War Office, trenchantly presented in the *PMG,* was that contrary to Gladstone's assurances, Gordon was in great peril and that the government should move immediately to authorize and dispatch a relief expedition to save him.[31] In providing the material for such arguments "with just the right nuance for the effect intended,"[32] Brett cautioned Stead (as he often did) to conceal the source. Thus when communicating confidential information on May 1, he wrote: ". . . please do not let the source of it appear English. If you put it in the *P.M.G.* let it come from abroad. . . ."[33]

By the end of April, Gladstone had had enough of Stead's hectoring criticism. He had helped facilitate the conversion of the *PMG* from a Tory organ and Stead's translation from the Darlington *Northern Echo* to the *PMG* in 1880 and, following Stead's assumption of the editorial chair from John Morley in 1883, expected loyalty from Stead.[34] Through his secretary, Horace Seymour, Gladstone remonstrated to Stead against his critiques of the government's Sudan policy and especially his severe criticism of Cabinet ministers. In his reply (which he had shown to Brett), Stead told Seymour that "the position of apparent antagonism to Mr. Gladstone . . . [had] . . . been forced by the carelessness of some of his colleagues" and that his criticisms were motivated by a sincere desire to assist in saving the Gladstone ministry from "imminent disaster" in Egypt and the Sudan. Indeed, said Stead, the situation is sufficiently critical to justify even more strenuous language than I have ever used in the *PMG*. . . ."[35] When Seymour asked for more precise particulars, Stead (after conferring with Brett) replied that among "the most wanton mistakes that the Cabinet made" was the government's refusal to permit Gordon to meet with the Mahdi and "Sarawak" the Sudan.[36] This exchange did not improve relations between Stead and the Gladstone camp. As Brett continued to provide hints and "useful information,"[37] which Stead used further to belabor the government, Stead's relations with Gladstone reached the breaking point.[38]

At this point Brett, aware that some members of the Cabinet and their staffs were suspicious of his relationship with Stead and fearing that he and Stead were pressing the government too hard, sought to moderate Stead's tone and "to keep him on the Liberal side."[39] As Stead prepared to demand a completely "new departure" in foreign and imperial policies from the government in early June, Brett advised him not "to lay too much stress upon that point" and (on June 10) "to save as much as we can out of the fire . . . [and] . . . (1) to reopen friendly relations with Downing Street and especially Mr. G. and (2) . . . to grant an armistice for a few days, while we can consider and settle the right and wise course for the future."[40] Brett's advice was reinforced by Stead's assistant editor, Alfred Milner, who, following a long talk with a prominent member of the government, advised Stead to "Be gentle with the Govt., if you write on Egypt, . . . Gladstone is awfully cut up and sore at the way he has been abused."[41]

Brett now assumed the role of mediator between Stead and Gladstone to resolve a conflict for which in a large sense he was responsible. Because Stead's exchange with Horace Seymour had even worsened the *PMG*'s relations with the government, Gladstone had his son, Herbert, complain to Stead on June 10 against his "reckless" denunciations of the government's policy on Egypt and the Sudan and his failure to obtain "authentic information" about the situation from Downing Street.[42] He accused Stead of wreaking "immense harm" on the government by publishing "shadowy and unsubstantial" charges and demolishing "explanations favourable to the government. . . ."[43] In his immediate reply Stead declared that if the government desired to be defended by the *PMG*, it must take him into its confidence, hitherto withheld from him by the prime minister. Editors who write on government policy, said Stead, must be afforded data on which to form judgments, and because no information was forthcoming from Downing Street, he had to seek it from other sources.[44] Taking advantage of what seemed an invitation to obtain "authentic information at headquarters," Stead wrote to Herbert Gladstone on June 13 requesting verification of intelligence received by the *PMG* that the government had asked the Turks "to undertake the permanent pacification of the Soudan."[45] Herbert Gladstone firmly refused to render "categorical replies" to both this query and to another that followed it.[46] Profoundly irritated by Stead's cavalier tone, Herbert Gladstone replied (on June 17) that the information requested could serve no good object except "for the honour and glory of the P.M.G. . . ."[47] To these strictures Stead responded curtly that "It is impossible to remain silent when all your contemporaries [in the press] are discussing questions supposed to be before the Cabinet" and that if information is not available and forthcoming from the Prime Minister's office, then it must and will be obtained elsewhere.[48]

At this point, Brett, who was kept appraised by Stead of his "tremendous row" with the Gladstones, intervened "to pour oil on troubled waters."[49] On the day (June 17) that Stead wrote his reply to Herbert Gladstone, Brett met with the younger Gladstone and offered to endeavor "to get Stead to be more reasonable. . . ."[50] But before fulfilling his role as a reconciler, Brett reviewed the "problem" with Hartington and what might be done "to soften the acrimony of the *Pall Mall Gazette*. . . ." Noting that even Hartington had previously remarked that the government was badly "managing" the press, Brett blamed Downing Street for the present difficulty. Gladstone had now asked him and Herbert "to see whether terms . . . [could] . . . be arranged with Stead," and he (Brett) thought that something could be done, "though . . . not all at once, to get rid of this regular evening assault upon the Govt." "I have come to hear of a means which will . . . be effectual . . . ," he explained to Hartington, ". . . [and] . . . commits neither Mr. G. nor you, nor the Govt. . . . It is, however, most desirable that no one should . . . say that Stead has been 'squared' for if any statement of the kind were to come to his ears all attempts at conciliation would be . . . futile."[51] Meanwhile, Brett had informed Herbert Gladstone that "Stead might be induced to alter the tone which he had hitherto adopted," but because that might entail "considerable difficulty," he must have prior approval from Gladstone for what he might have to do.[52] On the same day that the Gladstones approved Brett's "plan," he spoke to Stead and secured his "reluctant" assent to "an armistice for some days . . . to . . . carefully consider" the consequences of the possible fall of the Gladstone government at this time.[53] Having obtained Stead's cooperation, Brett returned to Herbert Gladstone and asked the prime minister to make the following concessions: (1) not to attack the *PMG* in the House of Commons; (2) to "consent to throw the spell of his personality over Stead, by giving him an interview on some early date"; (3) that Herbert Gladstone, or Gladstone's principal secretary, Edward Hamilton, or both invite Stead to call and discuss "the question of the hour"; and (4) to apprise Stead of "any gross inaccuracies or misrepresentations" in the *PMG* or other papers and communicate "the true facts not necessarily for publication." "The rest," added Brett, "I will endeavour to do, but . . . Stead . . . must be given some . . . time to withdraw . . . from a . . . position of hostility to the Govt. *into which he has got* . . . as Stead is not the sort of man who would allow it to be said . . . that he had been squared. . . ."[54] Brett now told Stead: ". . . the strong regard I have for you is one of the strongest motives in endeavouring to prevent you from establishing yourself too irretrievably in a position which might become irksome and painful to you."[55] On the next day (June 19), as Stead assumed a more friendly stance toward the government, Brett remarked to him: "No line could be better than the one you have taken tonight. *Let us make our stand in a new position*. . . ."[56]

During the following six weeks, an uneasy truce prevailed as Stead, at the arrangement of Brett, called at Downing Street (June 21) for a talk with Hamilton and heeded Brett's advice to avoid asking questions "too blank" and searching.[57] Hamilton was pleased with Stead's professions of friendship and pledge to comment on Gladstone's most recent pronouncement on Egypt "in the most favourable light and to make it palatable. . . ."[58] But by July, Stead's relations with Downing Street began to fray again. In reply to a "friendly expostulation" from Horace Seymour, Stead impudently declared that Gladstone would never extricate himself from the Egyptian and Sudanese "morass" until he got rid of Lord Granville at the Foreign Office and the British proconsul in Egypt, Evelyn Baring, and repudiated their course for Egypt and the Sudan.[59] But on these points Stead was again reflecting Brett's views.[60] Indeed, even during Stead's absence on holiday in the first part of August, his locum, Alfred Milner, regularly consulted Brett.[61]

While the fate of Gordon hung in the balance and the government was increasingly troubled by other foreign problems and by intraparty dissension, Brett and Stead made things worse for Gladstone by helping to launch a "Navy Scare" and agitation during September 1884.[62] Although H. O. Arnold-Forster, not Brett, inspired Stead to embark on the "Truth about the Navy" agitation, with Captain John Fisher, Brett supplied a large part of the inside information that Stead used in his campaign and, as usual, gave advice about the strategy of what to say and when.[63] Stead always acknowledged Brett's role in the campaign and repeatedly stated that "Without the assistance of . . . Fisher . . . and Brett, 'The Truth about the Navy' would never have been written" and that "No man was more helpful . . . than . . . Brett . . . when the truth about the Navy was being told in the *Pall Mall Gazette*. . . ."[64] In fact, Brett not only provided confidential information but wrote articles for the *PMG* and "Behind the scenes . . . did much to ensure that the arguments of the naval critics struck home. . . ."[65] Like many of the young Liberals, Brett shared Arnold-Forster's dislike of Gladstone's negelect of the empire and its first line of defense. For the past two years, Arnold-Forster had published articles on the obsolescence and inadequacy of the Navy but was unable to arouse much public interest in the problem. Much impressed by Stead's "Gordon for the Soudan" campaign in the press, Arnold-Forster approached Stead in August 1884 to undertake the publication of some sensational revelations about the weaknes of the Navy.[66] After consulting Brett, who arranged for interviews with the Sea Lords at the Admiralty, Stead agreed to undertake the campaign provided he was given pertinent technical data. Following consultations with friends at the Admiralty, Brett suggested Fisher and helped facilitate meetings between Fisher (who

Brett did not personally meet until 1886) and Arnold-Forster and Stead. In several clandestine meetings with Stead, Fisher provided exactly what Arnold-Forster and Stead sought,[67] and following the publication of a preliminary article by Arnold-Forster in the *PMG* on August 14,[68] Stead published the first of a series on "The Truth about the Navy" (September 15-23). This was followed by two articles on "The Truth about our Coaling Stations" (October 16-17) and several leaders (including one by Brett) on what was needed to strengthen the Navy, which assailed the government for the neglect and weakness of the Senior Service.[69] The impact of the articles and leaders on the press and public opinion exceeded the expectations of Arnold-Forster, Stead, and Brett, and the ensuing agitation and panic became an acute embarrassment for the troubled Gladstone government during the latter part of September and October.[70]

During the remainder of September and the first two weeks of October, Brett kept his head low, contacting Stead only to prevent publication of an alleged libel by a discarded mistress of Leopold II against the Belgian king (with whom Brett had connections through his wife's family) and to admonish Stead for his "exaggerated belief in the superior virtue of women. . . ."[71] But on October 13 Brett informed Stead that as a result of their agitation, the government was preparing "to spend at once about half the sum which will be required" to modernize the Navy.[72] Displeased with such half-measures and by now in disfavor again at Downing Street, Stead, with Brett's assistance, approached the Tory party leadership and obtained assurances that they would press Gladstone to do more for the Navy.[73] At this point, however, Stead seems to have heeded Milner's advice on October 22 to ease up on Gladstone.[74] Hence while continuing to publish articles on naval reform, during November Stead concentrated on Egypt, the Sudan (where Gordon was besieged and an expeditionary force was on the way to rescue him), and the government's relations with Bismarck.[75] Brett, as a result of his friendship with Bismarck's son, Herbert, was quite active in influencing the *PMG*'s line on Anglo-German relations.[76] Thus on November 12 he told Stead that he had received "interesting" intelligence from Herbert Bismarck and "should be glad if you could see your way to write an article on . . . relations with Germany. . . ." emphasizing the merit of German proposals for a settlement with Britain on conflicting claims in west Africa and on the use of the Suez Canal.[77] When Stead proposed going to Berlin to interview either Herbert Bismarck or his father, Brett requested the younger Bismarck to receive Stead and advised him that "some hints privately . . . would guide . . . [Stead] . . . through the next few months. . . ." Herbert Bismarck declined but hoped that Stead and the *PMG* would continue to be "very useful, if he only will pursue the same course. . . ."[78] It was just as well that the interview did not materialize because Stead had to deal with such important issues as Wolseley's relief expedition to extricate Gordon and the maneuvers of Gladstone and the first lord of the admiralty, Lord Northbrook, to provide less than what had been demanded by the agitation for the Navy.

On November 25 Brett asked Stead to drop Egypt and the Sudan for the time being and to "fire some final shots . . . in the Admiralty and the War Office," emphasizing the irreducible minimum for the Navy; how money could be obtained to be spent on the Navy; and that the responsibility of the War Office and Hartington for the nation's defense is almost as great as that of the Admiralty and Northbrook and "to blow out of the water the doctrine . . . that putting our first line of defence into order is in any degree a threat or an irritant to foreign powers. . . ."[79] During the following two days, Stead duly published leaders that included almost all of Brett's points and blasted the government's response to the defense "emergency."[80] Five days later (November 30), Brett informed Stead that because "Nothing is finally decided in the Cabinet" on the naval estimates, Hartington and Northbrook "want a touch of the spur" and that it would make "a better appearance to give it to them both equally." Also, added Brett, "an article about Egypt . . . would be very useful tomorrow" to deny Bismarck's opposition to the British presence in Egypt and "to discount before-hand" any statements by Gladstone or his ministers that Britain's "speedy retirement" from Egypt is intended or possible.[81]

Basically, the Navy agitation ended on December 2, when Lord Northbrook announced for the reluctant government that in addition to ordinary naval estimates, £5,500,000 would be spent during the next five years on warship construction, naval ordnance, and coaling stations.[82] Although this was much less than what the *PMG* and the agitators had demanded, Brett and Stead hailed the campaign as "a great success." "You will be pleased to hear," Brett reported to Wolseley in the Sudan, "that by its resolute campaign, the Pall Mall Gazette has managed to get 5 millions out of the Govt. for the Navy. . . ."[83]

By this time, Brett was already suspected as the source of the leaks from the Cabinet to the *PMG*. Gladstone had expressed concern to Granville in early September about matters discussed in the Cabinet appearing in the *PMG*,[84] and two months later, in November, Sir Charles Dilke informed Edward Hamilton of his "well-founded suspicions as to where the Pall Mall gets its news. . . ." and complained to Hartington of Brett's "indiscretions."[85] Nothing, however, was done by Hartington, who depended on Brett to do much of his work and to provide political intelligence and gossip.[86] For Stead the success of the Navy agitation had exacerbated his relations with Downing Street. The Government again complained about his recent treatment of them but, fearing a catastrophe in the Sudan, sought to avoid completely alienating the powerful editor.[87]

During January 1885, Brett continued to feed material to Stead and to suggest what the *PMG* should say about foreign policy (pro-Bismarck) and the disunity in the Cabinet.[88] Then, on February 5, the government's much feared nightmare—the death of Gordon in Khartoum—became a reality when at 2.30 A.M. Brett personally brought the news from the War Office to Downing Street,[89] having also informed Stead of the event. Almost a week later, Stead asked Brett to review a special leader on Gordon, which was a stinging condemnation of the Gladstone ministry for the disaster, prior to its publication on February 11, 1885.[90] Stead also consulted Brett when he was preparing the *PMG* "*Extra*," "Too Late!," for publication as a pamphlet on February 19.[91] It was, as Brett told Wolseley, "a terrible indictment against the Govt." for failing to support and rescue Gordon.[92] To Stead he confided that he could hardly abide Gladstone's apparent indifference to Gordon's demise.[93]

Brett's differences with the Gladstone government, his leaks to Stead, and his use of the influential *PMG* made his departure from the government inevitable. The break occurred in late March 1885 when Brett's conduct was brought before the Cabinet by Dilke and Lord Selborne, and Hartington was constrained to request Brett's resignation.[94] Although his relationship with Dilke was henceforth strained, Brett remained friendly with Dilke's close collaborator, Joseph Chamberlain, who made no secret of his intense dislike of Stead to Brett and others.[95] Yet Brett (with Chamberlain's knowledge) provided Stead with a major "scoop" when, in a "secret" communication on May 20, he informed Stead of the resignations of Chamberlain and Dilke from the Gladstone Cabinet immediately after the event.[96]

During the Anglo-Russian Penjdeh crisis in the spring of 1885, Brett prudently took no part in Stead's vigorous defense of Russia and his efforts to avert war between Great Britain and Russia over the disputed Afghan frontier.[97] In the midst of the crisis, however, Brett protested privately to the editor of *The Times,* G. E. Buckle, for imputing base motives to Stead for his role in the Penjdeh affair.[98] Nor did Brett, who was campaigning to secure a new Parliamentary seat at Plymouth during the summer and fall of 1885, become involved in Stead's greatest crusade in the *PMG*—"The Maiden Tribute of Modern Babylon" agitation in July and August and its aftermath.[99]

On behalf of the efforts of groups concerned with white slavery and child prostitution to compel an indifferent Parliament to enact the pending Criminal Law Amendment Bill raising the age of consent for females to sixteen, Stead undertook a personal investigation of juvenile prostitution in London and published the results of his probe in a series of sensational articles in the *PMG* during early July 1885.[100] The public storm evoked by these revelations compelled the new Tory government (the Gladstone government had fallen on June 9) to approve the bill but proved somewhat embarrassing for Gladstone who, although widely known for his "rescue" work among London prostitutes, had done nothing to support the measure. While preparing his articles for publication, Stead confided to Brett that in his investigations of brothels he was "horrified" to learn that Gladstone had frequented many of them and that he was pondering whether to publish the evidence that he had amassed on Gladstone's activities or "to keep it all to himself." In communicating this information to his friend, Lewis Harcourt, to be passed on to Gladstone and his staff, Brett indicated that what Stead might do depended on the line that Gladstone would take on the Criminal Law Amendment Bill. Speculating that if Gladstone continued to do nothing to support the bill, Stead might portray him as defending prostitution or, conversely, if he took a strong stand for the measure, Stead could very well denounce the Grand Old Man as a hypocrite, Brett and Harcourt concluded that Gladstone should, on account of an alleged throat condition, be forbidden by his physician to speak and absent himself from London.[101] Meanwhile, during the week following the publication of Stead's revelations, Brett objected to the "unfair" allusions in the Maiden Tribute articles to "Princes of the Blood and prominent public men" as the worst offenders of sexual morality. Such statements, he told Stead, set "class against class" and "I appeal to your sense of what is fair . . . to publicly disclaim an impression which you have never intended to introduce."[102] Similarly, he wrote to Stead: "Please do not think I am concerned to defend the Prince of Wales or Mr. Gladstone. But I think it unfair . . . to mention or to hint at any better known individuals."[103] Henceforth and especially during his trial (October 23-November 13) for the alleged abduction of a minor during his investigations, Stead heeded Brett's objection and advice and remained silent on the "prominent persons" alluded to in the Maiden Tribute series.

When Stead was sentenced to three months' imprisonment, Brett worked with Stead's *PMG* colleagues and others (including the Earl of Carnarvon and Lord Randolph Churchill) to have him treated as a first-class misdemeanant.[104] Following the end of the electoral campaign in November, in which Brett failed to secure the Plymouth seat, he visited Stead in Holloway Gaol, assisted him in the preparation of the long essay on "Government by Journalism," and alerted him to Gladstone's decision to offer a Home Rule Bill for Ireland.[105] He advised Stead against continuing the Maiden Tribute investigations and, in this respect, told the acting editor of the *PMG*, E. T. Cook: "Stead has done good in the matter, . . . but we want him for other things besides Virgins. . . ."[106] Indeed, in some quarters, "it was generally believed that . . . [Brett] . . . was conducting the Pall Mall in Stead's absence. . . ."[107]

Following Gladstone's return to power in late November, Stead had written to him from jail "to offer . . . whatever journalistic service the *PMG* can render" and was pleased with Gladstone's reply (duly passed on to Brett) that he would be glad "If conscience and conviction . . . [could once more] . . . bring the Pall Mall and myself on the same lines at a critical moment. . . ."[108] But there could be no complete rapport between Gladstone and the *PMG* because neither Brett nor Stead could accept all of Gladstone's Irish Home Rule scheme and Brett was certainly less for Irish home rule than Stead.[109] Although Brett and Stead often disagreed about the Irish home rule issue and in their attitudes toward Chamberlain, Brett continued to provide information about both topics, which Stead almost always used in the *PMG.* Thus he kept Stead *au courant* on the planning, strategy, and prospects (he predicted failure) of Gladstone's first Irish Home Rule Bill and tried hard to persuade Stead to accept the line that Chamberlain and Hartington were taking on the issue.[110] "If you attack my position," Brett told Stead on March 15, 1886, "you will not offend me, and . . . I am . . . always open to conviction. But at present I am confident that the scheme is damnable. . . ."[111] Brett, however, was no more successful in changing Stead's position on Irish home rule then he was in altering Stead's attitude and conduct toward Charles Dilke in the Crawford divorce case and scandal.

When the Scottish M.P. Donald Crawford sued his wife, Virginia, for divorce and named Dilke as corespondent in the midst of the Maiden Tribute agitation in August 1885, Stead reported the affair as "A Great Social Scandal."[112] Although no major mention was made of the case in the *PMG* until January 1886,[113] Stead was much interested in the affair not only because it seemed to substantiate his "Maiden Tribute" allusions to upper class immorality and appealed to his intense interest in sex but because of his long-standing distrust of Dilke ("I never trust him further than I see him. . . .") and Dilke's close association with Chamberlain (who Stead loathed).[114] Immediately after the court decision on February 12 granting the divorce to Crawford on the grounds of his wife's adultery with Dilke but dismissing the case against Dilke, Stead charged that Dilke (still pleading innocence) had not cleared his name and by not testifying on his behalf, indicated that he was concealing something about his past.[115] He continued to harass Dilke, demanding that he resign as M.P. for Chelsea.[116] Dilke appealed to Brett to intervene: "If you have any weight with Stead, . . . do what you can to stop him. I am absolutely innocent. . . ."[117] Brett immediately wrote to Stead: "I beg of you—as a favour—not to return to the charge. You have had your say. Let the matter drop now. . . ."[118] A day later (February 17), Brett argued that Dilke had avoided cross-examination in the trial because he would have had to incriminate persons who were not involved in the case and again urged Stead to let "your goodness of heart . . . temper your zeal as a reformer."[119] But Stead would not desist and now charged that Chamberlain was responsible for Dilke's situation because he had wrongly advised Dilke not to testify and engaged in an acrimonious public exchange with Chamberlain in the *PMG*.[120] Meanwhile, Chamberlain, while denouncing Stead's "ruffianism" to Brett, urged Brett: "Do not give up Dilke. He stands in dire need of any . . . help you can render. . . ."[121] Privately, like his old friend Rosebery, Brett doubted Dilke's innocence and told Stead as much when, following his arrangement of a meeting between Stead and Lady Emilia Dilke on March 2, he confided to Stead that he did not believe that Dilke was innocent and that he doubted if anything could be done to salvage his political career.[122]

On the advice of his friend, Cardinal Manning, Stead had previously met with Lady Dilke and, in response to her plea for understanding and assistance, he had advised that Dilke break with Chamberlain and set the queen's proctor in motion for a second trial in which to disprove Mrs. Crawford's assertions.[123] Now, in their second meeting, Lady Dilke again implored Stead to desist, but he refused until Dilke had withdrawn from public life and proved his innocence in court.[124] Again, Dilke appealed to Brett to restrain Stead, and Brett promised: "I will do what I can. But you must know . . . how difficult it is to move him upon such a matter."[125] Brett, however, did nothing, and Stead continued to hound his quarry in and out of the *PMG*.[126] Dilke's defeat in the general election in early July was followed three weeks later (on July 23) by a verdict against him. In the conflict of evidence with Mrs. Crawford, Dilke had proved an unconvincing witness.[127] Stead now felt vindicated and to the end of his life remained convinced of Dilke's guilt. As for Brett, like others in London Society, he had already distanced himself from the ruined politician.

Brett's close association with Stead continued during the last three years (1886-1890) of his tenure at the *PMG*. With easy access to the leadership of both parties and important contacts on the Continent, during 1887-1888 Brett provided Stead with much news and gossip on the trials and tribulations of the Salisbury government, Gladstone's Irish Home Rule plans, the complicated negotiations (in which Brett served as a major intermediary) between the Liberals and Chamberlain and his cohorts in the Round Table Conference, and Bismarck's high diplomacy; contributed several anonymous articles (under the pseudonym "XIII") on political subjects; and wrote private commentaries for Stead on the impact of *PMG* leaders.[128] When Stead journeyed to Russia in May 1888 to interview the Tsar Alexander III, Brett supplied letters of introduction for Stead's visits en route in Paris and Berlin but failed with Herbert Bismarck, who refused to receive "the over-bearing, conceited, bad mannered brute."[129] Several months later, even Brett could not dissuade Stead from publishing, anonymously, a bitter attack on "The Bismarck Dynasty" in the *Contemporary Review*.[130]

Brett's last involvement with Stead on the *PMG* concerned the Pigott forgeries and the ensuing Parnell Commission in 1888-1889. In June 1886 Albert Grey told Brett that he had been approached by a person who offered to sell some letters that revealed the complicity of Charles Stewart Parnell with the Irish terrorists responsible for the Phoenix Park murders in 1882. Grey asked Brett whether Hartington might be interested in purchasing the documents, which purported to compromise Parnell and his party, for £1,000. According to Brett, he told Grey that "no prominent public men could . . . embark on transactions of that kind, but that it was otherwise with newspaper Editors. . . ." Apparently on Brett's advice, Grey contacted Stead and pledging him to the "utmost secrecy," arranged for Stead to meet the mysterious vendor of the documents in Grey's rooms at Dorchester House.[131] Here Stead met the Irish journalist, E. C. Houston, who told Stead that he could provide conclusive proof of Parnell's involvement in the Phoenix Park assassinations from a person in Ireland for £1,000 and a guarantee of the person's safety. Stead said that he lacked the money and suggested that the incriminating material might be offered to the wealthy anti-Parnellite *Times*—unaware that Houston had earlier (in March) offered the documents to the editor of *The Times*.[132] According to Stead, he did not know that Brett had previously been approached concerning a possible purchase of the materials by Hartington and therefore told Houston that he might query Brett as to whether Hartington would be interested in the matter.[133] Pledged to secrecy by Houston, Stead did not see him again until the proceedings of the Parnell Commission.

The letters were finally purchased and published by *The Times* under the rubric "Parnellism and Crime" (March 7-14, 1887).[134] In response to Parnell's demands, the government conceded a special commission to determine the authenticity of the letters in *The Times* series, and hearings were held from September 1888 to November 1889. Stead sought to avoid involvement in the probe, but despite his request to Brett "not to say anything publicly about the source of the *Times* forgeries," quite uncharacteristically, Brett revealed in a speech during late July 1887 that the letters had been offered for sale to Hartington and properly rejected.[135] "You will now be summoned before the Commission," Stead complained to Brett, "and you will bring me in. And I shall . . . refuse to say a word . . . and get sent to gaol."[136] And, as Stead had anticipated, he, Brett, and Grey were subpoenaed in early October. When Stead insisted that he felt bound by a pledge of secrecy not to reveal his conversations with Brett, Grey, and Houston, Brett questioned Stead's "ethical position" with the remark, "what higher obligation has man to man, than to help save his life or . . . reputation . . . ?"[137] Stead accepted Brett's logic but only after he had consulted Cardinal Manning who advised him that because he had never received the documents, Stead was in no way bound by "the contract of secrecy" with Houston and others and could tell what he knew to the commission.[138]

Stead and Brett were in Parnell's corner throughout the commission's proceedings; Stead, in spite of the misgivings of the *PMG*'s proprietor, staunchly supported Parnell and lashed *The Times* while Brett was providing him with much inside information on the commission's work.[139] As the tide began to turn in favor of Parnell when the author of the forgeries, Richard Pigott, broke under sharp cross-examination in late February 1889 and rendered a full confession,[140] Brett exulted to Stead: "Bravo Titus Oates Pigott. How excellent it all is. . . ."[141] Stead, however, felt sorry "for the old reprobate" and following Pigott's suicide, helped launch a fund for Pigott's children.[142] As Stead prepared to celebrate the vindication of Parnell following the verdict of the commission, Brett cautioned him: "I say don't shout till you are out of the wood. . . ."[143] The fall of Parnell within two years after his triumph substantiated Brett's caution especially when Stead turned on the "adulterer" Parnell with a vengeance that almost equaled his persecution of Dilke.[144]

Brett and Stead rendered good service to each other during the two decades after Stead's departure from the *PMG* to found and edit *The Review of Reviews.* As a confidant and adviser of the old queen and the prince of Wales, Brett (who succeeded his father as Lord Esher in 1899) declined to accept any official position in the government until Rosebery persuaded him to accept the commissioner of works post in 1895. Later, while serving Unionist and Liberal governments as chairman of important military reform committees and as a member of the Committee of Imperial Defence, Brett acted as a military and constitutional adviser to Edward VII and his heir. During these years, Stead often turned to Brett for advice, and Brett facilitated Stead's interview with the prince of Wales and subsequent defense of the prince's life-style, discreetly protected Stead during his vehement and almost seditious opposition to the Boer War, helped rescue Stead from financial ruin following the failure of his *Daily Paper* venture, and regularly provided Stead with political intelligence. For his part, Stead unreservedly supported and espoused Brett's interests and projects by publishing special articles in *The Review of Reviews* and other periodicals and in the daily press of Britain and the United States. Indeed, Brett had good reason to mourn Stead's death in 1912 as the loss of a faithful and devoted friend.[145]

Of course, Brett was not the only person to use the New Journalism to advance and promote his (or her) policies and projects, but few used the press so adeptly. The combination of great personal charm and ability, advantageous political and social connections, and, above all, the availability of Stead and the *PMG* made it all possible for Brett. But an essential factor in Brett's *modus operandi* was perhaps the maxim that he often repeated to his family: "The only thing in life is not to be found out. . . ."[146]

NOTES

1. Peter Fraser, *Lord Esher: A Political Biography* (London, 1973), p. 1. Hardly one-fourth of Fraser's study deals with Esher's career prior to 1900. For additional information on the life and career of Brett/Esher, see M. V. and Oliver Brett, eds. *Journals and Letters of Reginald Esher* (London, 1934-1938), 3 vols.; the biographical sketch in the *DNB, 1922-1930,* pp. 106-109; and James Lees-Milne, *The Enigmatic Edwardian. The Life of Reginald, 2nd Viscount Esher* (London, 1986). See also an interesting view of Brett/Esher by his daughters, the artist Dorothy Brett and Sylvia Brooke (the Ranee of Sarawak), in Sean Hignett, *Brett: From Bloomsbury to New Mexico. A Biography* (London, 1985), passim; and Sylvia Lady Brooke, *Queen of the Head Hunters. The Autobiography of . . . Sylvia Lady Brooke* (London, 1971), ch. i.

2. Wilfred Scawen Blunt, *Gordon at Khartoum: Being a Personal Narrative of Events* (London, 1911), p. 369; J. A. Spender, *Men and Things* (London, 1937), pp. 35-36.

3. Sir Edward Hamilton to Horace Seymour, 16 December 1883, Gladstone-Glynne MSS., Flintshire County Record Office. Hereafter cited as G-GM.

4. Memoirs, Sir Charles W. Dilke Papers, British Reference Library (BL), MSS. 43933, f. 189. Hereafter cited as DP.

5. Richard Hough, *Admiral of the Fleet: The Life of John Fisher* (New York, 1970), p. 80; and Sir Frederick Ponsonby, *Recollections of Three Reigns* (London, 1951), p. 129.

6. Fraser, *Esher,* pp. 1-2.

7. Ibid., pp. 3-38.

8. Ibid., p. 40. On the life and career of W. T. Stead (1849-1912), see Frederic Whyte, *Life of W. T. Stead* (London, 1924), 2 vols.; J. W. Robertson Scott, *Life and Death of a Newspaper* (London, 1952), chs. vii-xx; J. O. Baylen, "The New Journalism' in Late Victorian Britain," *Australian Journal of Politics and History,* XVIII (1972), 376-385; and Raymond Schults, *Crusader in Babylon: W. T. Stead and the Pall Mall Gazette* (Lincoln, Nebraska, 1972).

9. Grant Richards, who worked for Stead on the staff of *The Review of Reviews* during the early 1890s, later reminisced that Brett had "the most lively belief in 'W.T.S.' and 'W.T.S.' had the most lively belief in him. He brought such . . . secrets . . . as it suited the Prince of Wales's entourage that 'W.T.S.' should hear, and he brought high argument and much useful information from the Devonshire and Rosebery households. I don't think 'W.T.S.' ever made up his mind on any important matter till . . . Brett had had his say. . . ." [Grant Richards, *Memories of a Misspent Youth, 1872-1896* (London, 1932), pp. 130-131] Following Stead's death, Esher told their mutual friend, J. A. Spender: "That brilliant and fervent man. . . . He was . . . truly A MAN." [Esher to Spender, 17 April 1912, *Journals and Letters of Esher,* III, 87]. To Mrs. Stead Esher declared: "No one loved and admired your husband more than I. . . . He

was one of the very few honest, very single-minded and really good men I have ever known. There was nothing he ever undertook which he failed to talk over with me. . . ." Esher to Mrs. Emma Stead, 20 April 1912, Ibid., p. 89.

10. Memoirs, DP, BL Add. MSS. 43933, f. 190; Blunt, *Gordon*, pp. 369ff.

11. Stead was also a great favorite of Brett's children. [Brooke, *Autobiography*, p. 9.] On Brett's affinity for handsome young men, see Hignett, *Brett*, p. 22.

12. W. T. Stead, "Who is Lord Esher?," *The World's Work*, XVI (1910), 141-142. See also Richards, *Memories*, pp. 130-131; and *Journals and Letters of Esher*, III, 89.

13. Esher's memorial to Stead in *The Review of Reviews*, XLV (1912), 480.

14. Fraser, *Esher*, p. 43; Charles Chevenix Trench, *Charley Gordon. An Eminent Victorian Reassessed* (London, 1978), p. 198; John Marlowe, *Mission to Khartoum: The Apotheosis of General Gordon* (London, 1969), p. 57. In his diary on 18 January 1884, Dilke noted: "Cabal at the War Office as to Khartoum . . . decided to send . . . Gordon to . . . report on the Soudan. . . ." [Diary, DP, BL Add. MSS. 43942, f. 69] Similarly, Wilfred Scawen Blunt accused Brett of collusion with Stead in provoking a clamor in the press to compel the government to send Gordon to the Sudan. See Blunt, *Gordon*, p. 162; also Lytton Strachey's charges (based on Blunt's assertions) in the much flawed *Eminent Victorians* (London, 1928), p. 253.

15. See Esher's "General Gordon," *Nineteenth Century*, LXIII (1908), 926; Lord Esher, *The Tragedy of Lord Kitchener* (London, 1921), pp. 6-7; Gordon to Lord Ripon, 6 and 22 July 1880, 1st Marquess of Ripon Papers, BL Add. MSS. 43626, ff. 172-74 & 184-186; Fraser, *Esher*, p. 43; Marlowe, *Mission*, p. 57. Stead later wrote: "To me . . . Esher stands out chiefly conspicuous because he was the friend of . . . Gordon. No two more dissimilar men ever existed. . . ." W. T. Stead, "Viscount Esher," *Coming Men on Coming Questions*, ed. W. T. Stead (London, 1905), p. 465.

16. As early as 1882, it was suggested that Gordon be sent to the Sudan. See Mekki Shibeika, *British Policy in the Sudan, 1882-1902* (London, 1952), pp. 146-147.

17. See Stead's leaders and "Occasional Notes" on the crisis in the Sudan, published in the *Pall Mall Gazette* (hereafter cited as *PMG*), 20, 22, 23, and 27 November (Sir Samuel Baker on the possible use of Gordon in the Sudan); 3, 10, 20, and 27 December 1883; 5 January (on Gordon), 1884.

18. Marlowe, *Mission*, pp. 119, 126; Trench, *Charley Gordon, p. 196.*

19. *"Chinese Gordon on the Sudan" and "Chinese Gordon for the Soudan," PMG*, 9 January 1884, also 10-12 January 1884; and *The Times*, 14 January 1884.

20. Trench, *Charley Gordon*, pp. 198-200; Shibeika, *British Policy*, pp. 152ff.

21. Stead to Blunt, 30 October 1911, Wilfred Scawen Blunt Papers, Lytton Collection, Fitzwilliam Library, Cambridge; [W. T. Stead], "Books of the Month. More about General Gordon and the Men who sent him Out," *The Review of Reviews*, XLIV (1911), 508-509.

22. Ibid., 509.

23. Brett to Stead, 29 January 1884, W. T. Stead Papers, Churchill College Library, Cambridge. Hereafter cited as SP.

24. Brett to Stead, 6 February (also 7 February), 1884, Ibid.

25. Brett to Stead, 16 February 1884, Ibid.

26. Brett to Stead, 19, 23, 25, 27, 28, and 29 February, 1884, Ibid.

27. Stead to Brett, 1 March 1884, 2d Viscount Esher Papers, Churchill College Library. Hereafter cited as EP. See also Marlowe, *Mission*, p. 125; *PMG*, 1 March 1884; Stead to Brett, 5 March 1884, copy, SP.

28. See *PMG*, 17 March 1884; Stead to Brett, 17 March 1884, EP; also Fraser, *Esher*, p. 50.

29. Stead to Brett, 26 March 1884; Brett to Stead, 27 March 1884, copy, EP. See also *PMG*, 18, 26, 28, 29, and 31 March 1884.

30. *PMG*, 10 and 29 March, 6 April and 6 May 1884. See also entries for 10 and 29 March, 6 April, and 13 May 1884, in the A. M.Cook Diary, 4 January 1881-10 July 1884, Bodleian Library, Eng. misc. e.170.

31. Stead to Brett, 21 April 1884, copy, EP.

32. Fraser, *Esher*, p. 50.

33. Brett to Stead, 1 May 1884, copy, EP.

34. See Stead to J. A. Godley, 14 September 1880, and Godley's and Gladstone's notes on Stead's letter, W. E. Gladstone Papers, BL Add. MSS. 44303, ff. 335-336. Hereafter cited as GP.

35. Stead to Harace Seymour, 26 April 1884, G-GM.

36. Stead to Seymour, 11 May 1884, Ibid.

37. See Brett to Stead, 19 May 1884, and Lord Rosebery to Stead, 20 May 1884, SP; Stead to Brett, 23 May 1884, EP.

38. Thus Gladstone remarked to Stead's confidante, Olga Novikov: "I am probably angry about Stead, but less angry than sorry. I do not forget his service to the cause of right. . . ." [Gladstone to Olga Novikov, 12 June 1884, in W. T. Stead, ed. and comp. *The M.P. for Russia: Reminiscences and Correspondence of Madame Olga Novikoff* (London, 1909), vol. II, p. 136.] She replied that "the poor fellow must be at this moment greatly sorry and distressed. . . ." [Olga Novikov to Gladstone, 12 June 1884, GP, BL Add. MSS. 44268, f. 292.] Later in commenting on Gladstone's remark, Stead declared that "The sorrow and anger were reciprocal, . . ." but he regretted that he had then not known that Sir Evelyn Baring, rather than Gladstone, should bear the major responsibility for Gordon's death. See Stead, *M.P. for Russia*, vol. II, p. 136.

39. Fraser, *Esher*, p. 50. As early as December 1883 Edward Hamilton and Horace Seymour regarded Brett as a ubiquitous intriguer. Thus Hamilton told

Seymour that Brett is "a very clever shrewd fellow [who] has wormed himself into the confidence ... of Hartington ... Harcourt and Dilke. ..." Hamilton to Seymour, 16 December 1883, G-GM.

40. Stead to Brett, 6 June 1884, copy, SP; Brett to Stead, 8 and 10 June 1884, copies, EP.

41. Alfred Milner to Stead, [June 1884], SP.

42. See Sir Charles Mallet, *Herbert Gladstone: A Memoir* (London, 1932), p. 101; 10 June 1884, Herbert Gladstone Diaries, G-GM; also Stead to Herbert Gladstone, 13 June 1884, Herbert Gladstone Papers, BL Add. MSS. 46050, f. 236. Hereafter cited as HGP.

43. H. Gladstone to Stead, 10 June 1884, as quoted in Mallet, *Herbert Gladstone*, pp. 101-102. This communication is neither in the Herbert Gladstone Papers nor in the Stead Papers.

44. Ibid., 102. This letter is neither in the HGP nor the SP.

45. Stead to H. Gladstone, 13 June 1884, HGP, BL Add. MSS. 46050, ff. 236-237.

46. 14 June 1884, H. Gladstone Diaries, G-GM; Stead to H. Gladstone, 16 June 1884, HGP, BL Add. MSS. 46050, ff. 240-241; Mallet, *Herbert Gladstone*, p. 102.

47. H. Gladstone to Stead, 17 June 1884, copy, HGP, BL Add. MSS. 46050, ff. 243-247.

48. Stead to H. Gladstone, 17 June 1884, Ibid., f. 242.

49. Concerning his letters from the Gladstones, Stead told Brett: "G.O.M. says I am a liar and a traitor, the most mischievous man in the country, and that I may ... upset the Govt. ... I say that he and his people would not tell me what was going on, that I must therefore get to know elsewhere ... that I hope to rescue the Country from a great danger and that he has only himself to blame if the Govt. is endangered. ... I wrote the leader in reply to Herbert ... as a conciliatory overture to the G.O.M. But my conciliatory efforts ... don't seem to conciliate. ..." Stead to Brett, 14 June 1884, EP.

50. 17 June 1884, H. Gladstone Diaries, G-GM; Mallet, *Herbert Gladstone*, p. 102; 18 June 1884, Esher Journal, 1881-1884, EP.

51. Brett to Hartington, 18 June 1884, copy, in Esher Journal, 1881-1884, EP.

52. 18 June 1884, Esher Journal, 1881-1884, EP; Brett to H. Gladstone, 18 June 1884, HGP, BL Add. MSS. 46050, f. 250.

53. 18 June 1884, Esher Journal, 1881-1884, EP.

54. Brett to H. Gladstone, 18 June 1884, HGP, BL Add. MSS. 46050, ff. 248-249, my italics; also copy in Esher Journal, 1881-1884, EP. Three days later, Herbert Gladstone informed Brett that his father "readily assents on the two points. ..." H. Gladstone to Brett, 21 June 1884, EP.

55. Brett to Stead, 18 June 1884, copy, EP.

56. Brett to Stead, 19 June 1884, SP, my italics. In his diary, Edward Hamilton noted: "Stead . . . appears to be desirous to extend his hand to the Government. . . ." 20 June 1884, Sir Edward Hamilton Diaries, Sir Edward W. Hamilton Papers, BL Add. MSS. 48636, vol. VII. Hereafter cited as EWHP. Also Dudley W. R. Bahlman, ed., *The Diary of Sir Edward Hamilton, 1880-1885* (Oxford, 1972), vol. II, p. 640. For a succinct comment on the Stead-Gladstone conflict and Brett's role in the affair, see Stephen Koss, *The Rise and Fall of the Political Press in Britain:* vol. I. *The Nineteenth Century* (London, 1981), pp. 258-259.

57. Brett to Stead, 20 June 1884, copy, EP.

58. Hamilton to Seymour, 21 June 1884, G-GM.

59. Stead to Seymour, 8 July 1884, Ibid.

60. See Brett to Stead, 3 August 1884, EP.

61. Milner to Stead, 3, 5, 6, and 7 August 1884, SP.

62. A recent study of the Victorian press asserts that the "Truth about the Navy" campaign is more an example of "the efficiency of a lobby . . . than the power of the press. . . ." See Lucy Brown, *Victorian News and Newspapers* (Oxford, 1985), p. 189. On the naval agitation of 1884, see Arthur J. Marder, *British Naval Policy, 1880-1905: The Anatomy of British Sea Power* (London, 1940), pp. 121-122; Hough, *Fisher,* pp. 80-84; F. W. Hirst, *The Six Panics and Other Essays* (London, 1913), pp. 41-58; Whyte, *Stead,* vol. II, ch. vii; Harvey Blumenthal, "W. T. Stead's Role in Shaping Official Policy: The Navy Campaign of 1884," Ph.D. dissertation, George Washington University, 1985.

63. Although a recent biographer of Admiral Fisher states that "it is not clear that [Brett] contributed anything substantial to the ["Truth about the Navy"] articles in the *PMG* [Ruddock F. Mackay, *Fisher of Kilverstone* (Oxford, 1973), p. 179], another biographer of Fisher takes an opposite view [*Hough, Fisher,* pp. 80-81]. In his study of Brett/Esher, Fraser asserts that he "played his full share" in the agitation [p. 52]. During this time, Brett's close friend, L. V. (Loulou) Harcourt, was convinced that Brett was not only involved in the agitation but might have written the "Truth about the Navy" articles for the *PMG* [14 November 1884, L. V. Harcourt Diary, L. V. Harcourt Papers, Bodleian Library]. Writing in 1904 about the Navy campaign in 1884, Stead declared that "Fisher and . . . Brett helped independently of each other. . . ." [Stead quoted in Henry Stead, "Admiral Lord Fisher," *The Review of Reviews for Australia,* XLIV (1914), 1010.] On Brett's role in the agitation, see also Esher to Fisher, 20 April 1912, Admiral Lord Fisher Papers, 569, Duke of Hamilton Collection, also in *Journals and Letters of Esher,* vol. III, 88; Esher to Fisher, 21 July 1918, in Arthur J. Marder, ed. *Fear God and Dread Nought: The Correspondence of Admiral of the Fleet Lord Fisher of Kilverstone* (London, 1953-1956), vol. III, 546; Fisher's remarks in his memorial to Stead in *The Review of Reviews,* XLV 494. Yet Brett later wrote that "Between them they [Fisher and Stead] initiated

and conducted in the *Pall Mall Gazette* . . ." the campaign to modernize and strengthen the Royal Navy. Esher, *Tragedy of Lord Kitchener*, p. 6.

64. Stead, "Viscount Esher," *Coming Men on Coming Questions*, 469; and "Who is Lord Esher?" *The World's Work*, XVI (1910), 142; also Stead as quoted in Henry Stead's "My Father, . . . II," *The Review of Reviews for Australia*, XLII (1913), 356.

65. Fraser *Esher*, 52. See also R. B. Brett, "The Responsibility of the Navy," *PMG*, 29 September 1884.

66. Cf. May Arnold-Forster, *The Right Honourable Hugh Oakeley Arnold-Forster: A Memoir* (London, 1910), pp. 54-61; Whyte, *Stead*, vol. II, pp. 146-147.

67. See W. T. Stead, "Character Sketch: Admiral Fisher," *The Review of Reviews*, XLI (1910), 115ff; Whyte *Stead*, vol. II, p. 150; Hough, *Fisher*, pp. 81ff; Marder, *British Naval Power*, p. 121 and n.; Taprell Dorling, *Men O'War* (London, 1929), p. 227.

68. H. O. Arnold-Forster, "More Ships for the Navy," *PMG*, 14 August 1884.

69. See the various leaders and "Occasional Notes" on the Navy in *PMG*, 15, 19, 20, 22, 23, 24, 25, 26, 27, and 30 September, 9, 14, 16, 17, 21, 22, and 25 October, 6, 12, 13, 14, 26, and 27 November, 3 and 8 December 1884.

70. See Hough, *Fisher*, p. 81; Marder, *British Naval Power*, pp. 121-122; Hirst, *Six Panics*, p. 52. Three days after the publication of the first article, Stead told Brett that he regretted not "having fired my first shot" many months before. Stead to Brett, 18 September 1884, EP.

71. Brett to Stead, 2 October 1884, SP. Eleanor Brett was the daughter of the Belgian ambassador in London and confidant of the Belgian royal family, Sylvain van de Weyer. See Fraser, *Esher*, p. 15; and Hignett, *Brett*, p. 11.

72. Brett to Stead, October 13, 1884, SP.

73. Stead to Brett, 22 October 1884, EP.

74. "I don't think I should declare war against Gladstone anent the navy. . . ." Milner to Stead, 24 October 1884, SP.

75. See Brett to Stead, 8 November 1884, copy, EP, and 11 November 1884, SP.

76. Fraser, *Esher*, p. 53.

77. Brett to Stead, 12 November 1884, copy, EP.

78. Herbert Bismarck to Brett, 24 November and 5 December 1884; Brett to Bismarck, 28 November 1884, copy, Ibid. See also Stead's leader on "Anglo-German Policy in Africa," *PMG*, 14 October 1884.

79. Brett to Stead, 25 November 1884, copy, EP.

80. "A Test of Backbone," and "Inside the Admiralty," *PMG*, 26 and 27 November 1884. "I thought today's article very good and I trust it will do some good. . . ." Brett to Stead, 26 November 1884, SP.

81. Brett to Stead, 30 November 1884, copy EP. See also Brett to Stead, 1 December 1884, copy, Ibid.; and leaders and notes in the *PMG*, 1 and 2 December 1884.

82. Marder, *British Naval Power*, pp. 122-123.

83. Stead to General Sir Garnet Wolseley, 5 December 1884, copy, EP.

84. See Gladstone to Lord Granville, 5 September 1884, 2d Earl Granville Papers, P.R.O. 30/29/29A; Granville to Gladstone, 7 September 1884, GP, BL Add. MSS. 44177, f. 88; also reproduced in Agatha Ramm, ed. *The Political Correspondence of Mr. Gladstone and Lord Granville, 1876-1886* (London, 1962), vol. II, pp. 248-249.

85. Dilke to Hamilton, [November 1884], EWHP, BL Add. MSS. 48624; 19 November 1884, Memoirs, DP, BL Add. MSS. 43938, vol. LXV, p. 304; and Add. MSS. 43939, vol. LXVI, p. 48.

86. For example, see Brett to Hartington, 1 January 1885, copy, EP; and *Journals and Letters of Esher*, I, passim. Wilfred Scawen Blunt was convinced that the "clever, but unprincipled . . . [Brett] . . . manages all Hartington's intrigues for him with the press" and that "Brett and Stead are the two he works through most. . . ." Diary, 30 January 1885, in Blunt, *Gordon*, p. 369.

87. Stead to Seymour, 31 December 1884, G-GM; 2 and 5 January 1885, Hamilton Diaries, EWHP, BL Add. MSS. 48638, vol. IX, pp. 107, 112; Hamilton to Granville, 5 January 1885, Granville Papers, PRO 30/29/129.

88. Brett to E. T. Cook, 23 and 26 January 1885, Sir Edward Tyas Cook Papers (courtesy Mr. Robin Duff); Brett to Stead, 25 and 27 January, 2 February 1885, SP.

89. 5 February 1885, Hamilton Diaries, EWHP, BL Add. MSS. 48639, vol. X, p. 37.

90. Stead to Brett, 9 and 10 February 1885, EP; *PMG*, 11 February 1885.

91. "Too Late!" *Pall Mall Gazette "Extra,"* no. 14 (19 February 1885), 32 pp.

92. Brett to Wolseley, 26 February 1885, *Journals and Letters of Esher*, vol. I, p. 109.

93. Brett to Stead, 20 February 1885, SP.

94. Memoirs, DP, BL Add. MSS. 43933, f. 190; 28 January 1885, Diary, Ibid., Add. Mss. 43939, f. 48; also Gladstone to Hartington, 23 March 1885, 8th Duke of Devonshire Papers, Chatsworth, 2nd Series, 340.1697. Fraser makes no mention of the real reason for Brett's resignation. See Fraser, *Esher*, p. 56.

95. Chamberlain to Brett, 14 April 1885, EP. On the Chamberlain-Brett friendship, see Fraser, *Esher*, p. 56.

96. Brett to Stead, 20 May 1885, SP; see also *PMG*, 22 May 1885. On Stead's activities during the Penjdeh crisis, see Baylen, "The 'New Journalism,' " pp. 380-382.

97. See *PMG*, 4, 5, 12, 27, 30, and 31 March, 11, 20, and 24 April, 4 and 30 May 1885.

98. Brett to G. E. Buckle, 5 April 1885, Archives of *The Times;* also copied in Brett's Journal, 1885-1886, EP.

99. On the "Maiden Tribute of Modern Babylon" agitation, see Ann Strafford, *The Age of Consent* (London, 1964); Deborah Gorham, "The 'Maiden Tribute of Modern Babylon' Re-Examined: Child Prostitution and the Idea of Childhood in Late Victorian England," *Victorian Studies*, XXI (1978), 350-379; Judith M. Walkowitz's *Prostitution and Victorian Society: Women, Class, and the State* (New York, 1979); and "Male Vice and Feminist Virtue: Feminism and the Politics of Prostitution in Nineteenth Century Britain," *History Workshop*, no. 13 (Spring 1982), 77-93; and Baylen, "The 'New Journalism,' " pp. 382-384.

100. See *PMG*, 6-10 July 1885.

101. 19 July 1885, L. V. Harcourt Diary, 8 July-21 August 1885, L. V. Harcourt Papers, Bodl. dep. 371.

102. Brett to Stead, 15 July 1885, copy, in Esher Journal, 1885-1886, EP.

103. Brett to Stead, 15 July 1885 (second letter on this date), copy, in Ibid.

104. Cook to Brett, 12 November 1885, EP; Lord Randolph Churchill to Sir Richard Cross, 11 November 1885, Viscount Richard Cross Papers, BL Add. MSS. 51274, pp. 131-132.

105. Stead to Brett, 16 November, 1, 6, and 21 December 1885, EP; Cook to Stead, 11 December 1885, Frederic Whyte Collection, University of Newcastle Library. See W. T. Stead, "Government by Journalism," *Contemporary Review*, XLIX (1886), 653-674.

106. Cook to Stead, [January 1886], Whyte Collection.

107. 12 January 1886, L. V. Harcourt Diary, 3-24 January 1886, L. V. Harcourt Papers, Bodl. dep. 376.

108. Stead to Gladstone, 17 December 1885; Gladstone to Stead, 18 December 1885, copy, GP, Add. MSS. 44493, ff. 361, 364-365; Stead to Brett, 21 December 1885, EP.

109. 12 January 1886, L. V. Harcourt Diary, 3-24 January 1886, L. V. Harcourt Papers, Bodl. dep. 376. See also Fraser, pp. 56-57.

110. 8 and 15 March 1886, Stead Journal, SP.

111. Brett to Stead, 15 March 1886, Ibid.

112. *PMG*, 8 August 1885.

113. Ibid., 11 January 1886.

114. See W. T. Stead, "Character Sketch: Sir Charles W. Dilke," *The Review of Reviews*, VI (1892), 135.

115. *PMG*, 13 February 1886.

116. Ibid., 15 and 16 February 1886.

117. Dilke to Brett, 16 February 1886, EP.

118. Brett to Stead, 16 February 1886, SP.

119. Brett to Stead, 17 February 1886, SP. Meanwhile Brett was advising Dilke to "unobtrusively appear" in the House of Commons and perhaps go to Italy for his health. Brett to Dilke, 19 February 1886, copy, Esher Journal, 1885-1886, EP.

120. *PMG*, 20, 22, 23, 24, 26, and 27 February 1886.

121. Chamberlain to Brett, 25 February 1886, EP. Chamberlain sent a copy of this letter to Dilke. See DP, BL Add. MSS. 49612A, f. 38.

122. Memorandum, 24 February 1886, Esher Journal, 1885-1886, EP; 26 February 1886, L. V. Harcourt Journal, 24 January-5 March 1886, L. V. Harcourt Papers, Bodl. dep. 377; 2 March 1886, Stead Journal, SP.

123. 23 February 1886, Ibid.; Betty Askwith, *Lady Dilke: A Biography* (London, 1969), p. 151; also 26 February 1886, L. V. Harcourt Journal, 24 January-5 March 1886, L. V. Harcourt Papers, Bodl. dep. 377.

124. 2 March 1886, Stead Journal, SP.

125. Dilke to Brett, 25 March 1886; and Brett to Dilke, 30 March 1886, copy, EP; Dilke to Brett, 31 March 1886, copy, DP, BL Add. MSS. 49612A, f. 66; Dilke to Brett, 1 April 1886, EP.

126. Stead even interviewed the witnesses and obtained statements from all but one of the witnesses who had been subpoenaed and not called to testify. See Dilke to Brett, 1 April 1886, EP.

127. See *PMG*, 21 and 24 July 1886. On the second trial, see Jenkins, *Dilke*, chs. xiii and xiv; and Askwith, *Lady Dilke*, ch. xvi. Not long after her divorce, Mrs. Crawford was befriended by Stead who employed her on the *PMG* and later on *The Review of Reviews* and his short-lived *Daily Paper* [See Scott, *Life and Death of a Newspaper*, p. 82 and n.]. On Stead's vehement opposition to Dilke's return to political life in 1891-1892, see Stead, "Dilke," *The Review of Reviews*, VI (1892), 135ff.

128. For example, see Brett to Stead, 5, 11, 15, 17, 21, and 26 January; 4 February 1887; 10 April; 27 June; 24 August; and 27 October 1888; 16 February; and 13 September 1889, SP; Stead to Brett, 17 June and 24 August 1888, EP. See article by "XIII" on Gordon's scheme for a "Secret Society" to promote Imperial concerns, in *PMG*, 22 February 1889. On Brett's role at the Round Table Conference, see Fraser, *Esher*, p. 64; and Michael Hurst, *Joseph Chamberlain and Liberal Reunion. The Round Table Conference 1887* (London, 1967) passim.

129. See Edward B. Malet to Brett, Berlin, 2 May 1888; and Herbert Bismarck to Brett, 2 May 1888, EP; Malet to Lord Salisbury, 9 February 1889, 3rd Marquess of Salisbury Papers, Hatfield House, A/62.

130. [W. T. Stead], "The Bismarck Dynasty," *Contemporary Review*, LV (1889) 157-78; also Malet to Salisbury 9 February 1889, Salisbury Papers, A/62; 9 February 1889, Carnarvon Diary, 4th Earl of Carnarvon Papers, BL

Add. MSS. 60932; Bramwell Booth to Stead, 15 February 1889, and Flora Shaw to Stead, 20 February 1889, SP.

131. Brett to Hartington, 21 February 1889, Hartington/8th Duke of Devonshire Papers, 340.2210; W. T. Stead, "Character Sketch. Mr. Charles S. Parnell," *The Review of Reviews*, I (1890), 104. Grey's version of the story was somewhat different from that of Brett and Stead. Thus he wrote to Brett: ". . . You seem to think Stead was only dragged into the affair after our conversation took place in *consequence* of Stead's communication to me. According to my recollection, . . . Stead told me a mysterious offer had been made to him . . . [of the documents]. . . ." Albert Grey to Brett, 2 November 1888, EP.

132. See Stead's detailed account of his meeting with Houston in Stead, "Character Sketch: . . . Parnell," 104ff; and what he later told Lord Carnarvon in the Carnarvon Diary, 14 February 1889, Carnarvon Papers, BL Add. MSS. 60932, f. 25. Historians of *The Times* are incorrect in asserting that Houston offered the Pigott letters to Stead *before* approaching Buckle. See Stead's account in his "Character Sketch: . . . Parnell," 106, and compare with *The History of The Times: The Twentieth Century Test, 1884-1912* (London, 1947), p. 64; Oliver Woods and James Bishop, *The Story of The Times* (London, 1983) p. 137; and W. D. Bowman, *The Story of The Times'* (London, 1931), pp. 288-291.

133. Stead, "Character Sketch: . . . Parnell," 106. See also Stead's remarks on why he spurned the Pigott letters in Stead to Sir Robert Morier, 8 October 1888, Sir Robert Morier Papers, Balliol College Library. Houston tried to contact Hartington who refused to have anything to do with him or the letters. See F. S. L. Lyons, *Charles Stewart Parnell* (London, 1977), p. 370.

134. On the purchase and publication of the Pigott forgeries, see Woods and Bishop, *Story of The Times*, pp. 136-141; and especially T. W. Moody, "The Tories versus Parnell and Co., 1887-1890," *Historical Studies*, VI (London, 1968), 147-175; and Stead's burlesque of the "Parnellism and Crime" series in the *PMG*, 10 May 1887.

135. Stead to Brett, 10 July 1888, EP; Stead, "Character Sketch: . . . Parnell," 106.

136. Stead to Brett, 24 July 1888, EP. Stead complained to Albert Grey: "I was very much put out by his making the speech because it brought me into it and you also. He ought not to have done it without consulting us. . . ." Stead to Albert Grey, 15 October 1888, 4th Earl Grey Papers, Department of Paleography, University of Durham.

137. Stead to Morier, 8 October 1888, Morier Papers; Stead to Grey, 8 October 1888, copy; and Grey to Stead, 13 October 1888; Brett to Stead, 17 October 1888, SP.

138. Stead to Brett, 22 October 1888, EP.

139. For example, see *PMG*, 16, 23, 27, and 28 February, 30 April and 22 July 1889; and Yates Thompson to Stead, 21 February 1889; Stead to Thompson, 21 February 1889; Thompson to Stead, 22 and 28 February 1889, SP.

140. Lyons, *Parnell,* pp. 420-422.

141. Brett to Stead, 22 February 1889, SP.

142. Stead to Lady Aberdeen, 23 February 1889, 1st Marquess of Aberdeen Papers, Public Archives of Canada; Henry Labouchere to Stead, 9 March 1889, SP.

143. 24 November 1889, Esher Journal, 1886-1890, EP.

144. Yet, as L. W. Brady notes, the vindication of Parnell seemed to be "justified by the extraordinary coming together of politics and journalism" and demonstrated the verity of Stead's and Brett's prognostications on "Government by Journalism." See L. W. Brady, *T. P. O'Connor and the Liverpool Irish* (London, 1983), p. 112.

145. See Spender, *Men and Things,* p. 26.

146. See Dorothy Brett's comments on her father as quoted in Hignett, *Brett,* p. 32.

7

John Goodbody

The *Star:*
Its Role in the Rise of the
New Journalism

". . .we have to consider the new voters, the democracy as people are fond of calling them. They have many merits, but among them is not that of being, in general, reasonable persons who think fairly and seriously. We have had opportunities of observing a new journalism which a clever and energetic man has lately invented. It has much to recommend it. It is full of ability, novelty, variety, sensation, sympathy, generous instincts; its one great fault is that it is feather-brained. Well the democracy, with abundance of life, movement, sympathy, good instincts, is disposed to be like this journalism, feather-brained."[1] Arnold's assault on the New Journalism as practiced by W. T. Stead in the *Pall Mall Gazette* preceded by almost a year the first edition of the *Star* in 1888. But the criticism would have been even more relevant to the *Star*, another London evening newspaper, because unlike the *Pall Mall Gazette*, the *Star* was aimed at a mass readership. Indeed, the *Star* was the first daily paper in Great Britain of what was termed the New Journalism, which was designed to be read by large numbers rather than the educated few.

Between 1888 and 1891, the *Star* occupied a unique position in the history of morning and evening newspapers: a daily London paper, dominant in circulation, which at the same time promoted radical socialism. The period was brief. Under proprietorial pressure the newspaper shifted its stance to align itself with the Liberal party. Yet the *Star's* significance in newspaper history remains not only because it anticipated the rise of popular journalism, whose leading proponent was to be Northcliffe, the proprietor beginning in 1894 of the *Evening News,* which was to be the chief rival of the *Star* and ultimately, in 1960, to take it over. We will see how the *Star* in its earliest days differed from other popular newspapers in its journalistic approach and philosophy. The *Star* at that stage was not the vehicle of commercial enterprise that it became with Northcliffe's arrival and has subsequently been the rule in British newspapers.

The remarkable early growth of the *Star* was, of course, the result of many of the factors that are familar to observers of late nineteenth-century newspaper history. In Britain there was a drop in the number of working hours, allowing more opportunity for reading;[2] technical innovations such as rotary machines and the Hattersley machines;[3] a higher standard of living, which benefited advertising;[4] the abolition of advertisement, stamp and paper duties (1853, 1855, 1861); and the passing of the Companies Act (1856).[5] In London in particular the tradition of buying street literature and the spread of transport aided circulation and allowed more people to read newspapers while they commuted.[6]

There was also the general effect of the 1870 Education Act. It has been argued that the conditions in which the New Journalism was able to flourish in Britain were not unduly affected by the act because there were already sufficient numbers of readers to make an extension of the newspaper public a viable entity. There are two important qualifications to this argument, however. First, until 1870, the areas of Great Britain, which were most difficult to provide for in any voluntary system of education, had high concentrations of literacy. The passing of the act ensured that the number of literate people in those areas would increase. Second, it was not necessarily the result of the act that was important. It was rather that the act focused entrepreneurial attention on the reservoir of public literacy that was available. Max Pemberton recalls Northcliffe saying about Sir George Newnes and *Tit-Bits:* "The Board Schools are turning out hundreds of thousands of boys and girls who don't care for the ordinary newspaper. They'll read anything that is simple and sufficiently interesting. The man who has produced this *Tit-Bits* has got hold of something bigger than he imagines. We shall try to get in with him."[7] Given all these factors, conditions were eminently suitable for the launching of an evening newspaper aimed at a different readership from those people who already bought either the penny newspapers or even existing halfpenny newspapers such as the *Echo* and the *Evening News.*

The *Star* owed a debt to the *Pall Mall Gazette* both for its handling of editorial content and layout—the combination of which was termed the New Journalism. Whereas the *Pall Mall Gazette* was in Stead's words "the paper which was read by the political and litaerary classes," the *Star* was aimed at a less socially elevated readership[8] The fact that its typography both reflected and reinforced the radical social concerns and lively reporting of dramatic events made the publication of the *Star* so significant. The *Star's* own handling of this material acknowledged that there was a wider reading public than the *Pall Mall Gazette* could reach. Stead himself recognized the role of the *Star's* first editor, T. P. O'Connor, when he wrote: "He and I may fairly claim to have revolutionized English journalism . . . we broke the older tradition and made journalism a living thing, palpitating with actuality, in touch with life at all points."[9]

Some of Stead's techniques were not original. His use of interviews had been employed before in Great Britain by Henry Mayhew and William Howard Russell and particularly in American newspapers. The insertion of maps followed *The Times'* example during the 1870 Franco-Prussian War. His insistence on signed articles was not new. Yet a radical campaigning approach and lively writing and layout were unprecedented as a combination. Stead was also the first editor to employ maps and cartoons on a regular basis, showing how they could enhance makeup. He published 134 interviews in 1884 alone and copied *Tit-Bits* by holding competitions.[10] He published daily puzzles stating: "It is the duty of an evening newspaper not only to instruct and advise but also to amuse."[11] He ran the celebrated campaign of the "Maiden Tribute of Modern Babylon" series to compel an indifferent Parliament to enact the pending Criminal Law Amendment Bill, raising the age of consent of young girls to 16.[12] His urgency and purpose also included a campaign for working-class housing and virulent criticism of the government for sending Gordon to the Sudan without adequate protection.[13] To those who scorned the New Journalism as mere sensationalism, Stead replied: "Sensationalism in journalism is justifiable up to the point that it is necessary to arrest the eye of the public and compel them to admit the necessity of action."[14]

The first person to be practically inspired by Stead was O'Connor. His career as an Irish M.P. and journalist had given him a suitable background for editing a newspaper that appealed to those Liberals who were worried that the 1886 split over Home Rule would deprive the Gladstonian majority of adequate expression in the London press.[15] Gladstone's secretary, Sir Edward Hamilton, lamented: "The question of the press is one of the most serious questions ahead for the Liberal Party; London is without a single good newspaper."[16] With a small circulation (12,000 approximately), the *Pall Mall Gazette* was sympathetic to

Liberalism, but the more popular *Echo* and *Evening News* sided with the Unionists. O'Connor approached several rich Liberals to support the proposed newspaper. He maintains that £40,000 was raised, but Alan Lee, in *The Origins of the Popular Press 1855-1914*, reveals it was registered in 1887 with nominal capital of £100,000, of which only £6,000 was called immediately. Among the backers were John Brunner, Thomas Lough M.P., Sir John Whitehead, lord mayor of London, John Morley, a leader of the Liberals, Jeremiah Colman, and a Cambridge professor James Stuart as chairman.[17]

The later problems of the *Star* were present at its birth. Different parties, although their interests overlapped, had different aims for the newspaper. O'Connor founded the *Star* to promote Irish Home Rule.[18] Despite a general attachment to radicalism, it was subservient to this commitment, the *Review of Reviews* saying of O'Connor: "Above all a patriot, a passionate nationalist to whom Ireland comes first, last, everywhere."[19] The directors wanted a medium to articulate "Gladstonianism," whereas members of the staff seized the opportunity for other approaches. Among the unusually talented journalists were H. W. Massingham and Ernest Parke, both later to edit the newspaper, George Bernard Shaw, Richard Le Gallienne as book reviewer, A. B. Walkley as theater critic, and a cluster of future Fleet Street editors. There were several Fabians among the staff and contributors (including Sidney Webb) and another contributor was H. M. Hyndman. It was their political writing that was to have such an impact on the newspaper—to the proprietors' distress.

But future friction was masked by the paper's flamboyant start. O'Connor had said an average 40,000 readers for the first year would be satisfactory, a reasonable figure in terms of expectation because it was the seventh London evening newspaper.[20] But the first day of publication brought 142,600 readers. The *Star's* first fortnight's sales averaged 125,000.[21] A front page "Confession of Faith" stated that the *Star* would be "a radical journal. It will judge all policy—domestic, foreign, social from the Radical standpoint. This, in other words, means that a policy will be esteemed by us good or bad as it influences, for good or evil, the lot of the masses of the people. The chairwoman that lives in St. Giles, the seamstress that is sweated in Whitechapel, the labourer that stands begging for work outside the dockyard gate in St. George's in-the-East, these are the persons by whose conditions we shall judge the policy of different political parties."[22] Early campaigns included Home Rule, condemnation of the sentences meted out to John Burns and R. B. Cunninghame Graham for their roles in the Trafalgar Square demonstrations, and consequent criticism of Home Secretary Henry Matthews, attacks on the concept of a House of Lords, the exposure of sweating and loopholes in the Factory Act, and corruption in Hackney.[23] But it offset its radical policy with less austere features. There was the "Mainly About People" gossip column, which consisted of brief paragraphs broken up by lines recording such racy items as Gladstone's being stuck in a snowdrift. O'Connor was the first contemporary editor to revive a daily gossip column after its popularity in the early nineteenth century. This was approved by even so cerebral figure as Shaw—"O'Connor rightly maintained that washerwomen are as keen on society gossip as Duchesses."[24] Mrs. O'Connor was made column editor and began her first contribution with the arresting line, "Lady Colin Campbell is the only woman in London who has her feet manicured."

There was a Woman's Column, predictably concentrating on fashion, and also a City Column that gratified O'Connor because it generated company advertising whose rates were higher than those for other advertisements.[25] Sport, particularly racing, was another feature the *Star* promoted consistently. The *Echo* had dropped racing tips because of the morals of its editor-proprietor,

Passmore Edwards, and the *Star* began to publish selections.[26] It was the first paper to offer probable runners and ultimately collected riding arrangements and added likely jockeys. Ross McGibbin has shown how popular horse-race betting had become by 1880.[27] He also says that it was only in the 1880s that a "large enough part of the working classes had sufficient income to bet even on the small scale they did."[28] Here is one way in which the improvement in living standards indirectly aided the rise of newspapers by providing prospective readers with sufficient money to enjoy an interest that newspapers could exploit. Its value to newspapers is evident. Some sporting papers' circulations frequently reached 300,000, and O'Connor estimated that London evening papers lost between one quarter and one third of their circulation at the end of the racing season.[29]

Football made less impact in the early days partly because of the absence of the "Pools" (betting coupons) and partly because of the relative lack of development of the professional game in London. The *Star* was the first London evening newspaper to print a weekly half-column about football, but even by 1909, when the Saturday Classified was publishing the full results of the afternoon's program, the *Star* contented itself to print on the eve of F. A. Cup matches only the program, not comments.[30] O'Connor, after taking advice from an Irish editor, determined to make sport a feature of the *Star,* but it never exceeded six percent of the total nonadvertising material in the first month of its existence. (Berridge listed percentages for 1886 of 2.8% of the content in *Reynolds' Newspaper* and *Lloyd's Weekly Newspaper* and 5.3% of the *Weekly Times*).[31] Newspapers certainly seemed sluggish to reflect the commonly expressed interest in sport noted by contemporaries such as W. T. Stead: "Athleticism is the sole religion of multitudes and there is no sign of it anywhere losing its hold."[32]

There were other innovative features in the first weeks of the *Star*—columns devoted to theatrical and musical gossip and book reviews and another, entitled "Labour World," detailing various trades and listing hardships. Cartoons were used regularly.[33] O'Connor also began a Stop Press, the first paper to do so. The rest of the coverage, apart from major political stories, concentrated on local London news with a bias toward the reporting of radical and socialist activities. One constant and anticipated exception was the interest in Irish affairs, events such as the demonstration for T. P. Sullivan and William O'Brien.[34]

In the first two years of publication, the stories that attracted most readers were the Jack the Ripper murders. A four-deck Page One head ("The Ripper Again/Surpasses himself in fiendish mutilations/His victim found in Cable Street Archway/The Legs cut off and Carried away") was followed by Ernest Parke's colorful description beginning "Another touch of lurid light is poured on the East End."[35] The following day's story juxtaposed the words" The story must be told and it's better to tell it than to hush it up. But no one realises better than the newspaper editors the dangers which beset the recital of these loathsome deeds," with the news that the previous day's circulation had reached a record 360,598. The event coincided with the Dock Strike, which, for once, did not receive its customary prominence. The tradition of street literature reached its peak on such occasions, and the *Star* used the public's excited fear of further murders to escalate its demands for the resignation of Police Commissioner Sir Charles Warren. Whereas a similar demand after the banning of Trafalgar Square demonstrations had little effect on the public, this time the *Star* got a more fruitful response.[36] Warren resigned on November 12. This combination of radical politics and violent crime had already proved popular on Sundays. After detailing the amount of court cases and violent crime in the immediately preceding period, Berridge maintains that "the mass readership was gained not through their radicalism and not entirely through the removal of press restrictions but by the satisfaction of the need for vicarious thrills felt by the mass of readers."[37]

If the contents of the early issues of the *Star* had sufficient interest to attract a wider readership then had been previously considered commonplace in London evening newspapers, its presentation was strikingly appropriate. Headlines often extended across two columns, crossheads were used extensively to break up the solid type, and leading articles were often intentionally restricted to half a column.[38] The contrast with the *Evening News*, which the day before the *Star's* first edition published a report in two columns solid, is startling. Later the *Star* used lower case for both secondary headlines and crossheads, neither of which had been seen before in British newspaper typography although they had been widespread in the United States.[39] The *Star* also varied the position of broken lines in subheads, whereas previously they had been centered. This technique allowed long second headlines that summarized the substance rather than pointed to the importance of the article. The headline, wrote Massingham, became a "shorthand description of the event." One celebrated heading was Ta-Ra-Ra-Boom-De-Ay after a contemporary music hall song to celebrate the 1889 London County Council election results.[40]

These changes were of immense significance in British newspaper history. Morison said of the first editions of the *Star* that it may "fairly claim to be regarded as the first whole-hearted determination to engraft the 'New Journalism' upon the stock of high Victorian tradition," whereas Raymond Williams said: "The essential novelty of the *Star* is that the new distribution of interest which the second half of the 19th century had brought about was now typographically confirmed. From now on the new journalism began to look what it was."[41]

Not only the editorial content was presented in a different fashion in the *Star*. Advertising was also undergoing dramatic changes. The growth of display advertisements was to transform the economic basis on which newspapers were to be published and their layout. The display advertisements in the first edition of the *Star* did not extend across more than one column. Editors had been rigorously against breaking across straight single columns, the accepted makeup style, until the advent of the New Journalism. Dicey says that "there was scarcely an exception" to the rule that all advertisements "should be printed in the same type and placed as nearly as possible upon a footing of equality."[42] Advertisers, increasingly aware of the available market, wanted to transfer poster techniques to newspapers. Editors, however, content to rely on finance from small circulations rather than advertisements, were able to resist their demands. Illustrated magazines were the first to permit display advertisements, and it took the *Star* only three weeks before it allowed the first genuine display ad (for Brooke's soap) across three columns.[43] The fact that display ads were admitted to the newspaper forced change in the rest of the layouts by breaking down accepted beliefs about how newspapers should look and forcing changes in editorial copy to blend with it. Advertisers were to get the exposure that their companies desired.

The advertisements primarily consisted of small luxuries aimed at those increasing numbers of people who enjoyed a budgetary surplus after the necessities of life had been satisfied. It was these people to whom the new multiple stores were catering.[44] There are several similarities when we compare the earliest editions with those twenty years later. There are the relishes, sauces, and beverages that enliven a working-class diet that has been described as "stodgy and monotonous . . . but certainly substantial."[45] Thus in 1888 we find regular single-column display ads for cocoa and twenty years later we find Lipton's Tea and Cocoa advertised every day.[46]

Berridge has noted the prevalence of self-medication and ads for such products continued in the *Star*.[47] Growing interest in hygiene can be seen from the number of soaps advertised. In 1888 there were advertisements for Scott's Emulsion and Cod Liver Oils and Soaps, Lung Tonics, and Pills and Plaster.[48] In 1908, in a sample week, we find cures for eczema and both Lifebuoy and Edwards Soap; cures for headaches and bronchial catarrhs; Dr. Williams Famous Pink Pills; more soaps and Clarke's Blood Mixture.[49] It is little wonder soaps were so popular: 30 percent of all children had flea bites in 1908. The low standard of health was shown in World War One, when only one-third of all adult men conscripted were classified as having a normal standard of health. A major growth area was tobacco, which was advertised daily, in a sample week, in January 1908 compared to no display references at all when the *Star* began publishing twenty years earlier.

The *Star's* political stance was announced in its first edition and was followed by appropriate articles. Yet almost immediately there were efforts to curb this radical socialism. George Bernard Shaw was the first subject of liberal annoyance. His early editorials reflected his own concerns—"My sole object in joining The *Star* being to foist Fabian municipal socialism on it."[50] O'Connor was so disturbed that he refused to print Shaw's articles. The Fabian Society instructed members to protest to the *Star*.[51] O'Connor then began to print Shaw's articles because he believed from the letters, which unknown to O'Connor had been orchestrated by the Fabians, that there was widespread support for the view when he faced criticism from the Liberals. "An extraordinary situation was created that a paper started by a Liberal and intended to advance the Home Rule cause found in its pages sometimes extreme tirades upon Liberal leaders," O'Connor recalled, singling out one attack about which John Morley spoke to O'Connor.[52] Shaw then offered to become a music critic — he eventually succeeded Belfort Bax, cofounder of the Socialist League. It was a subject that he approached in a whimsical manner with the blessing of O'Connor, relieved to have diverted Shaw's energies to a less politically controversial field.[53]

But Shaw's indirect influence on political features remained. There were also plenty of other Fabians on the staff — William Clarke, Clement Shorter, Percival Chubb — and contributors such as Webb, who wrote that the paper was "nominally radical but virtually socialist," to ensure that the *Star* remained faithful to its original intentions.[54] Thus during the Matchgirls' Strike of 1888, the *Star* was in the forefront of those who demanded the establishment of a trade union. It began the campaign by stressing that workers "might make their demands on capital without fear."[55] Alternating with attacks against the government's hostile attitude to the new Boer republics and the "indiscriminate ruffianism of the police" at a Trafalgar Square demonstration, the *Star* maintained its support of the matchgirls.[56] Theoretical background was not forgotten by the *Star* which asserted: "The right of capital to draw its dividends irrespective of the rights of Labour to enjoy the friuts of its work, the non-responsibility of the shareholder for the conduct of the directorate . . . have come up for eager, insistent questioning."[57]

The election of the first London County Council in January 1889 became the next target for the *Star*. The London Liberal and Radical Union announced its program in the *Star*, which focused on working-class housing and Council control of the police, gas, water, hospitals, and the poor law. The *Star* particularly supported three Social Democratic Federation members who were now standing against progressive Liberals.[58] The election resulted in a sound defeat for the Tories who found themselves in a minority of 50 in a council of 118. Paul Thompson has said of this period in London that "the real motive forces in the Liberal recovery were the *Star* newspaper and the trade union boom of 1889-92."[59]

And the *Star* itself was supportive of this "boom." The gas workers' and dock workers' strikes received editorial support from the *Star*. It declared:" In the first place union; in the second place union and in the third place union" and three days later maintained that "the careless individualism, which allowed the control of London's riverside accommodation to pass uncontrolled into private hands, has brought its own reward."[60] The *Star* opened a fighting fund for the dockers, which reached £5,000 within two weeks.[61] Yet the Trades Union Congress (TUC), meeting at the same time, voted the dockers £10 and Chairman George Shipton termed the strike a "very lamentable labour dispute." The *Star* urged the TUC to establish "an effective Labour representation in Parliament" and, eleven days later, spoke of future liberalism including the hereditary principle disappearing in the House of Lords, free education, communes in villages, and increased public relief, including old age pensions.[62] Shaw was delighted with the tone of the paper. He later recalled:" The Liberal leaders remonstrated almost daily, with "T.P." being utterly bewildered by what was to them a most dangerous heresy. But the *Star* articles got more and more progressive, then ultra-Progressive, then positively Jacobin; and the further they went the better London liked them. They were not, I beg to say, written by me but by Mr. H. W. Massingham."[63] Engels wrote: "The *Star* is the daily paper which is most read by the workers and the only one that is open to use however little."[64]

The proprietors of the *Star* became worried. Jeremiah Colman wrote, saying that the paper had a "vulgar tone" and telling O'Connor that "I cannot conceal from myself nor can I conceal from you the strong dissatisfaction which is felt by a section of the Liberal Party as to the lines which the paper has taken." He added that there could be "no permanent success if there was serious difference of view between editor and proprietors." Sir James Whitehead claimed that "the *Star* has done positive harm to the Home Rule cause."[65] Because O'Connor was an active M.P., he was unable to see everything before publication, and he said, in an otherwise kindly obituary of Massingham, that he was sometimes surprised to find "very nasty flicks at the Liberal Party and its leaders."[66]

Massingham might have been party to O'Connor's leaving— with a £15,000 gift. It is curious that Massingham should have stayed while O'Connor, closely linked with the Gladstonians, should have been the target for proprietorial ire. Even Massingham's biographer mentions the probability of a letter sent to the shareholders by Massingham in which questions were raised about O'Connor's journalistic diligence because of conflicting Parliamentary duties.[67] Shaw, then in the process of resigning, also suggests the existence of such a document in his letter to O'Connor.[68] Massingham and Stuart took over joint editorial control of the newspaper in the summer of 1890, but the partnership did not last long. Friction centered on the Eight Hours Bill which Massingham wanted to promote against Liberal policy (and against an 1890 [although not put forth until 1891] TUC motion). He wrote: "I am in the grip of Whig wire pulling and I shall never be quit of them, either till they have sucked all the blood out of me or I assert my independence."[69] The break occurred when J. B. Stuart wrote an editorial criticizing John Burns for his intervention in the Scottish Rail Strike. Massingham resigned. A subsequent letter disclosed that "the question at issue is of the policy, involving in my opinion the abandonment of the Labour policy of the *Star*."[70]

Massingham's resignation marked a turning point in the political direction of the *Star*. Stuart remained editorial director with Parke, an experienced journalist without profound political commitment, in charge of daily editing.[71] The proprietorial demand to cut costs lead to the estabishment in 1892 of the *Morning Leader,* a daily stablemate that was to share overheads with the *Star.* Stuart, as a Gladstonian Liberal M.P. who respected the desires of his fellow directors, aligned both papers' political stance with the Liberal party. Given the recent defection of the Liberal Unionists and the opposition of the increasingly powerful Tory press, it was understandable the the proprietors did not want to divert any energy from supporting a party that was still in opposition. It was not so understandable that the *Star* should have made its campaigning less vigorous.

An early example of the new policy of the *Star,* which Shaw described as having become "Gladstonised," was the 1892 London County Council election.[72] In a triumph for the "Progressives," the *Star* backed the Liberals and staunchly opposed any independent socialist candidates.[73] The following year, when the Fabians published their famous "To Your Tents O Israel," the *Star* editorially defended the government from an accusation that it "falsified its promises to the workers."[74] In the same year the Independent Labour party was founded, an event that Philip Snowden described as "the most important political event of the 19th century."[75] The *Star* was less impressed and closeted the information in four inches on page three.[76] The next day an editorial stated that "the mass of the working class and the mass of the Liberal Party have still too many interests in common and too strong a common enemy to fight to be able to afford to part company and both of them know it."[77] The *Star* particularly concentrated its attack on Keir Hardie, saying after the Liberals' 1895 general election defeat: "His splendid egoism is delicious. He, a political Ishmael, regards the fact that every man's hand is against him as a triumphant testimonial to his moral superiority."[78]

Two days later, the *Star* urged the Liberals "not to be dictated to in order to adopt new policies."[79] When one combines these attitudes with its lack of interest in 1900 in the formation of the

Labour Representation Committee, which was completely overwhelmed by the news of the relief of Kimberley and tucked away in three paragraphs underneath the Horse Racing Card from Lingfield, we must surely be surprised at the *Star's* own assertion that it had championed the Labour movement.[80] In an anniversary issue in 1908, the *Star* proclaimed: "In 1888 the leaders of Labour were hunted by police; today they sit by the scores in the House of Commons respected by all classes. In the organization of the quiet Revolution the *Star* has played its part. . . . Now that the Labour Party has been returned in strength to the House of Commons many London newspapers have discovered the Labour movement. The *Star* did not need this electoral success to enlighten it."[81]

Since 1891 there had clearly developed an editorial concern to view events not from the standpoint of the ultimate benefit of the working class but from what was expedient for the Liberal party, desperately trying to reconcile the traditions that it had inherited from the Whigs with the demands of the new franchise and the increasing power of the trade unions. But the task of the proprietors of the *Star* was made more difficult by the competition from the *Evening News.* What Stead and O'Connor had done was observed by Northcliffe, and whereas their views of the New Journalism had led them to make their papers radical and innovative alternatives to more conservative publications, Northcliffe created a popular journalism that was less interested in political and social action per se than it was by increasing circulation. Northcliffe provided the reader with short, lively articles that did not express a dedicated and consistent political stance. "We are a sort of Universal Information Provider," Northcliffe wrote in *Answers,* a compendium of items ranging from bicycling to the empire.[82] He did not peddle unsavory information, nor did he stimulate fresh ways of thinking or challenge accepted ideas. When one reader wrote to him, deploring the many references to the "Conservative gang," Northcliffe answered: "Politics play no part whatever in the management of this newspaper."[83] To boost readership Northcliffe used stunts and competitions, which had already been employed successfully by *Tit-Bits*.

In 1894 Northcliffe bought the *Evening News*. He changed its character immediately, using many of the techniques that he had already tested. Instead of one leader, he followed the *Star* and printed three or four different leaders. Staid political reporting was stopped. Kennedy Jones, his manager, asked him once, when he had lifted articles from his magazine: "God man, you're not trying to turn the paper into an evening *Answers* are you?"[84] The *Evening News*, Jones observed subsequently, "addresses tired minds, at the end of a long day's work, desirous of amusement and relaxation."[85] There were headlines across two columns, and on January 15, 1895, there appeared a front-page banner headline. The Women's Column was expanded to a whole page. Competitions began with a weekly prize outlay of £5. Many of Northcliffe's moves forced the *Star* to expand its equivalent features.

Northcliffe's approach had a direct effect on the circulation and thus on the newspaper's ability to command advertising. Because of the comparative lack of sophistication in reader analysis, that would have provided details on which social and economic strata were buying particular newspapers, companies advertising products and services were more easily influenced by sheer circulation figures than they have been in the twentieth century. It was not that Northcliffe stressed the value of advertising. It was that instead of regarding a newspaper as an organ of concerned opinion, he produced reading matter for the public and then sold it in the same way as any other article of commerce. Northcliffe's extension of the New Journalism was less journalistic than economic. As Jones told Liberal politician John Morley: "You left journalism. We made it a branch of commerce."[86] The effect made by the *Star* was so striking that it ensured that the paper would never return to the radical campaigning approach that it had adopted in its first three years of publication. It had to compete with the *Evening News* on Northcliffe's own terms in the struggle for readers in the halfpenny market. Northcliffe ensured – although not necessarily deliberately – that the choice of newspapers would become more restricted and the range of expression would be less varied.

For three years the *Star* had shown what the New Journalism could be in Great Britain. Its decline in status and the change in the New Journalism were foreseen by the *Workman's Times* in 1891, when it lamented that it is "impossible to run an honest democratic newspaper financed by big capitalists and directed by office-seeking politicians." The *Workman's Times* wrote the epitaph for the *Star:* "The old *Star,* the fearless champion of the people, no longer exists."[87]

NOTES

1. Matthew Arnold "Up to Easter," *Nineteenth Century,* CXXIII (1887), 638-639.

2. E. H. Phelps Browne and Margaret H. Browne, *A Century of Pay* (London, 1968), p. 173; Paul Thompson, *The Edwardians* (London, 1977), p. 283.

3. Alan J. Lee, *The Origins of the Popular Press, 1855-1914* (London, 1976), p. 57. For a more detailed discussion of changes in nineteenth-century printing techniques, see Ellic Howe and Harold E. Waite, *A Centenary History: The London Society of Compositors* (London, 1948), pp. 202, 230.

4. Peter Mathias, *The First Industrial Nation* (London, 1969), p. 377; Browne, *Century of Pay,* p. 55; Phyliss Deane and William A. Cole, *British Economic Growth, 1688-1959* (Cambridge, 1962), p. 282.

5. George Boyce, James Curran and Pauline Wingate, eds., *Newspaper History: From the 17th century to the Present Day* (London, 1978), pp. 68, 151.

6. "Street News Boys of London," *Chambers Journal* LI, (1874), 113-115; T. B. Browne: *The Advertisers ABC* (London, 1889), p. 240; Donald J. Olsen, *The Growth of Victorian London* (London, 1976), p. 316, 317, and 319; John R. Kellett, *The Impact of Railways on Victorian Cities* (London, 1969), p. 369. See also letters to the *Star,* 30 January 1888 and 6 February 1888.

7. Reginald Pound and Geoffrey Harmsworth, *Northcliffe* (London, 1959), p. 54.

8. Raymond L. Schults, *Crusader in Babylon* (Lincoln, Nebraska), 1972, p. 15.

9. W. T. Stead, "Character Sketch: Mr. T. P. O'Connor, M.P.", *Review of Reviews,* XXVI (1902) 478-479.

10. Schultz, *Crusader in Babylon,* p. 61.

11. Ibid. p. 196.

12. *Pall Mall Gazette,* 6, 7, 8, and 10 July 1885.

13. J. O. Baylen, "The New Journalism in Late Victorian Britain," *Australian Journal of Politics and History,* XVIII (1972), 367-385.

14. W. T. Stead, "Government by Journalism," *Contemporary Review,* XLIX (1886), 653.

15. On O'Connor, see T. P. O'Connor, *Memoirs of an Old Parliamentarian,* 2 volumes (London, 1929) and Hamilton H. Fyfe, *T. P. O'Connor* (London, 1934).

16. Sir Edward Hamilton Diary, 18 January 1888, cited in Stephen Koss, *The Rise and Fall of the Political Press in Britain* (London, 1981), vol. I, p. 344.

17. Lee, *Origins of the Popular Press,* p. 83; Stephen Koss, *Sir John Brunner: Radical Plutocrat* (Cambridge, 1970), p. 157; Lawrence W. Brady, *T. P. O'Connor and the Liverpool Irish* (London, 1983), p. 104.

18. O'Connor, *Memoirs,* vol. I, p. 254.

19. *Review of Reviews* (November 1902), p. 479.

20. Wilson Pope, *The Story of The Star* (London, 1938), p. 17.

21. *Star,* 30 January 1888.

22. Ibid., 17 January 1888.

23. Ibid., 21 and 27 January 1888, 1 and 18 February 1888.

24. George Bernard Shaw, *Sixteen Self Sketches* (London, 1949), p. 110.

25. O'Connor, *Memoirs,* vol. I, p. 259.

26. *The History of The Times:* vol. III, 1884-1912 (London, 1947), p. 99; *Star,* 21 January 1888.

27. Ross McGibbin, "Working Class Gambling in Britain, 1880-1939," *Past and Present,* no. 82 (1979), 147-174.

28. Ibid., 148.

29. Cited in "W. J. K.," "Betting and Gambling," *Westminster Review,* CXL (1895), 146; *Sell's Dictionary of the World's Press, 1906,* pp. 104-105.

30. *Star,* 17 January 1909.

31. Virginia S. Berridge, "Popular Journalism and Working Class Attitudes, 1854-1886: A Study of *Reynold's Newspaper, Lloyd's Weekly Newspaper* and The *Weekly Times,*" Unpublished Ph.D. thesis, University of London, 1976, p. 141; O'Connor. *Memoirs,* vol. I, p. 255.

32. W. T. Stead, "The Press in the 20th Century," *Great Thoughts,* 9 March 1895, 362.

33. See the *Star*, 2 February 1888 for the first cartoon.

34. Ibid., 11 February 1888.

35. Ibid., 10 September 1888.

36. *Star*, 25 January 1888 and 11 September 1888.

37. Berridge, "Popular Journalism," p. 189.

38. *Star*, 17 January 1888.

39. Stanley Morison, *The English Newspaper* (Cambridge, 1932), p. 291.

40. *Star*, 18 January 1889.

41. Morison, *English Newspaper*, p. 283; Raymond Williams, *The Long Revolution* (London, 1961), p. 198.

42. Edward Dicey, "Journalism New and Old," *Fortnightly Review*, LXXVII (1905), 20.

43. *Star*, 6 February 1888.

44. Charles Wilson, "Economy and Society in Late Victorian Britain," *Economic History Review*, XV (1965), 190.

45. Edward H. Hunt, *British Labour History, 1815-1914* (London, 1981), p. 87.

46. *Star* 18 and 28 January, 3 February 1888, and the week from 17 January 1908.

47. Berridge, "Popular Journalism," p. 271.

48. *Star*, 17 January, 3 and 4 February 1888.

49. *Star*, 13, 14 and 16 January 1908.

50. Shaw, *Sixteen Self Sketches*, p. 112.

51. George Bernard Shaw, "The Fabian Society: What It Has Done and How It Has Done It," *Fabian Tract 41* (London, 1892), p. 26; Shaw, "In the Days of Our Youth," *Star*, 19 February 1908.

52. O'Connor, *Memoirs*, vol. II, p. 266.

53. Hesketh Pearson, *Bernard Shaw: A Biography* (London, 1942), p. 132.

54. Ely Papers, Letter from Sidney Webb to Richard Ely, 1 February 1889, cited in "The Influence of Socialist Ideas on English Writing and Political Thinking," Myra S. Wilkins, Unpublished Ph.D. Thesis, University of Cambridge, 1957.

55. *Star*, 11 July 1888.

56. Ibid., 3 and 17 July 1888.

57. Ibid., 18 July 1888.

58. Ibid., 15 August 1888; 7 and 10 January 1889.

59. Paul Thompson, *Socialists, Liberals and Labour: The Struggle for London, 1885-1914* (London, 1967), p. 97.

60. *Star* 16 and 19 August 1889.

61. Ibid., 6 September 1889.

62. Ibid., 5 and 16 September 1889.

63. Ibid., 19 February 1908; letter, 6 December 1889, from Shaw to Jules Magny, in *George Bernard Shaw: Collected Letters*, ed. Dan Laurence (London, 1965), p. 233.

64. Letter, 11 May 1889, from Engels to Lafargue in *Friedrich Engels, Paul and Laura Lafargue: Correspondence*, translated by Y. Kapp (Moscow, 1960), vol. II, as cited in Yvonne Kapp, *Eleanor Marx: The Crowded Years (1884-1898)* (London, 1976), vol. II, p. 301.

65. Fyfe, *O'Connor*, p. 152.

66. *Daily Telegraph*, 19 August 1924; See also Koss, *Brunner*, p. 158.

67. Alfred F. Havighurst, *Radical Journalist: H. W. Massingham* (London, 1974), p. 31.

68. Letter from Shaw to O'Connor, March 4, 1890, in *Shaw: Collected Letters*, p. 244.

69. Havighurst, *Massingham*, p. 33.

70. Letter from Massingham to Sir Edward Cook, 13 January 1891, Cook Papers, cited in Koss, *Rise and Fall*, vol. I, p. 309; see also H. W. Massingham, *The London Daily Press* (London, 1892), p. 190.

71. James B. Stuart, *Reminiscences* (London, 1912), p. 252.

72. *Fabian Tract 41*, p. 18.

73. *Star*, 4 and 6 February 1892.

74. Ibid., 30 October 1893.

75. Philip Snowden, *An Autobiography* (London, 1934), vol. I, p. 53.

76. *Star*, 13 January 1893.

77. Ibid., 14 January 1893.

78. Ibid., 20 July 1895, and see also 25 June 1894.

79. Ibid., 22 July 1895.

80. Ibid., 28 February 1900.

81. Ibid., 19 February 1908. The *Star* eccentrically ran its twentieth-anniversary issue thirty-three days late.

82. *Answers*, 16 February 1889.

83. Pound, *Northcliffe*, p. 100.

84. Ibid., p. 175.

85. Kennedy Jones, *Fleet Street and Downing Street* (London, 1919), p. 130.

86. Ibid., p. 173.

87. *Workman's Times*, 10 October 1891.

8
Aled Jones
The New Journalism in Wales

The New Journalism, as Philip Elliott has observed, "meant not only breaking up the old material with new types of layout," but also the introduction of "new material for new audiences."[1] In Wales this process led to the disruption of older patterns and practices of journalism and to the emergence of different concepts of audience. The impact of these developments on newspaper production in Wales was profound, and their implications for Welsh society were far-reaching. Briefly, there are three levels at which the New Journalism in Wales can be discussed and understood. First, it is not difficult to identify the new elements of style that were introduced into layout, language, coverage, recruitment policies, economic organization, and marketing strategies in the newspaper industry in Wales in the 1890s. The presence of a New Journalism can thus clearly be demonstrated, and the crosscurrents or style can be located and identified. Second, it is also evident that the New Journalism in

Wales was predominantly, though by no means exclusively, English in language. Important sections of Welsh-language journalism, for reasons that I shall explore, resisted these innovations in style and for that reason failed to address new audiences. Third, the New Journalism, exemplified by such Cardiff-based papers as the *Western Mail,* succeeded in constructing a new and crucially undifferentiated audience that was conceived of as being essentially *Welsh* in character. The introduction of the New Journalism in Wales then had significant cultural and political dimensions. These are, of course, closely related themes, but they need to be examined separately.

But, first, I shall say something about newspapers and their history. The newspaper press in Wales was a creation of the nineteenth century. Papers in both Welsh and English languages appeared during the Napoleonic Wars and in the years immediately following them. The periods of most sudden growth, as might be expected, were the mid-1850s for the weeklies, the years between 1859 and 1872 for the mornings, and the ten years between 1883 and 1893 for the evening papers. By 1879 there were about sixty-one newspapers in Wales. The vast majority of these titles were penny or twopenny weeklies, though their circulation was increasingly being threatened by the popularity of the new dailies. Thirteen of the weeklies were in Welsh, and forty-eight were in English. By 1893 the number of Welsh-language papers had risen to fifteen, but the number of English newspapers had increased from forty-eight to eighty. By the mid-1880s halfpenny papers had made an appearance, and the era of the cheap daily press had effectively begun. The two great morning papers, both published in Cardiff, were the Liberal *South Wales Daily News,* begun in 1872, and the Conservative *Western Mail,* started three years earlier, in 1869. In addition, by 1893 there were six evening papers. For this mainly English-language daily journalism, emerging in the rapidly expanding society of urban and industrial South Wales, the late nineteenth century was a time of growth and experimentation. The Welsh-language papers, on the other hand, remained primarily under the control or the influence of the nonconformist denominations and espoused a sectarian, Liberal, even Radical, politics. Their response to this new world was cautious to say the least.[2]

Early commentators often identified the New Journalism with movements of the left. Henry Cust, editor of the *Pall Mall Gazette,* remarked in the *National Review* in 1893 that "it is the mouthpieces of Socialistic Radicalism—*The Star,* more lately *The Daily Chronicle*—that have shown how attractive the flamboyant style is to the public, because to their public no other style is acceptable."[3] And Sidney J. Low, editor of the *St. James's Gazette,* went so far as to advise Tory journalists "to emulate the remarkable financial, social, and commercial triumphs of the Radical organs of the 'new journals.' "[4]

In Wales, however, Radical Liberalism was divided on the issue. It is one of the peculiarities of the Welsh that in an over-whelmingly Liberal and nonconformist country, it was a Conservative newspaper that first broke through to mass circulation. This historical phenomenon demands an explanation.

I shall begin by describing those elements of the New Journalism that can be identified in papers published in Wales during the 1890s. Any description of so varied a subject must necessarily be partial and impressionistic, and no doubt my selection of examples reveals the assumptions that I have made regarding the defining features of the New Journalism. I shall focus mainly on one newspaper, the *Western Mail.* It was started in 1869 in the usual way by a rich local magnate in the heat of an election campaign. The Conservative coal owner, the marquess of Bute, spent many thousands of pounds in the early years of publication to keep his new Cardiff daily paper alive. But the most influential figure in the paper's management was its first subeditor and later managing editor and part proprietor, Lascelles. Carr. A Yorkshireman who had served his apprenticeship on the *Liverpool Daily Post*, Carr was a Tory democrat and an unorthodox, resourceful, and energetic editor. Like many of his peers, Carr was active in local politics, serving as a Cardiff town councillor and a J.P. before his retirement in 1901. It was he who guided the *Western Mail* away from its sectarian origins toward a broader readership, and his innovations increased the daily circulation of the paper from 13,000 in 1874 to the 100,000 or so that it enjoyed by 1916.

Changes in the paper's format, content, and management were undertaken during the early 1890s. The paper's offices were partially destroyed by fire in 1893, when many of the early records were lost. Within a matter of weeks, Carr reorganized the enterprise, purchasing new rotary presses and pushing through typographical innovations. It would be a mistake to suggest that the New Journalism came to Wales by way of an accident, for some of these changes had already been instituted before the tragedy occurred. Carr, it seems, knew well the kind of paper that he wanted to produce; the fire was both a challenge and an opportunity. Carr was closely involved with the managerial and technical side of the paper's production. According to Lord Riddell, Carr was one of the first to suggest that newspapers could be printed on continuous rolls of dry paper, and the *Western Mail* was one of the earliest papers to use a linotype press. It was also one of the first papers to illustrate its columns with half-tone blocks, and to possess its own block works. Carr had apparently stumbled on this idea while on an earlier visit to the United States. By the mid 1890s, the *Western Mail* carried a six-page women's supplement, and the paper itself included a wide range of articles and features, with excellent first hand reports of events in London, and with access to the Parliamentary Lobby. It was a bright and lively penny daily, often provoking controversy, but never dull.[5]

Its principal rival, the *South Wales Daily News,* had by 1895 also attempted to enliven its image. It carried 'special features' including 'Bright Tittle Tattle', 'Welsh Tit-Bits', 'Queer Stories: Grave and Gay: True and Otherwise', 'A woman's letter to women — by a Lady Journalist', and a children's column. It claimed to be 'The Largest, Brightest and Best Journal Published in the Principality.[6] By comparison with the *Western Mail,* however, the format was less bold and experimental, retaining many features of the more conventional block-column format. Its coverage of local and national news was impressive, though much criticised by radical Welsh Liberals and representatives of the labor movement.[7] Owned by the Duncan family, this paper also made vigorous attempts to reach a popular readership, and to compete in the same mass market as the *Western Mail.* From the late Victorian through to the Edwardian years, it is evident from the robust vitality of these and other papers that the market for daily newspapers was buoyant. This was a period of exceptional and unprecedented industrial expansion, a time of dramatic growth in population, immigration, community building and popular political activity which produced a cosmopolitan, 'American,' Wales.

Papers like the *Western Mail* flourished in this environment thanks to their ability to bridge the gap between sectarian and mass markets. Carr's paper did so by satisfying the requirements of at least two target audiences, and there is ample evidence that the "coal owners' paper" was widely read not only by the Cardiff Conservatives, but also by nonconformists and trade unionists in many other parts of Wales. Increasingly, the journalism of the *Western Mail* came to resemble a broad church, which balanced political, industrial and financial news with leisure, reports of cultural activities and general interest stories. The editorial line

was Conservative, but never uncritically so, and Carr was careful
to place alongside his columns of comment regular articles penned by such leading Welsh Liberals as miners' leader William
Abraham, Cochfarf (Edward Thomas), and other Welsh
language literary figures. Carr, the Yorkshireman, was eager to
maintain close contacts with the Welsh cultural establishment and
the trade unions. The *Western Mail* actively sought a reputation
as the 'national' Welsh newspaper – a subtitle, incidentally,
which it continues to carry. It was no longer relevant to their
marketing strategy whether their target readers voted Liberal or
Conservative, were members of a certain church, or were native
Welsh or English speakers. The paper was read and written for
by individuals who represented each of these constituencies, and
its early success was partly assured by the support and participation of Liberal and nonconformist writers and readers. Another
competitor, the *South Wales Star,* launched in Barry in March
1891, also carried a social column and a children's club, and an
increasing number of the new dailies began to exhibit the same
general tendencies. These developments marked a distinct change
in style and format from those prevailing a decade or so earlier.
In Wales this journalism was regarded with some justification as
being new.[8]

The adoption of the rhetoric of 'nationality', and the appeal to a
broadly conceived Welsh audience, explains, for example, why
so many of the ambitious Liberal nationalists of the North were
so eager to be associated with this and other popular English
language Southern publications. One should bear in mind that
what might be described as the New Journalism was introduced
into Wales at a critical moment in its recent history, when
discourses of modernization, of Young Wales, coincided with the
emergence of a powerful Welsh Liberal presence in British
Parliamentary politics bent on constructing a new democratic
Welsh state underpinned by a politicized public.[9] The press, in

short, was regarded as a means, indeed *the* means, of projecting and articulating a new kind of corporate or national indentity, and of familiarizing readers, many of whom were only recently enfranchised, with the structures of a new political language. T. E. Ellis, Liberal M.P. for the Northern constituency of Merioneth, interviewed by the editor of the *South Wales Star* in the National Liberal Club in London in May 1891, was asked what 'our young leader thought of the future of Welsh nationalism; whether he still believed that we shall see (to quote his own words) the national Parliament elected by the womanhood and manhood of Wales and responsible to them alone. I am, he answered', and continued, 'It is our new writers which are bringing to the minds of the Welsh people that they have a part and are a nation . . . to bring this about, Mr. Editor, should be your work'.[10]

For those editors or managers who were intent on transforming the production, format, and purpose of their papers, however, the recruitment of experienced staff as journalists and administrators from Wales could prove difficult. Much of the evidence indicates that David Davies, editor of the *South Wales Daily Post,* was right to complain in 1897 that "the staffs of our daily newspapers are recruited chiefly in England."[11] As was the case in other parts of Great Britain, newspapers in Wales were dependent on syndicated news reports, and the stereotype services of the news agencies. T.P. O'Connor, for example, wrote a regular Parliamentary column for the *South Wales Daily News,* [12] and "scoops," which first appeared in the London papers, were often quoted and discussed at length in the Welsh papers of both languages.[13] Individual lines of connection between English and Welsh journalism may also be drawn in the other direction. David Lloyd George, the moving force behind a newspaper syndicate in North West Wales, was writing a weekly column for O'Connor's *Star* by 1892 and for the *Manchester Guardian* in

1893. In 1895 he and Samuel Storey attempted to launch a livelier Liberal daily to rival the *South Wales Daily News*. They failed, and Lloyd George had to content himself with the London *Daily News*, of which he became a proprietor in 1900, and the *Daily Chronicle*, which he purchased in 1918. It is evident that many of the journalists who were associated with the newspaper press in Wales at the close of the nineteenth century were not unfamiliar with the New Journalism of the English metropolis and that some, like Carr, were eager to apply the formula. Though few of these journalists admitted to being practitioners of a much criticized new method of newspaper writing, it is clear that many of the papers for which they worked aimed at a "national" relatively well-off readership, were increasingly integrated into the commercial life of Wales through advertising, and recruited professional journalists, often from England and Scotland.

With few exceptions, the Welsh-language press was dominated by the religious denominations, primarily the Calvinistic Methodists, the Wesleyans, the Baptists, and the Independents. It was their intellectuals who supplied this sector of the industry with its journalists, editors, fund raisers, and distributors. In the early 1880s many of the Welsh denominational newspapers were regrded as "modern," in tune with developments in the English-speaking world. In 1884 *Y Goleuad*, a paper run though not directly owned by the Calvinistic Methodists, was hailed by T.E. Ellis, later to be the Liberal chief whip in the House of Commons, as the Welsh version of the *Pall Mall Gazette*, and in 1886 another reviewer compared it favorably with the *Spectator*.[14] By the 1890s, however, the management of virtually all the denominational papers was in full retreat from the New Journalism. John Davies, a prominent Welsh-language journalist,[15] complained bitterly of the increased space given in recent years to scandal, adultery, and crime and of the vividnesss with which they were reported. Not long after, the Calvinistic Methodists passed a motion at their conference in Newport in which they condemned the new trends in journalism. A Cardiff editor typically replied that he would gladly print any material that he deemed to be newsworthy or that his readers found interesting or important.[16] In terms of journalistic ethics and taste, this editor and his Calvinist critics inhabited two very different moral worlds.

One of the objections put forward by the denominational papers was that an increasing amount of space was being devoted to sport. It was regarded not simply as trivial news unworthy of readers' attention but also as being dangerously corrupting to public morals. There was little serious sports coverage in Welsh-language papers until the twentieth century, when nonconformist ministers began to take an interest in the redeeming qualities of rugby football. Where ministers led, correspondents followed. In sharp contrast and more in step with the changing patterns of public leisure, the South Wales Echo, a halfpenny evening, frequently carried one or more full pages of sports news daily from the mid-1880s.[17]

By the late 1890s the distance between the English- and Welsh-language papers had become greater. David Davies, editor of the South Wales Daily Post, remarked in 1897 that

there is something of tragedy in the ineffectiveness of the Welsh people in relation to the prosperous press which uses English when account is taken of the wealth of thought gracefully expressed, thrown into the scarcely visible press that moves with lingering feet in a circle ever threatened by the deepening shadow of the irresistable English language.[18]

An Anglican reviewer, writing in Welsh in the literary journal Y Traethodydd in 1898, was less wistful. "Our weekly newspapers," he wrote, "are too narrow and sectarian in tone . . . in them we have far too many biographies and obituaries of people who are as often as not of no consequence. The English papers compare very favourably with our own."[19]

The Welsh-language papers, he suggested, were dull and full of irrelevances. Similarly, the newspaper-reading public, whatever their native languages or sectarian loyalties, residual or otherwise, had come to expect liveliness and topicality in their print media. Like the popular Sunday press, daily newspapers could now be read for pleasure as well as for the acquisition of information essential to the management of everyday life.

As notions of what constituted the "news" were redefined in the 1890s, doubts began to be expressed about whether the Welsh-language papers were newspapers at all in the modern sense. According to David Davies (in the same article in 1897), "The influences which have transformed the British press and given it a wonderful vitality have in truth passed lightly over the Cymric newspapers. For them the revolution in the mechanical means of production has meant little, and the telegraph and the telephone are to them as if they were not."[20] Davies suggested two reasons why this was so. First, he argued, the Welsh papers were "primarily instruments for giving publicity to views—in this regard, resembling the French journals in which felicity of expression, and grace of form are esteemed of greater importance than the bald records of great events in the outer world."[21] Second, he attributed their failure to expand to their "noncultivation of the commercial side of the newspaper. The chief sources from which the English press draws its breath of life in the forms of revenue have been consistently neglected."[22]

There were obvious exceptions to this general and critical analysis. Thomas Gee's *Y Faner,* Lloyd George's *Genedl* syndicate, and Coplestone's *Herald* papers were in relative terms lively, technologically-advanced, and commercially-sound enterprises.[23] But some newspapers measured their success in terms other than the commercial. For such denominational papers as *Y Tyst* or *Y Goleuad,* survival could best be ensured by meeting the needs of small but consistent and specific audiences that frequently breached class though only rarely doctrinal divisions.[24] A newspaper run by and for Methodists, for instance, was able to count on the help of voluntary or low-paid correspondents and distributors organized in Wales and beyond through a network of Methodist ministers and chapels and funded by the contributions of sympathetic readers. The editors of such papers objected on moral and, for lack of a better term, "organizational" grounds to a journalism that offered "new material to new audiences."

Increasingly, however, English-language papers began to reach for this Welsh-speaking market, particularly in the industrial south. Some, like the *South Wales Star,* published regular columns in Welsh, and others included weekly review articles on the contents of the Welsh papers.[25] Readers could then be kept in touch with Welsh journalism wholly through the medium of English. By the late 1890s the balance between Welsh- and English-language journalism had been seriously disturbed, and the distance between the two cultural forms had increased still farther.

Ironically, Welsh nonconformity finally succumbed to the New Journalism in 1904. In that year Welsh Wales was shaken by a volcanic religious revival, a convulsion of collective born-again Christianity that sent its shock waves through urban and rural communities alike. Among the most vivid and sympathetic accounts of this revival were ones that appeared in a series of newspaper articles published in English in the *Daily Chronicle* in December 1904. Their author was W.T. Stead. Furthermore, Evan Roberts, the revival's young and charismatic leader, expresses his Welsh Christian fundamentalism directly and eloquently in English by means of a series of interviews.[26] Despite their rejection of the form, at a critical moment even the militant nonconformists were grateful for the publicity that the doyen of the New Journalism provided. T.P. O'Connor once said, half-jokingly, of Stead that "he was too good a fanatic to be a real journalist, and too real a journalist to be a good fanatic."[27] Had the editors of the sectarian Welsh newspapers pondered that dilemma, perhaps they might have begun to think of themselves as journalists as well as activists. A distinctive Welsh-language New Journalism might then have been conceivable.[28]

Although I have concentrated on developments in the 1890s, the processes that I have described continued and intensified. With few exceptions, the titles that survived the First World War became the properties of a dwindling number of proprietors. By 1918 D.A. Thomas, Lord Aberdare, was chief proprietor of a host of old, previously-independent titles, including the *Western Mail, Evening Express, South Wales Journal of Commerce, Y Faner, Y Tyst, Tarian y Gweithiwr, Cambrian News, Merthyr Express*, and a series of titles in Pontypridd. Many were later transferred to his brother, Lord Kemsley. In 1928 the Duncan family sold the *South Wales Daily News*, the *Echo*, and the *Cardiff Times* to their erstwhile competitors and political rivals, the proprietors of the *Western Mail*. By the end of the 1920s virtually all the South Wales titles belonged to Kemsley, and in the early 1960s these were in turn purchased by the present owners of the *Western Mail*, the Thompson Group. But the developments that had presaged and made possible this concentration of ownership had occurred in the 1890s, when the pace of change in the newspaper industry in Wales had suddenly and decisively accelerated.

It is now time to draw together the loose ends of my remarks into something that resembles a conclusion. The question I asked myself when I began to research this paper was "why and in what sense is it useful to talk of a New Journalism in late Victorian Wales?" The argument thus far suggests that changes in style, new forms of economic organization, and an altered concept of audience, which I assume to be characteristic of the New

Journalism in London, the United States, and elsewhere, were introduced into Wales unevenly and that in general terms that unevenness accentuated the cultural difference between the English- and Welsh-language press. The gulf between them was more than stylistic: It was also moral and ideological. The contrasting modes of presentation were rhetorical and typographical expressions of that difference. The two journalisms cannot adequately be explained by referring to the geographical divide between a rural north and an urban south, nor can they properly be understood in terms of the exclusive political and cultural dynamics of separate language groups. Not enough is known about the readership to sustain sociolinguistic theories of this order, although sufficient evidence is available to suggest that tensions not infrequently emerged within the Welsh-speaking portion of the reading public regarding the kind of periodical literature to which they desired access. But what can be argued is that the Welsh variant of the New Journalism and the hostile responses that it invited revealed the coexistence of radically different approaches to the production of newspapers. The areas of disagreement centered principally on the ways in which journalists defined their medium and explained its purpose.

Essentially, the editors of the sectarian papers perceived their audiences as being highly fragmented in terms of religious affiliation or, more precisely, of doctrinal polarities within nonconformist denominations. Being homogenous in belief, the readership was assumed to be heterogeneous in social class and to include relatively poorer workers and tenant farmers as well as shopkeepers, teachers, academics, and other professionals. By providing for this kind of market, which was limited but relatively constant, editors were reasonably certain that funding would remain adequate. In this way they could remain free of the mechanisms of the mass market and could avoid the financial and ethical complexities induced by dependence on commercial advertising. Furthermore, the primary function of their papers was to maintain and extend standards of virtue and to propagate certain cultural and religious values, among them being the solidarity of the sect. Ranged against them in the new marketplaces of the streets, the newsagent shops, and the railway stations was an expanding, mainly English-language press that was heavily dependent on commercial advertising and sought to reach a numerically-large audience among the skilled working class and the metropolitan middle-income and mercantile groups irrespective of their religious or political loyalties. Its function was to provide news, in its many forms, as a commodity that had been gathered and edited by professional journalists and represented in a way that accorded with a consensual, capitalist, and "progressive" world view. But despite the fact that new material was being presented to new audiences beginning in the 1890s, the implications of the New Journalism, for Wales as elsewhere, were ambivalent. It created some possibilities and frustrated others; it diversified content but concentrated ownership and control; it reduced the price of newspapers but pushed up operating costs. It was populist in sentiment but authoritarian in structure. Yet the uncertainties, anxieties, and excitement that accompanied the New Journalism suited the mood of an expanding industrial society at a time when a new and more dynamic idea of Wales was being formed. The making of this new Wales and the introduction of the New Journalism were two dimensions of the one social process.

NOTES

1. P. Elliott, "Professional Ideology and Organisational Change: The Journalist Since 1800," in G. Boyce, J. Curran, and P. Wingate, *Newspaper History from the Seventeenth Century to the Present Day* (London, 1978), p. 179.

2. Saunders, Otley and Co., *The Newspaper Press of the Present Day* (1860), pp. 95-97; J. Parry and J.O. Jones (eds.), *Y Gwyddoniadur Cymreig*, (Gee, 1896), vol. VII, p. 64; *Y Traethodydd*, XXXIX, 1884, pp. 192-193. See

also MS 3.348, Cardiff Public Library, Cardiff; P. Davies, *Atgofion Dyn Papur Newydd* (Liverpool, 1962), p. 131. For a more general treatment of this theme, see Lucy Brown, *Victorian News* and *Newspapers* (Oxford, 1985), pp. 271-272. In the 1880s, Welsh-language periodical publishing reached impressive proportions. Seventeen weekly newspapers enjoyed a joint circulation of 120,000, and a further 150,000 copies of Welsh magazines were also circulating. See the evidence of Beriah Gwynfe Evans to the Royal Commission on Education, 1886-87, Par. 42,576, in J.E. Southall, *Bi-lingual Teaching in Welsh Elementary Schools* (London, 1888).

3. H. Cust, "The Tory Press and the Tory Party, II – An Answer," *National Review*, XXI (1893), 364-365.

4. S.J. Low, *Ibid*, p.374; F. Gardner complained that the Tory papers were dull by comparison with "the London Radical papers, with their smart interviews, suggestive headings, rough cartoons and portraits, signed articles, interesting chit-chat, and general up-to-dateness." "The Tory Press and the Tory Party, I – A Complaint," *National Review*, XXI (1893), 357.

5. Lord Riddell, *The Story of the Western Mail* (Cardiff, 1929), pp. 1-9; J. Davies, *Cardiff and the Marquesses of Bute* (Cardiff, 1981), p. 13; K.O. Morgan, *Rebirth of a Nation: Wales 1880-1980*, (London, 1981), p. 45. For Carr's dealings with his staff, see also Minutes of the Provincial Typographical Association, Report of the Cardiff Deputation, 29 August 1887, pp. 99-100, University of Warwick Modern Records Centre, MSS 39A/TA/1/3. For the political engagements of Victorian editors, see Derek Fraser. "The Editor as Activist: Editors and Urban Politics in Early Victorian England," in Joel H. Wiener, (ed), *Innovators and Preachers, The Role of the Editor in Victorian England* (Westport, Connecticut, 1985), pp. 121-142. The commercial and administrative structures of the *Western Mail* and other successful newspapers deserve further attention and impinge directly on the concerns of this paper. The relationship between mode of production and style, however, must be explored elsewhere.

6. *South Wales Daily News,* for example, 21 August 1895.

7. Thomas Halliday, leader of the Amalgamated Association of Miners, reviled the *South Wales Daily News* in 1874 in these terms: "This so-called Liberal organ . . . is the lickspittle of the masters . . . a rag, or little better than a rag . . . well up with the large masters of South Wales." Not unexpectedly, this outburst from a public platform was reported without comment in the *Western Mail,* 17 August 1874.

8. *South Wales Star,* for example, no. 1, 20 March 1891. For explorations of "American" and "Imperial" South Wales, see G.A. Williams, *The Welsh in Their History* (London, 1982), chapter 7, and Dai Smith, *Wales! Wales?* (London, 1984), p. 152 ff.

9. K.O. Morgan, *Wales in British Politics* (Cardiff, 1962), chapters 3 and 4.

10. *South Wales Star*, 22 May 1891. Despite its claims to be a "national"

paper, the *Western Mail* failed to make much headway in North Wales, where the Welsh edition of the *Liverpool Daily Post* enjoyed—and continues to enjoy—a healthy circulation.

11. D. Davies, "The Journalism of Wales During the Victorian Era," *Young Wales*, 31-32, August 1897, p. 187.

12. J. Duncan to T.E. Ellis, 14 August 1886, T.E. Ellis Papers, MS 369, National Library of Wales, Aberystwyth (N.L.W.).

13. For example, the report of Gladstone's impending resignation, which appeared in the *Pall Mall Gazette* on 31 January 1894, was hotly debated in Gee's *Y Faner* the following week.

14. T.E. Ellis to Williams, 27 September 1884, N.L.W. MS 10851B/13; letter from E.W. Evans, dated 21 January 1886, N.L.W. MS 10851B/9. The best study of this paper available in English is R. Buick-Knox, *Wales and 'Y Goleuad"* (Caernarfon, 1969). Evidence of the distribution network of the Wesleyan press may be found in the Wesleyan Archives, MS 977C, N.L.W.

15. John Davies (Gwyneddon), 1832-1904, was editor of *Cronicl Cymru*, founding editor and owner of *Y Goleuad* in 1869, and a leader writer for *Y Genedl Gymreig*. He had a seat on the Board of Directors of the Welsh National Newspaper Company, was a leading temperance advocate, and an active member of the North Wales Liberal Federation (N.W.L.F. Minutes, N.L.W. MS 21,171D).

16. J.E. Hughes, "Dylanwad y Wasg Newyddiadurol ar Fywyd Cymdeithasol y Genedl," *Y Traethodydd*, LXV (Medi/September 1910), p. 397.

17. *South Wales Echo*, no. 1, 13 October 1884; *South Wales Daily News*, 6 August 1895. See also D. Smith and G.W. Williams, *Fields of Praise* (Cardiff, 1980), pp. 6-7, and Brown, *Victorian News*, p. 245-246.

18. Davies, "Journalism of Wales," p. 184.

19. J. Myfenydd Morgan, "Diffygion y Cymeriad Cymreig," *Y Traethodydd*, LIII (Tachwedd/November 1898), 472.

20. Davies, "Journalism of Wales," pp. 185-186.

21. *Ibid.*

22. *Ibid.*

23. Details of the Welsh National Press Co., for example, may be found in the W.J. Parry Correspondence, N.L.W. 8816c/74.

24. The economics of small circulation newspapers, in this case, the radical unstamped papers of the 1830s, are described by James Curran, in James Curran and Jean Seaton, *Power Without Responsibility: The Press and Broadcasting in Britain* (London, 1981), pp. 54-55.

25. *South Wales Star*, 20 March 1891; *South Wales Daily News*, "The Welsh Press," for example, 6 August 1895, or *South Wales Echo*, "What Welshmen Think" by "Adolygydd," for example, 28 October 1888.

26. W.T. Stead, *The Revival in the West: A Narrative of Facts* (London, 1905), pp. 23, 41-54. "Where Stead was an innovator was in the systematic use

he made of the interview." Brown, *Victorian News*, p. 162.

27. T.P. O'Connor, *Memoirs of an Old Parliamentarian* (London, 1929), vol. 1, p. 303.

28. New departures that were made in Welsh-language journalism at this time require further examination. See, for example, the Prospectus of the Welsh National Press Co., in *Y Werin*, 24 June 1892. *Y Faner* and *Yr Herald Cymraeg*, both extant, deserve separate treatment, as do the periodicals. O.M. Edwards, for example, began to publish *Cymru*, a successful monthly magazine, in 1891.

PART THREE

SUBJECTS AND AUDIENCES

9
John M. Robson
Marriage or Celibacy?:
A Victorian Dilemma

On 30 July 1868, a leading article in the *Daily Telegraph* began:

If the public has watched with an amused wonder the flood of letters poured upon our columns by the spinsters, bachelors, wives, husbands, widows, widowers, and old maids of the community, we have ourselves shared the astonishment and interest. We frankly own that we did not know what was coming when we threw open the gates of publicity for the discussion of "Marriage or Celibacy?" We have been like the fisherman in the *Arabian Nights,* who caught the simple-looking silver box in his net, and opened it to behold issuing forth a mighty cloud, which rolled right across the sky and filled the blue vault, turning at last into a Djin of tremendous dimensions, who had been locked up ever since the time of Solomon. Or, to choose a still more suitable analogy, it has been with us as with the schoolmaster in the Norse story, to whom the water-elves sent a letter. A damp feeling about the epistle, together with its curious look, made him open it out of doors; whereupon flowed from it, first a stream which filled the yard, then a torrent which inundated the street, then a river which washed the town away, and finally there remained a huge lake which hid the entire countryside. It was a letter that set open the flood-gates of all our amazing correspondence; and the public have seen only so much of the flood as we could turn forth again; the fact being that, for every epistle which has seen the light, twenty at least were of necessity relegated to an oblivion not always deserved.

Very different is the content and tone of a leading article in the same paper six weeks earlier:

There comes to our knowledge every now and then the evidence of a trade so infamous, horrible, and pitiless, that its prosperity is due to its hateful character. Society will not contemplate the hideous traffic. Justice does not wield against the plague a weapon stern and unsparing enough to use with any effect; the eyes of the kind and good turn from the proof of the evil with a loathing too strong for the sense of duty and action, and after each outburst of irrepressible disclosures, we conspire together to forget the event, lest the open mention of the abomination should make the air of public discussion too foul for Virtue to breathe . . . . The slave trade, which has cost this sad and guilty earth so many tears, so much gold to pay for them afterwards, so much blood to wash them away, was innocent in comparison with the fiendish buying and selling of which we mean to speak plainly. The slave trade only dealt in the bodies of human creatures: this deliberately traffics with their souls, and consigns the womanhood of helpless and friendless creatures to "death in life," as "per invoice," and for "value-received.". . . Again, we say that murder, like the slaver, only assails the body, and "after that has no more which it can do." But these hellish commercial speculations, and the people who are the *commis-voyageurs* and consignees, murder the spirit, kill with cold, butcherly lust of money, the life of a woman's soul, slay the hope in her, destroy her womanly right to be a happy, honest mother, and to live and die in a home, impair the sweetness and sacredness of her existence, and leave it to rot with guilt, remorse, and self-scorn, into that ghost of God's work and purpose, which we call, to keep ourselves up in the practice of wit and irony, "a daughter of pleasure." But what we describe is only half the murder, although the direst half. The human or inhuman devils, who feed the maw of a bestial vice with victims, do not stop short at the soul of a woman. Indirectly they finish the job, and murder her body too. Some night—after many dreadful nights and days, it may be more or less—since the Antwerp or Calais boat has delivered the commodity, as per invoice, it goes back to sea—does the "commodity." But it goes upon the tide, a ghastly, festering corpse, with its hair muddy and washing about the face, when the beauty which ruined it is withered. This is their work—these butchers of a sister's soul! Or the policemen for a short time leaves his ordinary "beat," to bring the body of a girl, all but speechless with poison, into the accident-hall of the hospital, and she gasps out a word of a foreign tongue, and dies, while the surgeon seeks to aid her in the misery that is her lot. This is their work—these merchants on the Exchange of Hell; these men who break up souls and bodies to make a harlot, and then a corpse. . . .[1]

Different as these two leaders are, they are part of one story, which began not with a letter but with a news report on 15 June, under "Police Intelligence. / Mansion House," concerning a needlewoman from Antwerp, who had been persuaded to come to London, passage paid, to become a waitress. She had been told to apply to Miss Page at a house in Somerset Street, Portman Square, where, in fact, she was to be entrapped into prostitution. The lord mayor, to whom she had applied, correctly interpreted the facts, and it was arranged to send the woman back to Belgium.

The news report prompted the leading article on the sixteenth quoted above, which in turn brought a letter published on the seventeenth under the title "The Procuress," from a surgeon, John W. Miller, commenting on the case as illustrative of the problem. Another leading article on the subject appeared on the nineteenth, along with letters, again headed "The Procuress," from a Mr. Nicholas (saying he would put down money right away for the cost of prosecuting Miss Page), from Harriet Barnett (offering 50£. for prosecution), and once more from Miller (offering to convene a meeeting for the purpose). On the twentieth "One Sorrowing for her Sex" offered 20£., and then the subject lapsed until the twenty-forth, when views of "A Barrister" on the causes of prostitution were published. He commented in part:

The principal root of the evil lies in the exaggerated notions of luxury that pervade our social system, and put an almost impassable bar upon early marriage, in the middle and wealthier classes. For nearly half a century a custom has been growing up, and is now fixed, that young men, when they marry, are expected, if they mean to maintain their social *status*, to live in almost the same style as their parents and the circle in which their parents move.

There is nothing unusual in the record to this point,[2] though the individual items are valuable as evidence both of perceived fact and attitudes. And the subject probably would have disappeared had not a letter appeared on the twenty-sixth, still under the same heading, signed "R.P.C.," that picked up the Barrister's theme:

I am a young man of the class named by him [Barrister], and my parents have kept their carriages. Years ago I entertained the opinions of your correspondent with regard to the social evil, its cause, and the means of reduction, and have endeavoured to show an example to my fellow young men by marrying at 24 years of age, with an income of 130£. per annum; and, though happy in a little family, can still find an occasional half-crown to go to the Opera, and shall undoubtedly have a vote under the new lodger franchise. Now, if I had listened to the advice of my friends, in all probability I should by this time be equally gay as the friends of my boyhood now are, and in the course of a dozen years have married the lady of calculation, instead of having by my side one whom I know does not wear false hair, and whose bloom of face the baby cannot kiss away. I have another source of pride in my young wife: she believes me to be thoroughly honourable in my detestation of the means by which so many of our sisters are brought to the streets. Do our parents think of these horrible things when they tell us to be worldly, and say that we must not marry till we have earned 500£. a-year, and lost all our young feelings of admiration and devotion for the fairest prize of our life?

This letter prompted the *Daily Telegraph* to publish yet another long leading article on the same day, saying in part:

There is no doubt that the letter which we lately printed from our correspondent, "A Barrister," laid bare one main root of the awful evil which we have exposed and denounced in these columns. The outrageous expectations of parents in behalf of their marriageable daughters, and the inflated sumptuary ideas of the young ladies themselves, are, past all question, a cause—and a cardinal cause—of this cruel traffic in the souls and bodies of foreign women.

And that comment started the flood of correspondence. On the twenty-seventh, a Saturday, under the provocative title that was maintained throughout the series, "Marriage or Celibacy?", two letters were published, from "Benedick" and "One Who Has Tried It." Nothing appeared on the Monday following, but on Tuesday, the thirtieth, "Masterfamilias" and "Solon Smiff" picked up the theme that was for the next month to cover an astonishing part of the *mentalités* and *realités* of the period.

In the twenty-five publishing days in July there was a total of 270 letters on the subject—or, rather, as will become evident, subjects—that is an average of more than ten letters each day. (If we are to accept the concluding leader at face value, twenty letters were received for each printed, and so more than 5,000 were sent to the newspaper on this subject.) In addition to the leading articles on the sixteenth and nineteenth, there was one on the twentieth and the one on the thirtieth (quoted above), which explicitly cut off the series. Many of the letters were far longer than any now printed in newspapers, running a full column of very small type, and very few were as short as one paragraph; in fact, including the leaders, the series amounts in transcription to almost 600 double-spaced pages, or close to 150,000 words.

Here is an unexamined mine of information about the period. Of late, there has been a vogue for "history from the bottom up" to counteract the decades of wicked "history from the top down"; perhaps I am dealing in "history from the middle out"—or, to steal another top-of-the-pops phrase, "the bourgeois experience," though this manifestation comes without the Viennese center. Thomas Carlyle was often wrong, but he was certainly right when he said: "Courage, reader! Never can the historical inquirer want pabulum, better or worse: are there not forty-eight longitudinal feet of small-printed History in the Daily Newspaper?"[3] He was not referring to letters to the editor, but now that social history is given the recognition that he called for and it deserves, his remark has even more point not least to anyone who has tried to interpret after transcribing accurately several hundred feet of tiny print. Also pertinent is a comment by Gilbert Murray, speaking at the opening of the British Museum Newspaper Library at Colindale, that "from the historical point of view the newspaper" is "not so much a record of contemporary facts as a picture of the feelings of the time." "Facts," he continued, do "not become known until long after."[4] It is mainly the "feelings of the time" that I am concerned with, though some of the elusive facts can also be found.

The *Daily Telegraph* was the first successful cheap daily, attaining what certainly was seen in its own time as mass circulation. It cost one penny from September 1855; by 1861 it was selling almost 150,000 copies and in the next year had a circulation almost equal to that of all the other London morning papers combined. Initially Liberal and supporting Gladstone, a broad franchise, and social reforms, it became Conservative only in Disraeli's second administration. There was little substantive experimentation in its early years, and one may perhaps infer that the desire to emulate marked both the readers and the proprietors (who were also the main editors). My judgment is that initially the departures from earlier journalistic practice can be seen in the correspondence and in the leading articles, which were more directly tuned to the broad middle and lower-middle classes than were those of its major competitors.

Of course, the *Daily Telegraph* was not the first newspaper to print letters to the editor or even the first to have several letters in successive issues on the same topic.[5] I, however, know of no example earlier than "Marriage or Celibacy?" of a sustained series, under the same heading, consisting of scores of letters from a broad range of readers, taking up common points in expository, argumentative, hortative, and interrogative modes, with dashes of humor and lashings of self-interest. In short, a series providing a quite unusual glimpse into the opinions and behavior of a literate mass audience, if that is not an oxymoron.

In his tantalizingly vague history of the *Daily Telegraph,* Lord Burnham, grandson of the founder of the newspaper, comments on the "special and worthwhile silly-season correspondence," saying: "Topics were not unusually silly in the months of August and September, nor for that matter were readers, but it is difficult to-day . . .to realize quite how dead things became at the end of July when the contents of newspapers were mainly political and there was no autumn season and the long vacation of the courts was both long and real."[6] So in the "last twenty years of the century" correspondence features, "usually coming in with the grouse and going out with the pheasant, . . . were the stand-by. . . ." The implication here is that the editors relied on their readers to fill the gap and stimulated them to do so. Burnham says nothing, however, about the methods, though it is obvious that catchy headings and prompt publication for promising letters and occasional promptings in leaders played an important part.

Burnham lists, without date, several series that were "slight and short": "The Age of Love"; a titleless series "on the continuance of engagements when affection is dead"; "Are Appearances Worth Keeping Up?"; "The Slavery of Drink"; and "The Art of Losing Fat." He says that "some were of deeper purpose and more enduring appearance," the first "big subject" being "Is Marriage a Failure?" in 1888 (the only specific date he gives), prompted by an article in the *Westminster Review* by the actress, Mona Caird; it was discussed in a leading article in the *Daily Telegraph* on 8 August, which brought forth a total of 27,000 letters (not all of which, I need hardly say, were printed). The leader does not explicitly invite letters but certainly is a come-on, and the series, which began on 10 August, ran for more than a month and a half. Usually it occupied three columns, not all of the last being filled. Burnham makes it clear that this series was in some way controlled by John Le Sage, then subeditor, who broadened the scope by sending the paper's Paris correspondent to interview Zola and Dumas fils. He refers to one more series, "Do We Believe?," calling it an even greater success.[7]

Burnham, in writing of the last two decades of the century, seems unaware of any earlier parallel to these series. Newspapers notoriously have memories as short as they are exculpatory: the model for this particular manifestation of the New Journalism can be found in "Marriage or Celibacy?" in 1868. One link between the earlier and the later series is provided by the annual recurrence of the "silly season." The *Daily Telegraph*, following another practice of the time, during the series picked up a passage from the *Spectator* that anticipates Burnham and continues the hydrological imagery:

The journals are tapping the rock early this year, and we cannot wonder at it. There never was for journalists such a wearisome year. There have been few incidents except the Abyssinian expedition, and that allowed of but little writing; and all alike, proprietors, editors, contributors, reporters, penny-a-liners, and readers are bored to exhaustion by the Irish Church. . . . The *Telegraph* has been the first to bring out the pipes, and has struck into a social stratum which does not yield much water; but which was worth investigation, because it lies below the regular watershed.[8]

The New Journalism suggests a descent "below the regular watershed," involving a different perception of newspapers by their readers and by newspapers of their readers. And in this instance we have in the published letters and the leading articles, which are all we have as evidence,[9] a close match between expectation and intention. The *Daily Telegraph* offers its space to serve the public interest; the readers thank it, often expressing their gratitude in the opening sentences of their letters. On 6 July, for instance, A Bachelor says: "I cannot but appreciate the generosity which induces you . . . to afford space for the discussion of this important matter"; A Would-Be Reformer admits to having been "much interested in reading the various and conflicting opinions set forth in the letters you so kindly admit into your paper on this subject"; and A Simple Country Girl judges that it "is, indeed, good of you to throw open your columns to letters on the matrimonial subject, and I am sure you have the gratitude of many thousand English girls." In L.C.J.'s letter of the tenth, the note is one of appeal as well as admiration: "As the ever-ready champion of the weak, can you spare a few inches of your valuable space in the cause of assailed and libelled womanity . . .?" Their unstated assumptions are that the space is valuable and that somehow the *Daily Telegraph* is responsible for the discussion. It is clear that such letters were irresistible invitations to the newspaper to reinforce and broaden its image as a newspaper concerned with justice and impassioned if rational discussion, concentrating on social issues of major importance, and reflecting the lives and beliefs of the solid middle and lower-middle classes.

The *Daily Telegraph* knew its readers in general – but we are less fortunate in particular, having no satisfactory answer to the question, Who wrote the letters? In accordance with the practice of the period, most used pseudonyms, and those who did not had special reasons. Many assume that what they have to say is more important than who is saying it and use signatures appropriate to the subject and indicative of the point of view or tone or both that often suggest membership in a group or class that has special interest in the matter under debate.

A few examples are provided only to illustrate the types (which, of course, are found with variations in all such correspondence in the period). Names reflecting status in relation to the central controversy include Benedick, One Who Has Tried It, Materfamilias, Never Say Die, Nil Desperandam, One Who Married on 120£ a Year, A Happy Nine Years' Wife, Paterfamilias, A Plain Girl, Charlie's Wife, A Simple Country Girl, A Welsh Bachelor Pro-Tem, A Pilgrim of Love, A Few True Girls of the Period, One Who Looks Before He Leaps, Vieux Moustache, A Real Help-Meet, Pegging at It, Un Français qui n'a plus 20 ans, et qui a fini ses études (one of three letters in French – imagine such a phenomenon in the 1980s!), An Ordinary-Looking English Girl, One Who Speaks from Experience, Cassio, A Lover of a Quiet Home, Home-Made Bread, Comfortably Single, A Match-Maker (Matrimonial, not Lucifer), An Eldest Daughter, An Anxious Father, Bread Winner's Wife, A

Young Man of the Period, A Disciple of Malthus, A Woman but not a Slave, "They Also Serve Who Only Stand and Wait," One Who Can't Help It, One Who Is Waiting, A Contented Old Maid, Unfortunate Husband, and that constant favorite, A Bachelor Curate.

Several names may be assumed to be real and identifying: Therese Picot, Edwin C. Booth (Late Inspector of Settlement to the Government of Victoria), George Francis Train, W. Frank Lynn, and W. Parker Snow; there are the forenames and nicknames, real or fictional, but not identifying, such as Lucy, Flo, Penelope, Jane, Allie, Hannah, Joseph, Nellie, Miles, and (but why) Bunny. Penelope, of course, may be a literary allusion (as may Joseph), like Erastes, Enemoplem and Emolas (both to be read in reverse), Giglio, Nachod, and Fabius. I know not where to fit in Solon Smiff, M.E. (whom we shall meet in a moment).

Some express the attitude and tone of the writer: Preceptor, A Would-Be Reformer, Plain Truth, Moderation, Spes, Humanus, A Philanthropist, A Plain Man, Prudentia, Veritas, Espero, Pro Bono Publico, Amicus, Self-Help, Vestigia Nulla Retrorsum, Caution, Lex, and The Best of Things. Others reflect the writers' status in relation to one major solution to the dilemma, emigration: Colonista, Antipodes, Would-Be Emigrant, Perth (W.A.), An Old Colonist, Colonial Tom, Traveller, Roamer Returned, Pioneer, Five Years' Colonist, A South Australian, Pampas, Huron, Kangaroo, Kentucky, An Intending Emigrant to Natal, Canadian J.P., A Colonial Clergyman, and (one of the pessimists) Returned Emigrant.

Finally (excluding a miscellaneous group and the large number signing with initials), there are those, like some already seen, that indicate occupational status: A Young English Governess, A London Mechanic, A Clerk, A Clergyman (aetat 47), A Draper, An Anxious Worker, Professional, Hammer and Nails, Life

Assurance, Accountant, A Married Priest, An Undergraduate, Mariner, Scotch Civil Engineer, and A Poor Tutor.

Although the sex of all the correspondents cannot be determined by the content or signatures, it would appear (including probables) that 211 of the correspondents are men and 63 women; marital status is less easy to determine, but (again, including probables) 75 signal that they are (or were) married; 113 that they were single (of these a few indicate that they are engaged to be married). There is a marked difference between the two halves of the series: Most of the letters from women appear in the first half of the series, and indications of marital status are fewer in the latter half.

	Men	Women	Married	Single	Married Men	Single Men	Married Women	Single Women
To 16 July	101	51	56	67	33	42	23	25
From 17 July	110	12	19	46	11	42	8	4

The reason for these differences (assuming that the editors of the *Daily Telegraph* chose indifferently as to sex and marital status) is that the topic turned from the conditions of marriage to the desirability of one escape hatch from the dilemma—emigration. (Emigration is mentioned in 23 letters up to 16 July, in 99 letters thereafter.) This subject seems to have meant automatically to all concerned that the opinions of single males had weight over any others—or, perhaps less tendentiously, that emigration was more clearly a choice for single males than for any others, whereas opinions on marriage were equally open to all. Interestingly, most of the letters signed by initials—suggesting a lack of bias—involve emigration, and most were evidently written by single men.

On the major initial topic, which can be stated as the likelihood of a successful marriage on an annual income of less than 200£., sex and marital status influence opinion: Up to 16 July, of the males, fifty-two say no to marriage on the stated terms; twelve say yes. Twenty males indicate that circumstances should determine the decision. Of those who say no, twenty are evidently married, twenty-three single; of those who say yes, seven are married, two are single. Of the females, seventeen say no to marriage on the stated terms; twenty say yes. Nine females indicate that circumstances should determine the decision. Of those who say no, ten are evidently married, seven single; of those who say yes, eight are married, twelve are single. On and after 17 July, of the males, twenty-two say no, two yes; of the noes, six are married, fifteen single; of the yesses, one is married, one single. Four say circumstances should dictate. Of the females, ten all of whom are married say no; none says yes. One only says circumstances should dictate. So to some extent, though not fully (and examination of the exact wording qualifies the judgment even further), the stereotype is upheld: In the words of M.T.M., "while unmarried girls are unanimous in saying 100£. or 150£. a year is sufficient, the men almost unanimously agree that married life on such a sum is impossible" (10 July).

A great deal can be inferred from explicit statements about the motives of the letter writers. Although some are lighthearted and some satirical (among them many of the most interesting), gratitude is expressed several times to specific writers for bringing up practical issues. The series was seen as a channel for offering and receiving practical and moral advice. An example is the account given by Paterfamilias on 4 July:

The reasons, I believe, why we are able to make our means [under 300£. per annum] stretch so far, are these. I am, though I trust I shall not be considered immodest for saying so, never idle! I always find so much to do in my house that I have scarcely a moment to spare to think about what we commonly call "amusements." When not employed with extra work from the office, I am cutting my grass, sticking my beans, doing carpenter's work, drilling my children in music, or mending their toys. My wife, also, is never idle. Our washing is not done out, but at home, by a charwoman; and my wife is not too proud to assist in ironing some of the light articles, to lend an eye and hand to the cooking department, to make many of the children's dresses, to trim her own bonnet, and darn her husband's hose. Keeping but one good servant, my wife feels it her duty, and therefore a pleasure to do all she can to preserve the home as one of comfort.

One of the goals of the correspondents is to put down nonsense, especially pernicious nonsense. Indeed, some of the writers are quite angry, perhaps most typically when attacking those false notices of the proper education for young women that lead to silly behavior. For example, A Country Girl (on 10 July) identifies a major reason against marriage as "the great want of rational topics of conversation." She adds that she speaks only "from short experience, and would not condemn all for the sake of a few," but continues the indictment:

Take a sample of the conversation I have heard among the ladies at an ordinary friendly call, or an evening party, as the case may be: Mrs. E's dress, how elegant it looks! Miss C.'s ornaments, what are they worth? the cut of a Marie Antoinette, the length of a skirt, the exquisite style of Mr. A.'s moustache, the bad taste young Wilson always shows in his neckties, the last new thing in trimmings, the lovely complexion of Miss D., — the last remark followed up by the whisper, "Ah, but do you know she uses rouge and pearl powder?" — the size of Miss K.'s chignon, and the false curls Mrs. L. delights to wear.

But complaints are not the only or even the principal burden of the correspondence. Not a few of the writers pride themselves on offering a service through instruction and information about, say, openings for emigration; these are not always selfless, for the writers are identified (or identifiable) as agents for governments and emigration companies; or are perhaps, like "Natal," just enthusiasts: "If any one of your correspondents would like to settle in Natal, on a free grant, I shall be glad to cooperate with him. All applications for free grants are subject to the consideration of the Commissioners" (28 July); or the extremely well-informed "Kentucky": "I am a professional man, residing in Kentucky, but not a naturalised citizen of the United States. Before I settled in this beautiful region — the garden of the United States — I had served as surgeon in passenger and mail steamers, and had been in India, Mauritius, Natal, the Cape Colonies and Free State, in Brazil, River Plate, Chili, Bolivia, and Canada. Briefly let me tell you my experiences of these various countries." (25 July.) And he does just that.

There are fewer letters specifically asking questions; those that do usually have the aim of relieving uncertainty about the wisdom of plans and actions.[10] C.A.J. complains, inviting an informative response: "Though greatly interested in the subject just now occupying so much of your space, I am somewhat disappointed that your correspondents have confined their remarks to the discussion of whether marriage or celibacy is best for London clerks. Now, as I am neither a Londoner nor a clerk, and as your valuable paper is read by thousands of young men in my position in life, I should have been gratified had some kind contributor given us his experience or advice on the subject of matrimony or celibacy for country tradesmen." (11 July) His plea did not go unanswered.

Very evident in the letters is the common Victorian (and, of course, not only Victorian) interest and delight in the war of the sexes; correspondents writing in that vein give more than a hint that they are practicing their expository and argumentative skills, that is, in John Stuart Mill's phrase, writing because they have to say something rather than because they have something to say. And without question they assume that there is a debate. Indeed, one of the strongest justifications for considering this material as one series is the constant interplay between the letter writers: In virtually every letter there are references to the opinions and facts offered by others. Erastes, for instance, undoubtedly has a point of view and appreciates debate but obviously also wants to exercise his pen: "I throw a glove down against your thoughtful and able correspondent, 'Benedick,' and, with your permission as master of these lists, I mean to splinter an argumentative spear upon his shield. . . . Now, sir, I have challenged this doughty champion of the celibates because here is the best aspect of this huge mischief of our time put in the fairest and most plausible manner. . . . But . . . I must ride straighter and strike fuller to unhorse your correspondent. . . . He wields a sharp lance. . . . I drive my lance full against his visor. . . . (1 July)

More obviously sincere, but equally evidently practicing, is A London Mechanic: "As the class to which I belong . . . have not yet been represented by your numerous correspondents, and as I know that many of my fellow workmen are deeply interested in this question, in the absence of some abler pen I beg leave to occupy a little space in your paper; and, as I am but a plain speaker, I must use plain words to express my thoughts. The subject under discussion, Sir, is one of the—I might say 'the' most important in connection with our social life. The marriage state is the union of the lives, the affections, the habits, and desires of two persons, and the inevitable consequence (unless physically incapacitated) the production of more or less children. Now, Sir, very few of your correspondents have, to my mind, treated this subject, to say the least, with sufficient gravity." (10 July)

These few examples suggest a few of the large number of topics opened to scholars by the series. One is the astonishing level of literacy. As always (and this is a necesssary caution throughout), I assume that these are the letters that arrived unsolicited at the editor's desk; although it is likely that among the flood of others that did not get printed there were many less articulate, the series is evidence that the middle class was more literate than is often assumed and higher than it now is (judging by the letters in our newspapers). Another matter open to comment is the kind and variety of references, literary and contemporary: In conjunction with Mill one finds Malthus, and appearances are made by Darwin and Dickens, Browning and Tennyson, Ruskin and Carlyle, Shakespeare, of course, and *a fortiori* the Bible.

The longest and the most entertaining set of references is to Mill, and quotation from a letter on 27 June by Solon Smiff—

much discussed and criticized later—seems obligatory. Smiff has, to his regret and with the aid of Mill's *Principles of Political Economy,* concluded that, "in a highly-civilized State, a happy marriage—that is, a marriage free from the mean dread of absolute want—is an impossibility for all but the rich. . . ." Mill, he notes, has argued that "when early marriages and large families are looked upon with the same abhorrence and contempt as excessive drunkenness we may hope for existence upon easier terms . . .; and startling as this may . . . seem, he goes on to prove it in the most cool, clear, logical and unanswerable way. . . ." Smiff, however, has had the misfortune of being smitten:

I suppose every man has his *beau idéal,* and here I found mine: a lady born and bred; not rich, but highly cultivated, intelligent, and, to my eyes, the loveliest creature on the earth. John Stuart Mill's philosophy begins to fail me. I make frantic efforts to steady myself by the light of cool dispassionate reason. I never go out without his *Principles of Political Economy* in my pocket. . . . His book is always open on my office table; but I read it like a semi-drunken man. . . . I cannot keep away. John Stuart Mill and his philosophy sternly forbid me as a man of honor to propose. Last week I had the supreme happiness of spending a few hours in her society, and the utter misery of seeing an undeniably neat and well dressed fellow paying her too much attention. . . . Her face and figure haunt me. I see them among drawings of cogwheels, sawframes, and boilers [Solon is a mechanical engineer]; she is everywhere. I sit down with a dogged determination coolly and dispassionately, . . .and I take down John Stuart Mill and begin to read. I read on, until I see the well-known features of the honourable member for Westminster before me. I hear his grave voice, addressing me personally. He says, "Solon, Solon, avoid it. . . . You have your own way to make, it is as much as you can do to keep yourself. Leave her in peace, like an honourable fellow, to your well-dressed and well-to-do friend, she is not for you." But gradually the features of the honourable member for Westminster change. His nose shortens until it is a fair delicate Roman nose. His head becomes covered, by a wig that would surprise the House. It is a wig of fair flowing hair, taken off the brows, done up into a "chignon," with a "horse tail" which floats over his shoulders. His eyes change until they become of a dark violet hue. The whiskers disappear and the face fills out until it is a lovely face, blooming and fair, with a delicate colour, which never needs protection from the sun, much less any of Madame Rachel's protection, and the lilies and the roses are ever fighting for the mastery.

The necktie and coat of the honourable member vanish, and a lovely throat and heaving bust, protected by a dainty white dress edged with blue, appear. The voice, so well known in Westminster, changes to a soft and rich contralto, which thrills through one whenever it is heard. Seated in my dingy office, my head sinks upon my hands, and the vision and preaching of the honourable member for Westminster are changed into a glorious day dream, [which] . . . is broken at length. A strange step is heard ascending. I awake, and push the hateful *Economy* away, exclaiming, "O, glorious Lucrece! If this be but a client of the very smallest type; if he brings but the very remotest chance of a job to give me warrant, I will end this wretched struggle between passion and reason as soon as the interview is over; I will hasten to thy feet, oh, darling girl, and learn whether I may venture to hope or must undergo a period of wretched and painful disappointment, which, at any rate, is better than anxious suspense."

The step approaches. A man enters who says: "Mr. Hodl's *[sic]* compliments, Sir, and says your name and assistant's have been wrote up fourteen months, and you always been away or out of town, and he wants that little account for painting of it up settled to-day particular." I turn around, and from my fast diminishing stock pay the account, and sit me down again to John Stuart Mill and his hateful political economy with a sigh.

Following that, it seems appropriate to mention the detailed advice that comes in the form of budgets. One of special interest came on 4 July from E.F.H., who, following Solon Smiff, professes an adherence to Mill's philosophy. He has, however, an old and valued friend (a.k.a. "my O.A.V.F."), who admires not Mill, but a "fair young lady, whose accomplishments" are "only eclipsed by her radiant beauty and her mental acumen." When he proposes, admitting that his income falls just short of 200£. per annum, he receives a billet from her containing this account:

Housing rent	30	0	0
Living for three people, at 4s. per day	72	16	0
Dinners for you in town	25	0	0
Expenses to and from town	10	0	0
Servant	10	0	0
Laundress	15	0	0
Taxes	5	0	0
Gas	5	0	0
Coals	5	0	0
Dress for both	30	0	0

Sundries 5	0	0
Water rate 5	0	0
	217 16	0

His O.A.V.F. is now trying to raise his income to this minimal level.

In general the budgets give clear and comparable figures about the cost-of-living expenses of couples who have and do not have families, and of single men; there is also some information about expenses in the countries to which people were immigrating. Of course, there is subjectivity, but many of the data are instructive. In the budgets, as elsewhere in the series, assumptions have been made about the differences between classes in economic expectations and satisfactions; it is quite clear that descriptions of the "poverty line" (to use an anachronism) for young married couples would require a set of class discriminators. When the main discussion switches to emigration, it becomes evident how aware people were of the importance of class not only in expectations and satisfactions at home but also in estimating the chances of success abroad; there is considerable doubt about the clerks having the strength of body and will as well as the potential skills needed for success in pioneering communities—it is generally conceded that the working classes (artisans can be inferred) have advantages if they are not tempted by that great bugbear of the period, jealous emulation of those of higher social status. A related theme is the need for capitalists in the colonies: in short, precisely those who are creating the pressure for emigration, the lower-middle classes, are those who are the least promising as emigrants.

Another theme is thought-provoking: In what circumstances do young women and men meet and get to know one another? In the words of H.B. (10 July), who admits to having read all the letters, "the greatest bar to marriage seems to me scarcely to have been touched upon. It is the difficulty young men have to get a real knowledge of a young lady before marriage." But when he wrote, he had not had a chance to read the answer offered on the ninth by A London Girl: "There are many who act up to my ideas, and would make really good, industrious, loving wives; but as there is such a prejudice against us, I much fear that many are induced to trust to outward show, which they find so attractive to men, as it is only by seeing girls often and in their own homes that their good qualifications as wives can be discovered." This view accords with that of A Real Help-Meet (7 July), who gives the essential details:

The girls nowadays think they have to do nothing but dress and read novels; happily, there are some exceptions. Men admire girls much more when they can take their share of the household duties. My husband made up his mind to propose to me when he saw me washing up the breakfast things one morning when we were a servant short. He thought he would wait a few days before taking the eventful step. He did so, and caught me a few mornings after, paring potatoes. "Ah! that's the wife for me; I'll propose at once."

In the country, a bachelor tells us, things are arranged somewhat differently.:

Young men usually do not go about seeking a wife. The most ordinary way amongst country young men is accidentally to meet at some friend's house with a nice girl, probably from some other town. The two are pleased with each other's society, and find that their tastes and inclinations are similar, and a friendship springs up . . . [which ends] in mutual love, and a determination to share life's joys and troubles together. (C.A.J., 11 July)

A dominant concern of the correspondents is "The Girl of the Period" (and her counterpart, the "Young Man of the Period," similarly vain and feather-headed and possessing more sinister and debilitating habits). Eliza Lynn Linton's "The Girl of the Period," reprinted in penny pamphlets that generated enormous sales and were kept alive by controversy, as well as by a *Girl of the Period Almanack* and *Miscellany,* by satires (I specially like the series "Mrs. Punch's Letters to Her Daughter"),[11] and by parasols and articles of clothing, caused an immense fuss.[12] One indication of the relation between a manifestation of the craze and "Marriage and Celibacy?" is worth citing. In *The Girl of the Period Miscellany*, no. 7 (September 1868) there is a satirical account of "How I Managed My House on 200£. a Year," by Mrs. T. Wilkins, *neé* Warren. The fictional "Mrs. T. Wilkins" had a real mother, Eliza Warren, whose *How I Managed My House on 200£. a Year* (1864) was another best-seller.[13] Mrs. Wilkins includes, in order to demonstrate its inadequacy, "Mamma's account" from that work:

Rent and Taxes per annum	25	0	0
Coals, candles, and living for married couple, baby and servant, 27s, per week, or	70	0	0
Wages for servant	10	0	0
Insurance for £1000	25	0	0
Clothes for Papa	20	0	0
Clothes for Mamma	15	0	0
Clothes for Baby	5	0	0
Washing	10	0	0
Doctor's bills and unforeseen exigencies	20	0	0
	200	0	0

To Mrs. Tom this is quite ridiculous! Where in London could one live properly for 25£.? And the living expenses are as inadequate as the provision for servants and dress. There is no need for insurance. When she married Tom, his income for five years had been 200£. annually, his expenses 800£. To economize, they very sensibly stayed with friends, although this practice has caused some expense. It has been necessary, therefore, to look a little into things and draw up a budget:

Billiards, bets, cigars, theatres, newspapers, periodicals, etc.	52	0	0
Tips to servants	8	0	0
Travelling expenses	30	0	0
My millinery—paid on account	60	0	0
Tom's clothes—also paid on account	30	0	0
	180	0	0

Surplus to be devoted to renewing accommodation bills, and staving off other difficulties	20	0	0
	200	0	0

Of course, she comments, for them there is no baby or other such nonsense. On this system they have spent in ten months only 166£. and 13s. and so saved four pence on their "legitimate" outlay. (p. 10)

Although a lot of fun (for good or ill) was connected with "The Girl of the Period," it is evident in the letters to the *Daily Telegraph* that the topic was genuinely disturbing to those who agreed with Linton that young girls were all too apt to be fast slang-talkers, apers of the demimonde in costume and manner, who wished to marry only for money and the silly pleasures it can bring, and disturbing equally to those who thought Linton alarmingly wrong. One sample letter only, whose formal tone does not obscure the strong feeling expressed.

As to the "girl of the period," she is a creature of the men's own seeking; their folly has called her into existence; she is a deformity and a libel upon her sex; and, now the men themselves are becoming somewhat disgusted with her, she will, perhaps, ere long disappear, and carry all her meretricious arts and grotesque trickeries with her. . . . But there are thousands of girls good and true—true to their own pure woman-nature; which is not small praise. Whom, I ask again, can they wed without certain misery before them? The "men of the period" are not so short-lived as the "girls" whom we have just dismissed; the follies and vices of fast life are too deep-rooted; they are a part of the very nature of man, and, unless early training be such as to correct the evil in him, he most undoubtedly grows up vain, self-indulgent, and autocratic; so, when he does marry, he seeks rather to exercise dominion over others than to bring his own passions and predilections under prescribed control. ("***," 11 July)

Yet another matter worthy of investigation is what can be inferred about the sources of public knowledge on certain issues: The large number of letters concerning emigration suggests that the facts about this often desperate remedy were little known in spite of the vast amount of information that had been written about the subject during the preceding thirty years and the wide experience of its practibility as well as its difficulties that had accumulated especially during the last two decades. Similarly, so much had been published about the actual cost of living in the United Kingdom—not least by the formidable Mrs. Beeton—that one assumes would have been available to people who possessed knowledge and sophistication evident in these letters.

With reference to emigration schemes, the view of the places most suited for those without hope at home is wider than might be anticipated: Of course, most references (more or less in the order of frequency of mention, though it should be indicated that not all references are favorable) cite Canada (some refer to the rest of British North America), Australia, the United States, and New England, but quite a few cite South America (especially Argentina, Brazil, and Paraguay), a considerable number cite South Africa, a few refer to India, and a couple refer to Mexico and other parts of Central America. (Although there are several indications of the value of settling in places that have a similar culture, there is only rare reference to the problems of losing British nationality in the United States and elsewhere.) The main values associated with emigration are, of course, economic: The assumption is that there is no hope of gradual improvement in status at home for individuals, whereas there is every hope in the new countries. An associated topic is the general and genuine interest shown in "association" and "cooperation," giving more indication of the importance of such notions in the high Victorian period. This discussion, as already indicated, is very much male dominated; although there is some indication that improvement in family conditions is the main desideratum, the bias is that of the male patriarch; only one letter writer asks about the prospects for single women.

One final impression: There is an overwhelming sense that London is awash with clerks, fixed in status, having meager chances other than small increases in wages, competing desperately for underpaid positions, and fearing illness and dismissal.[14]

This impression is so dominant that I cannot do better than quote in conclusion the end of the leading article that brought the series to a close on 30 July. The *Daily Telegraph* must be content, the writer says, with having set forth "the general character of a discussion which has been very creditable . . . to the literary skill of the public, and clearly demonstrative of the fact that, whatever be the just philosophy of the question, the broad fact is that England is no longer big enough for her inhabitants."

NOTES

1. Daily Telegraph, 16 June 1868.

2. I am reminded of the mock newspaper report of the coroner's inquest in *Our Mutual Friend* that ends with "a rapturous admirer, subscribing himself 'A Friend to Burial,' " sending "eighteen postage stamps and five 'Now Sir's' to the editor of the *Times*" (Chap. iii).

3. Carlyle, "On History Again" (1833), *Miscellaneous Essays*, 7 vols. (London, 1872), vol. IV, p. 215. By 1868 the *Daily Telegraph* had many more than 48 feet—more than 100 in its six-column, twelve-page format—and during this series, more than one-half page was given to letters and leaders.

4. Quoted in *The Times*, 24 August 1932.

5. Although one would not wish to ignore them, one cannot consider as competition the spoofs initiated by Matthew James Higgins, the most famous being his writing in 1862 to *The Times* about "the pretty young horsebreakers" (i.e., courtesans, especially Catherine Walters, or "Skittles") who were supposedly causing such admiration that the traffic was held up in Hyde Park. I cannot ignore, however, the possibility that he, under one or more of his aliases (such as "Paterfamilias"), took part in "Marriage or Celibacy?", though he was ill at the time and died the next month. There is no question, of course, that some of the letters in that series were intended, as his were, to draw counterfire from the naive.

6. Lord Burnham, *Peterborough Court: The Story of the Daily Telegraph* (London, 1955), p. 88.

7. *Ibid.*, pp. 146-147. Lawson mistakenly says that the series "Is Marriage a Failure?" was prompted by a letter from Mona Caird, thereby closely duplicating an error made by the leader writer about "Marriage or Celibacy?"

One cannot tell from Lawson's account who was responsible for editing the paper in 1868, let alone for choosing correspondence or planning a series of letters. Thorton Hunt could be considered the editor, but Edward Lawson, later first Lord Burnham (the son of J.M. Levy, the first proprietor), who changed his name after his uncle Lionel Lawson Levy changed his "for business purposes," was generally responsible. John Le Sage was not yet (on this evidence) in a position to be responsible, though he was hired in 1863 as personal assistant to Lawson (*Ibid.*, p. 3)

8. *Daily Telegraph,* 7 July, quoting "How to Save" from the *Spectator.*

9. I am too stodgy to swing deconstructively into the gap opened by a commentator at a seminar at the Institute of Historical Research in the spring of 1986: "I realize that there are evidentiary problems in getting through to what Francis Place doesn't say, but...."

10. Having wondered about the authenticity of the desire for information, I was pleased to come across an annoyed comment that points to the prospect of the modern personal column: "I cannot help remarking . . . that some of your young unmarried correspondents have written for themselves some unexceptional testimonials and recommendations, and that the only drawback is that the private address of each is not placed in the left corner by the side of the date. Can you kindly, Mr. Editor, procure for some of us the interesting intelligence of their whereabouts when they are at home?" (A Lover of Home, 13 July) And at least one correspondent regretted having given his address: "When, in your issue of Monday last, you kindly allowed me space in your columns for the purpose of warning your correspondents against 'drifting into danger' with reference to emigration, I quite forgot the possibility of getting into mischief myself. This, I fear, I have managed to do, for every day since I have received letters in such numbers as to make it utterly impossible for me to reply to them separately. My correspondents are all readers of *The Daily Telegraph,* and, doubtless, in their circumstances and designs, represent a large class of persons." (Edwin C. Booth, 28 July)

11. "Mrs. Punch's Letters to Her Daughter," *Punch,* 4, July 1868, pp. 7-8; 11 July, pp. 12-13; 25 July, p. 44; and 1 August, p. 46. Judy outlines to Judiana "The Rights of Men," the third of which is: "To see that his wife or *fiancée* is properly taught the rudiments of arithmetic, so as to be able to do such sums as these:

"B.'s income is 600£. per annum, but B's wife cannot, with the strictest economy, keep house under 800£. per annum. Subtract the last sum from the first, and what remains to lay by for the education of the boys, and for the dress of the girls, poor things?

"If this does not answer, a man is justified by the laws of his country to quote Adam Smith, Jeremy Bentham, and other learned authorities, demonstrating that two and two make four."

Judy also proposes "a grant millinery and drapery Mart where ladies could buy costumes exactly proportionate to their husbands' incomes."

"Let us begin," she says, "with the 300£. per annum department. Straw bonnets, of any colour, trimmed with ribbon, no flowers nor veils, except Shetland veils worn on hygienic principles to prevent tic-doloureaux, Linsey dress for winter, serge for Sundays; cotton and alpacas for summer, with cloth or alpaca mantles.

"Next let us take the 500£. per annum department. Plain net bonnets for summer, plain velvet for winter; dresses as before, with the addition of black silk, and mantle of same material for summer.

"700£. per annum department. Bonnets as before, with the addition of neat flowers and one small feather; grey silk for summer, silk mantle trimmed with jet, French merino or black silk for winter; choice of mantles from 3£. to 5£."

12. *Saturday Review*, XXV (14 March 1868), 339-340. Originally anonymous, it was republished under her name as a pamphlet, with wide circulation (40,000 copies by one publisher, and there were several), and it appeared (also in 1868) in a volume of thirty-seven essays from the *Saturday Review*, entitled *Modern Women and What Is Said of Them*. For a summary of the subject, see Merle Mowbray Bevington, *The Saturday Review 1855-1868* (New York, 1941).

13. See the later work by "Mr." Warren (obviously a pseudonym), *How They Mismanaged Their House on 500£. a Year* (1878). Another connection with "Marriage or Celibacy?" should also be mentioned; "In the Editorial Sanctum," *Girl of the Period Miscellany*, no. 1 (1868), we find: "Let us get it recognized, say some people, with Mr. Mill at their head, that marriage is not the sole, or even the chief end of women. . . . She [modern woman] may become a powerful man of business; she may be like Julia Pastrana, or Hercules, or Mr. Mill himself, and be no more fit for a wife or mother than he is." (p. 6) The writer quotes the passage to which Solon Smiff had referred on "wife and mother" from the *Principles of Political Economy* Book IV, Chap. vii, Sect. 3; *Collected Works*, vol. III, pp. 765-766.

14. There are only a few parallel references to that other group of the desperate, the governesses. One letter from a governess, however, says things are not as bad as they have been painted.

10

Kate Flint

The Philistine and the New: J. A. Spender on Art and Morality

J.A. Spender turned artistic and literary controversy into front-page news. After the sale of the *Pall Mall Gazette* in September 1892, George Newnes launched a new liberal evening paper, the *Westminster Gazette* and Spender was among the former *Pall Mall Gazette* journalists who joined him. From the publication of the first issue, at the end of January 1893, until 1896, when he took over as editor, Spender worked as assistant editor under E.T. Cook, writing leaders, book reviews, and notices of art exhibitions. "Art News and Gossip" was also regularly supplied by "M.H.S.," probably Marion Harry Spielmann, an adherent of Ruskin who was a frequent contributor to the *Pall Mall Gazette* in the 1880s.

The showing of Degas's *L'Absinthe* at the opening exhibition of the Grafton Gallery in February 1893 gave Spender the opportunity to attack new trends in art and art criticism. The *Studio* commented that "A more typical work than "L'Absinthe" for the new and the old schools to fight over could not have been found."[1] Spender describes the canvas briefly in his initial review of 17 February: "A man and a woman, both of the most degraded type, are seated on a bench in a wine-shop, their backs reflected in a glass screen behind them." Degas's paintings — *The Rehearsal* was also on show — are not, he opines, art: ". . . supposing, that is to say, art is still concerned with what is beautiful."[2] What angered him above all was not so much their exhibition, but the fact that the *Spectator's* art critic, D.S. MacColl, chose to single out *L'Absinthe* for praise. Both its content and its Impressionist style displeased Spender, yet MacColl, in the *Spectator* of 25 February, claimed that the painting provided a lesson: not of morality, but of formal beauty. He wrote of it as one might describe a symbolist poem, rather than the moral narrative that formed the unspoken analogue to more old-fashioned critics' habits of "reading" a picture: "Exactly as a man with a just eye and comprehending mind and power of speech could set up that scene for us in the fit words, whose mysterious relations of idea and sound should affect us as beauty, so does this master of character, of form, of colour, watch till the *café* table-tops and the mirror and the water-bottle and the drinks and the features yield up to him their mysterious affecting note." This "inexhaustible picture," said MacColl, "sets a standard."[3]

In the second leader of March 9, Spender, writing under the pseudonym "The Philistine," took issue with MacColl, claiming to be surprised that such views were put forward in the *Spectator,* "so moral and so reputable in all other relations of life."[4] He was not alone at the time in finding MacColl's views strangely out of place in the newspaper's conservative columns: the Scotsman himself found the opportunity of addressing the *Spectator's* "very large public . . . a remarkable one, as if a heretic had been offered the pulpit of St. Paul's."[5] Spender's sobriquet might ostensibly seem to be borrowed from Matthew Arnold's categories in *Culture and Anarchy:* ". . . my admiration for that remarkable man was barely this side of idolatry," he wrote in his autobiography[6]; although it is strange that Spender ignored or, alternatively, chose to exploit the derogatory emphasis in the appellation "Philistine." Moreover, the remainder of his criticism shows that his cultural ideals were hardly as boorish as the deliberate use of the term suggests. Only a few days earlier, on 3 March, the *Westminster Gazette* carried a rhapsodic review of Walter Pater's *Plato and Platonism:* "lectures full of a golden wisdom full of a golden humour."[7] But the editorial of 9 March was turned to a double purpose in its effort to play upon popular feeling: it spoke against elitism in art and suggested the danger of separating art from morality. As Spender said in his editorial, the dispute was not between one specific style of painting and another — between, for example, Impressionism and the anecdotal genre — but "it touches the whole question of artistic ideals."[8] D.S. MacColl replied to him in two considered *Spectator* articles, "The Standard of the Philistine" (18 March) and "Subject and Technique" (25 March), in which he elucidated many of the tenets of what became known as the New Art Criticism, of which he and R.A.M. Stevenson were the foremost practitioners who developed a technical yet accessible language for talking about new practices in painting and prepared the way for the formalistic criticism of such writers as Roger Fry and Clive Bell.[9]

The "Philistine" believed that certain key criteria should be maintained when criticizing works of art. His values were the orthodox ones of the mid-nineteenth century, which still determined the conservative exhibition policy of the Royal Academy and which derived much of their authority from Ruskin. Spender had himself studied drawing and art appreciation under Ruskin when he was at Oxford, during the term of the latter's second Slade professorship, and greatly admired his views. First, for Spender, subject mattered more than technique in the sense that the latter became an issue only when it had moral connotations. At its crudest, this meant an alertness to value to be rendered for money to be paid, the acknowledgement of labor as pointing to the higher worth of mankind. Ruskin was appealed to here as an authority: "In flourishing periods, whether of trade or art, the dignity, whether of operatives or artists, was held to consist in their giving, in every sense, good value for money and a fair day's work for a fair day's wages."[10] The notorious Whistler/Ruskin trial, the precursor of the *L'Absinthe* controversy, had, of course, pivoted around this issue.

After value for money came the necessity for comprehensibility. The more progressive art critics like MacColl complained continually that "The English public only like pictures of familiar subjects, and only understand painters who see such subjects with the same vulgar unthinking eyes as they themselves are accustomed to contemplate common objects."[11] They ridiculed the taste of suburban mothers and Manchester cottonmongers for using art as they might use cheap tea or tobacco, as a stimulus: "Even so," lamented MacColl, "does the cheap Baby or Bishop or poodle act as a symbol, pull strings of association in the heads of those for whom the visible world does not exist except as a gaudily ticketed catalogue of sentiments."[12] For Spender, art should not require translation into verbal forms in order to be understood: It should not be "unintelligible to the public,"[13] that broad, unspecialized, and unspecified mass for whom he wrote. This point of view was in direct opposition to the New Critics, who were convinced that not everyone has the ability to recognize the formal qualities inherent in "good" works of art. MacColl claimed that the "Philistine" speaks as "one of the 'populace,' and resents the idea that a picture should be painted which is not addressed to a level of popular understanding. . . . The plain and wholesome truth, of course, is that fine painting, like any other fine art, music or literature or drama, is only to be appreciated by a special endowment, assiduously cultivated."[14]

Third, and most important for Spender's journalistic purpose, he emphasized the interrelationship between art and morality. This was another unmistakably Ruskinian concept. "Great art," Ruskin maintained in the third volume of *Modern Painters*, "is produced by men who feel acutely and nobly; and it is in some sort an expression of this personal feeling."[15] In later writings, Ruskin extended this view to the perception of art as reflecting not only the moral condition of the individual who produced it but also of the society in which it was executed. For Spender, the two were indistinguishable. This emphasis on morality covered both content and form, for it supported teaching through example by means of the stories and scenes narrated and reflected a belief that beauty and decency should be projected on the canvas in order to counteract the ugliness of modern life. It was one of the culturally conservative critic's self-appointed functions to draw attention to the acceptable and to point with a horrified finger to that which transgressed acceptable standards of social behavior, such as the "study of human degradation, male and female," as Walter Crane described *L'Absinthe*, entering the debate on the letter page of the *Westminster Gazette*.[16] This kind of moral criticism worked, moreover, to reinforce the assumption that art could, and should, be easily comprehended by those who have no special training in the field. This, of course, was the audience to whom Spender was appealing. The leader of March 9 describes the position from which he speaks: "we (and I am one) who count ourselves ordinary people.'[17] Yet for the New Art Critics, as Oscar Wilde's Gilbert articulates in *The Critic as Artist*, the "first condition of criticism is that the critic should be able to recognise that the sphere of art and the sphere of Ethics are absolutely distinct and separate."[18]

Spender's editorial engendered a heated correspondence. At first, this was slow in developing, taking second place to a debate over how to interpret Mrs. Solness's feeling for her "nine lovely dolls" in Ibsen's *The Master Builder*. MacColl and Spender fired a few shots at each other. "The affliction that he parades is indeed incurable; he will never know what painting is," complained MacColl of the "Philistine" on March 10[19]; "When a work like this is set up as a standard of beauty, I think I discern the cause of the vulgarities and flippancies which are spoiling many young painters," replied Spender the following day.[20] On 15 March the debate broadened as Harry Quilter, who had been writing splenetic and proudly individualistic art criticism since 1876, joined in, condemning the absurdity of MacColl's "lucubrations," his irreverence for standards that had been built up by his elders, and for expressing enthusiasm, throughout his criticism, only for paintings produced by members of the New English Art Club. He strengthened Spender's editorial hand in what was to become, during the next few years, something of a moral crusade for the *Westminster Gazette,* when he reminded its readers that "people are apt to take their opinions from their newspaper as well as their facts."[21] With the exception of further communications from MacColl, setting Quilter straight on factual points, the *Westminster Gazette* printed little in the way of support for Degas. The painter Charles Furse on 18 March did speak of *L'Absinthe's* qualities of draftsmanship, design, and color, "its delicacy of selection, the subtlety and research of its drawing"[22], and Walter Sickert, who, as he pointed out in his letter, knew the work of Degas well, maintained that "much too much has been made of "drink," and "lessons," and "sodden," and "boozing" in relation to the picture and hazarded the conjecture that the painting's title is not *L'Absinthe,* but the far less sensationalist "Un homme et une femme assis dans un cafe."[23] Among the authoritative voices raised in support of Spender's views were Walter Crane, who stated that the work manifested "the outward and visible signs of the corruption of society which are characteristic of the most modern painting,"[24] and W.B.

Richmond. Richmond, fashionable portrait painter and friend of
Spender and his wife, put forward the notion that *L'Absinthe's*
claim to be spoken of as a painting was in itself dubious: "It is a
novelette—a treatise against drink. Everything valuable about it
could have been done, and has been done, by Zola." Zola, Richmond said, was a clever man, "but curiously enough his
cleverness is literary far more than pictorial."[25]

II

Spender, writing as a journalist, was far more concerned with
the topic of morality than was MacColl. It had popular appeal,
unlike the theoretical questions about how the autonomous
language of painting could be translated into the verbal structures
of prose, which were currently intriguing the *Spectator's* critic.
When the "Philistine" resumed his defense of standards, it was in
order to deal with specifically literary issues.

During the next two years, Spender periodically grumbled
against contemporary fashions in literary criticism, which, he
believed, praised that which was new and experimental, irrespective of merit. He proved himself an heir to Robert Buchanan in
his strictures against the decadence of Selwyn Image, Arthur
Symons, W. B. Yeats, and John Davidson. Early in 1895 the
combination of the appearance of a number of works of "new"
fiction and the publication of the English translation of Max Nordau's *Degeneration* gave Spender both the occasion and an
emotive vocabulary with which to revive the aura of a moral
crusade, of common-sense decency, which he had built around
L'Absinthe.

Degeneration—"a very remarkable book"—was given a
serious, commendatory front-page review in the *Westminster
Gazette* of 25 February 1895. Its contents were summarized:
Nordau applied to literature and art the theory of "degeneracy"

which had been developed by Lombroso and others in relation to criminology and sociology. Lombroso saw crime and lunacy as forms of organic degeneracy, but, continued Nordau, "degenerates are not always criminals, prostitutes, anarchists, and pronounced lunatics; they are often authors and artists."[26] Emotionalism, mental weakness and despondency, and mystical delirium can be found, according to Nordau, in all these categories. The *Westminster Gazette* review is not devoid of criticism. It points out that Nordau has misinterpreted Ruskin, has been conspicuously unjust to Walt Whitman, and has given a primarily mythical account of Oscar Wilde. But the conclusion is entirely in keeping with the German's spirit: "The great need of the day is to preserve the sane and wholesome remnant from con- tamination. . . . Under these circumstances a great responsibility devolves upon the critics. Their duty, according to our author, is to call a spade a spade. Unfortunately they are too much given to finding plausible reasons for calling spades 'agricultural in- struments,' dirt 'art,' and disease 'courage.' "[27]

The reviews of *Degeneration* in more established publications tended to be less kind to Nordau. The *Spectator's* literary critic found in the author "one of those signs of disease which he so elo- quently depicts—a tendency to baseless exagerration"[28]; the *Saturday Review* noted the book's potential for short-term popular appeal: "It comes, appropriately, before the beginning of the season, and will provide society with a subject that might last as long as the present Government."[29] Hugh E.M. Stutfield, in two articles in *Blackwood's Edinburgh Magazine,* and Janet E. Hogarth, writing in the wake of the "Philistine," in the *Fortnightly Review,* were among the few who, like him, attempted to link Nordau's theories with contemporary literary movements: for Hogarth, the *fin-de-siècle* authoress, complaining against "the slavery of the marriage yoke," had "the instinct of a true degenerate . . . the delirious fancies of the victims of sex mania."[30]

Spender's articles on "The New Fiction" ran for a week, from 5-9 March, and were followed by a correspondence even more lively than that which accompanied the *L'Absinthe* controversy. The two debates, together with Spender's pieces on decadent poetry, were reprinted in 1895 in volume form that had a "flaming red cover embellished with a vigorous drawing of a frantic young woman by Mr. Arthur Rackham"[31] In his introduction to this volume, Spender drew together modern trends in art and literature.

Just as the "new" artists despised the picture that touched, the picture that taught, and the picture that pleased, so did the "new" writers profess to despise "the common affections," "the common sentimentality," and the "common morality." This led naturally in two directions. In the first place, there appeared a vast deal of "purple and gold stuff" in prose and verse which was immediately hailed as comparable to the greatest things in literature, but which seemed to the Philistine to say little or nothing, with a ruinous expenditure of precious words. This was "art for art's sake." In the second place, the maxim that art has nothing to do with morality was extended to mean that "art has a positive preference for the immoral," as ordinary people understand the word. [32]

In the first of his articles on the New Fiction, Spender claimed that since the prosecution of Henry Vizetelly for publishing several of Zola's works in translation, the police court had ceased to be operative against undesirable fiction. The *Westminster Gazette* proposed itself and its readers as replacement moral vigilantes: "We Philistines must assert ourselves."[33] Spender shows himself to have Nordau in mind as he asks in what respect current literature can be called advanced "unless in pruriency, morbidity, degeneracy," and attempts to gain credibility for his argument by not condemning all controversial fiction out of hand: He finds literary merit in Sara Grant's novel that dealt with the potentially shocking subject of venereal disease, *The Heavenly Twins,* in "Iota's" feminist *A Yellow Aster,* and in Grant Allen's *The Woman Who Did.* But he singles out, as representative of what he calls the "Revolting Woman" class of fiction, a far more technically experimental volume, from which moral didacticism, as Spender understood it, is conspicuously missing: George Egerton's second collection of short stories entitled *Discords*. He condemns Egerton for what he identifies as a relentless preoccupation with sexual matters: This, he asserts with the authority of pseudosciences to support him, is "the way of the neuropathic egoist."[34]

On subsequent days the "Philistine" railed against the "defiant man" novel, similar in being governed by impulse, sentiment, and "hysteria" to the New Woman fiction but, he claimed, even more cynical. It was typified for him by G.S. Street's short stories, which depict, he told his readers, a world peopled exclusively "by licentious men and faded women, whose life is a round of intrigues, betrayals, and irregular connexions."[35] This article was followed by one on the "morbid" and "lurid" classes of fiction, such as Thymol Monk's *An Altar of Earth,* in which a woman suffering from an incurable disease submits, it seems, to the sexual demands of an unappetizing builder in order to save a piece of woodland so that a community can enjoy the countryside's beauty, and Arthur Machen's even more preposterous tale, *The Great God Pan.* This tale features a physician who has the power to liberate from a woman's brain a spirit that turns out to be a she-devil incarnate, driving men to suicidal despair, and finally, having killed herself, dissolves into a black amorphous jelly: "an incoherent nightmare of sex," comments Spender, after recounting the wildly absurd plot at some length, an example of "sex-mania" which has always revelled in the contemplation of imaginary inarticulate horrors.[36] In addition, in that day's article, the Philistine attacked George Egerton's translation of Ola Hansson's work partly because this gave him the opportunity to deride the "decadent Nietzsche's 'triumphant doctrine of the ego,"[37] of which Egerton talks in her Preface. Spender mistrusted what he read as Nietzsche's asocial individualism and his interest in forces that lie below the surface of the human personality. In his journalism, Spender expressed a deep suspicion of anything that was not unambiguous, open to straightforward interpretation.

In the Philistine's final piece, "Recapitulation," Spender posed some rhetorical questions that he answered in the tone of "common-sense," which was his hallmark. "Is Sex Mania 'Art'?": "A Philistine has always a wholesome suspicion when he is told that a thing which is repugnant to ordinary taste is 'Art.' " He reiterated his point that art is inseparable from morality. "Is Sex Mania 'Life'?"—not, he thinks, for any but a small fraction of the population, and in any case, it must be so physically debilitating that such a life would be a short one: "Life it may be, but it is also 'death' to ordinarily-constituted human beings." Decadent art must be a prerogative of the rich and idle. Others have families to keep, businesses to pursue, more diverse interests to follow: "Nature, art, literature, sport, friendship, hospitality, travel, politics, philanthropy." Having provided a synopsis of his paper's contents, he was moved to ask: "Is Sex Mania 'Modern'?" No, it was rather a relapse into savagery. He concluded by reiterating that it is the duty of the Philistine to speak up, to challenge the ideas that are currently and thoughtlessly fashionable in criticism.[38]

Without wishing to question the good faith of Spender's expressed moral beliefs, the great detail that he provided in relating the plots of this New Fiction suggests that the Philistine's journalism contained something of what Richard Hoggart, in the context of twentieth-century popular Sunday papers, has called a "pseudo-moral Janus glance."[39] The readership could enjoy a mild titillation of scandal while remaining on morally safe ground. The debate was less popular in other quarters, however. In his autobiography, Spender tells how "art critics who, in spite of their advanced ideas about the handling of paint, were irreproachably family men, complained bitterly of being mixed up with the exploiters of the new fiction." John Lane told Spender how his intervention had "killed the *Yellow Book* and spoilt the sales of some of his favourite writers." The energetic correspondence between writers, publishers, and supporters of the Philistine's point of view had to be brought to a close, according to Spender, for "our correspondents were beginning to say outrageous things about each other."[40]

Public events, however, played straight into Spender's hands. In early April 1895, Oscar Wilde was unsuccessful in bringing an action for libel against the Marquess of Queensberry, in connection with the latter's exposure of details concerning the relationship between Wilde and Lord Alfred Douglas, the marquess's son. The *Westminster Gazette* professed to debate the rights and wrongs of reporting the details of the case before noting them in minute detail. Alongside Wilde's homoerotic poetry and suggestive correspondence, nothing could have served the Philistine better than his reply to the judge's question: "You don't concern yourself about the morality or immorality of a book?" – "I don't believe any book or work of art produces any effect on the conduct."[41] The day after the not guilty verdict was delivered, the paper's main leader dealt with "the decadent doctrine of 'Art for Immorality's sake.' " It recalled Spender's recent articles and used the case to demonstrate the perniciousness that could emanate from separating art from the demands of responsible social conduct. Luckily, explained the leader writer, the slide toward decadence had not gone too far in England:

for the Philistine element is strong enough to check the excesses of the artistic temperament. But it has gone far enough, and the crushing exposure which has come in this case will, we hope, give pause to some who have followed, either in sheer thoughtlessness or in the perverted notion that they have a mission to emancipate 'Art' from the discipline of civilised mankind.[42]

At no time does Spender challenge the paradox of equating

"Philistinism" with "civilization." The critical debates that he engineered helped establish the tradition, in popular journalism, of praising art and writing that not only uphold widely-held moral values but are immediately intelligible to audiences that do not possess specialized knowledge or understanding. Inevitably, this leaves no room for innovation, whether at the level of content or of form. Spender, unlike the New Critics whom he attacked, made no attempt to educate his readership. Instead, he was interested in aesthetic issues only to the extent that they could be turned into journalistic copy, feeding off the public's inherent suspicion of elitism and their conservative expectations of artistic and literary representation. Cultural experimentation, for the Philistine and his journalistic successors, was invariably treated as a highly suspicious activity.

NOTES

1. "Laodicean," "Studio Gossip," *Studio* I, (1893), p. 36. For an earlier discussion of the reception of *L'Absinthe* in England, see Ronald Pickvance, "*L'Absinthe* in England," *Apollo* LXXVII, (1963), pp. 395-398.

2. *Westminster Gazette*, 17 February 1893, p. 3.

3. D.S.M. "The Grafton Gallery," *Spectator*, 25 February 1893, p. 256.

4. *Westminster Gazette*, 9 March 1893, p. 1.

5. D.S. MacColl, *Life, Work and Setting of Philip Wilson Steer* (London, 1945), p. 43.

6. J.A. Spender, *Life, Journalism and Politics* (London, 1927), p. 41.

7. *Westminster Gazette*, 3 March 1893, p. 4.

8. *Ibid.*, 9 March 1893, p. 1.

9. See Introduction, *Impressionists in England: The Critical Reception*, edited by Kate Flint (London, 1984).

10. John Ruskin, "Whistler v. Ruskin," *The Works of John Ruskin*, edited by E.T. Cook and Alexander Wedderburn (London, 1903-1912), vol. XXIX, p. 587.

11. "At Whistler's," *The Picture Gallery Boy*, II, 4 May 1886, p. 123.

12. D.S.M., "The Royal Academy—I," *Spectator*, 7 May 1892, p. 642.

13. *Westminster Gazette*, 9 March 1893, p. 2.

14. D.S.M., "The Standard of the Philistine," *Spectator*, 18 March 1893, p. 357.

15. Ruskin, "Modern Painters III," *Works*, vol. V, p. 32.

16. *Westminster Gazette*, 20 March 1893, p. 2.

17. *Ibid.*, 9 March 1893, p. 1.

18. Oscar Wilde, "The Critic as Artist," *Intentions* 1891, reprinted in *The Artist as Critic*, edited by Richard Ellman (London, 1970), p. 393.

19. *Westminster Gazette*, 10 March 1893, p. 2.

20. *Ibid.*, 11 March 1893, p. 3.

21. *Ibid.*, 15 March 1893, p. 3.

22. *Ibid.*, 18 March 1893, p. 2.

23. *Ibid.*, 20 March 1893, p. 2.

24. *Ibid.*

25. *Ibid.*, 16 March 1893, p. 2.

26. *Ibid.*, 25 February 1895, p. 1.

27. *Ibid.*, p. 2.

28. Unsigned review, "Degeneration," *Spectator*, 2 March 1895, p. 291.

29. Unsigned review, "A Teuton Come to Judgement," *Saturday Review*, 9 March 1895, p. 323.

30. The articles by Hugh E.M. Stutfield, are "Tommyrotics" *Blackwood's Edinburgh Magazine*, CLVII (1895), 833-845, and "The Psychology of Feminism," *CLXI* (1897), 104-117; The quote by Janet E. Hogarth from "Literary Degenerates" is in *Fortnightly Review*, LXIII (1895), p. 591.

31. Spender, *Life*, p. 58. This collection of journalism, *The New Fiction (A Protest Against Sex-Mania) and Other Papers* (London, 1895), has the name *The Philistine* on the title page and the initials J.A.S. at the end of the introduction. These initials led to the wrong attribution, in both the British Library and National Union Catalogues, given to J. Ashby-Sterry.

32. J.A.S., Introduction, *The New Fiction*, pp. vi-vii.

33. *Westminster Gazette*, 5 March 1895, p. 1.

34. *Ibid.*, 6 March 1895, p. 2.

35. *Ibid.*, 7 March 1895, p. 2.

36. *Ibid.*, 8 March 1895, p. 2.

37. *Ibid.*

38. *Ibid.*, 9 March 1895, pp. 1-2.

39. Richard Hoggart, *The Uses of Literacy* (London, 1957), p. 176.

40. Spender, *Life*, p. 58.

41. *Westminster Gazette*, 3 April 1895, p. 6.

42. *Ibid.*, 6 April 1895, p. 1.

11

Deian Hopkin

The Left-Wing Press and the New Journalism

On the face of it the juxtaposition of the New Journalism and the left-wing press appears somewhat improbable. The left-wing press surely has nothing to do with the sort of milieu in which the New Journalism is conventionally seen to function. There are two reasons why one might say this. First, by definition it was part of a political press whose audience was differentiated by belief. In the second place, moreover, this particular political press existed to oppose those very forces of commercialism and profit making that constituted the foundations of the mainstream press. Indeed, as one might expect, most left-wing journalists disavowed any connection with the commercial press; they claimed, moreover, that the existence of the commercial press and its propensity to distort the truth and manipulate opinion constituted their own *raison d'etre*.[1]

Yet, however loud the protestations, to a greater or lesser extent, the left-wing press was deeply influenced by the general developments that occurred in the press in the last decade or so of the nineteenth century. This brief survey attempts to examine three features in particular: the role of personality, the range and character of editorial content, and the nature of the financial organization. An examination of each of these features demonstrates how pervasive was the influence of the New Journalism in this most unlikely quarter.[2]

First, let us be clear what we mean by the left-wing press. Broadly speaking one means those papers that espoused socialism or one of its variants and generally regarded themselves as politically on the opposite side, so to speak, of the conventional press. One could be a good deal more specific, but however this section of the press is defined, the actual numbers of papers were quite considerable.[3] Although Great Britain never developed the kind of mass circulation socialist press that emerged in Germany or the United States, there were nevertheless several hundred papers, ranging from dailies to quarterlies, published between 1890 and 1914. The majority were short-lived, but some actually lasted for many years. For example, the Independent Labour Party produced about 100 local and national papers, the Social Democratic Federation about 15, the Labour Party itself about 30, and the various syndicalist and anarchist groups another 20 or so. The vast majority were published in a small geographical area, usually a town or even part of a town, and with a few notable exceptions, lasted at best a year or two. The exceptions are interesting because they raise all sorts of questions about the ingredients necessary to produce a successful long-running socialist paper. For some the answer is simple and very conventional – the *Barry Herald,* begun by Marxists in 1896, lasted until the 1970s because it changed hands and became nonpolitical. More problematically, why did the *Huddersfield Worker* last for twelve years or so, the *Sheffield Guardian* for twenty years, and the Leeds *Weekly Citizen* for more than seventy years while cities such as Manchester or Birmingham, Cardiff or Bristol, where there was a viable socialist movement, failed to develop a long-running socialist press? There is some indication, though necessarily impressionistic, that those papers or groups of journalists that subscribed to the ideas of New Journalism, both in content and in organization, showed greater resilience than those that did not.

The early socialist papers showed no sign of having progressed from their Chartist predecessors except in the way they were actually printed, which involved the comprehensive reporting of speeches and details of meetings, the lack of features, the almost total absence of illustration and advertising. Around 1890 a change occurred that eventually affected the socialist press in general in four ways. The starting point for the change was the establishment of a private socialist weekly paper, the *Clarion*.[4] It was founded by journalists, one of them, Robert Blatchford, a highly paid and successful Fleet Street journalist who gave up a salary of reputedly more than £1000 in order to enter the very uncertain world of fringe socialist journalism. Before the appearance of the *Clarion,* it is doubtful whether any socialist paper had sold more than a few thousand copies. In a sense the *Clarion* was the first mass-circulation socialist paper. But it was also different from its predecessors in some important ways: in the use of typographical innovation, like two- or three-decker headlines, crossheads and illustrations; in the personal editorial comment built around the personality of the editor and his senior staff; through the variety of apolitical features, including the serialization of novels and short stories; columns for special-interest groups such as cyclists; and finally in the funding of the paper through share ownership and mortgages together with selling advertising space and maximizing circulation, including devices such as supporters' clubs and even free gifts and insurance.

The *Clarion* managed to combine a distinctly left-wing political stance and a good deal of heavyweight political comment with a substantial amount of lighter material. Indeed, the paper was noted for its humor, something that was not exactly commonplace in the socialist movement. But it was around the personality of Blatchford himself that the paper basically revolved, and it was his energy and dynamism that captured the attention of many thousands of readers. Blatchford never won an election, but he influenced a great many by his writing. More important from the point of view of press history, the *Clarion* became a yardstick by which other socialist papers were judged.

Less attractive and certainly less humorous was the *Labour Leader*, a weekly paper owned and edited by Keir Hardie, the first chairman of the Independent Labour Party, but because of that it was an equally important paper. The paper adopted decked headlines, illustrations, and crossheads, and a number of the features were similar to Blatchford's paper.[5]

Both the *Clarion* and the *Labour leader* were built around personalities, not only the editors, who in both cases dominated the papers (in the case of Keir Hardie, he actually wrote most of the paper, though he did take the precaution of using a variety of bylines, including "Lily Bell" of the women's page) but also journalists such as Mont Blatchford, "Marxian" (George Samuel) and the "Bounder" (E.F. Fay). These journalists became celebrities in the socialist world. They were not perhaps typical. On the whole, socialist journalists were shadowy figures, and in this respect they do not accord with the typology of editors of the New Journalism. The reason for their reticence is clear enough. It was a combination of genuine humility, a belief that it was difficult to square individualism with socialism, and more than a little personal anxiety or even fear. Socialism has never been terribly popular with employers. The exceptions, of course, were those men and women who wanted to base a career on their socialism.

They were certainly not reticent. Men such as Philip Snowden, who became a disastrous chancellor of the exchequer in 1929, and women such as Katherine Glasier and Margaret MacMillan, had everything to gain from the publicity that their journalistic activities gave them. Writing columns in the socialist press and public speaking were two sides of the same coin, and one also suspects that if the journalist Robert Blatchford was a politician manqué, so Keir Hardie was a journalist manqué.

There was nothing new in the way in which radical politics and journalism were combined. One needs only consider the function of the press in the Chartist movement or the early trade union movement or, indeed, the world of which Joel Wiener has written so eloquently, the radical unstamped press.[6] The difference, I would argue, is the degree to which the personality of the author became part of the substance of the journalism. Pamphlets and books as well as newspapers were sold on the strength of the names of Blatchford, Hardie, Snowden, and others. The content of the socialist press, however, revealed the impact of the New Journalism as a genre. This is a difficult aspect to quantify or, indeed, to demonstrate fully here, but my general point is that although the prime purpose of the socialist press was to provide a distinct view and policy on issues of the day as part of a process of political proselytization, many features from the contemporary press made their way into the pages. The role of such features in the commercial press, however, was altered in the left-wing press.

At one extreme, for example, some papers attempted to enter the risky world of the expose. Following closely W.T. Stead's revelations about the white slave traffic in London, Keir Hardie ran, over ten years, several series of articles exposing various corruptions, malpractices, and examples of humbug, ranging from straightforward documentary pieces exposing bad conditions and low wages in the Post Office, the Army and Navy stores, Lipton's grocery chain, and other multiples to exposes of immoral conduct in Glasgow's West End; unfortunately, although Hardie was pretty good when throwing abuse at well-known public figures, like the famous Sabbatarian Lord Ouverton who forced all his employees to work on Sunday, he was not so effective at digging around the dirt. His series on the West End scandal in Glasgow is a case in point. This was a widely publicized case of brothel keeping in which the girls involved had their names published but their clients remained anonymous. Hardie argued that this was not merely a matter of discretion, but a reflection of divisive capitalist society in which the poor and underprivileged are always unprotected, while the rich get away scot free to continue their immorality elsewhere. He threatened but utterly failed to name the men concerned; in this respect he fell short of the achievements of the New Journalism. One suspects, in fact, that Hardie's journalism was the product of a fertile imagination combined with some local knowledge, rather than the persistent investigative journalism that was so characteristic of modern journalism. Nor is this in the least surprising; investigative journalism required a considerable effort of manpower and money, neither of which was available to Hardie. But the expose was a means to an end, the target chosen because of its political significance; the arguments deployed were political more than moral, although it is difficult to disentangle the two.

The socialist press did not generally become involved in this kind of journalism. Nor, indeed, did the exclusive story or the "scoop" have any real place in a periodical press whose objective was the long-term conversion of the electorate. Besides, the socialist press was not in any sense competing in itself. Nevertheless, socialist papers were concerned to reveal the most damaging aspects of capitalism, and this most often took the form of attacking local employers or public figures. Unfortunately, the law on libel does not make fine distinctions between moral and commercial purpose, and socialist papers fell foul of the law quite often. Hardie lost a number of printers because they did not wish to become involved in some of his more outspoken writing. Indeed libel became a serious threat to socialist journals.[7]

On the other hand, campaigning journalism became the stock in trade in the socialist press. In the 1890s many socialist papers became involved in the campaigns being waged up and down the country to free public parks and spaces for political rallies and speeches but which incidentally gave excellent copy. The adventures of Hardie and Mrs. Pankhurst, the pioneer suffragette, in Boggart Ho' Clough park in Manchester provided the *Labour Leader* with weeks of instant copy, plenty of illustrations, and good headlines.[8]

News was always a means to an end. In this respect, the socialist press differed fundamentally from the contemporary commercial press for which news was usually an end in itself. At the same time, local newspapers had a somewhat different role to fulfill from their celebrated national contemporaries. Indeed, in many respects, there is little difference in news coverage between Bradford or Blackburn local socialist papers and their local contemporaries; local news stories in both cases were usually culled from the transactions of local governing bodies or the police courts in which socialist papers took as much interest as other papers. The one difference is that, like their national counterparts, local socialist papers usually accompanied their reportage with some moral lesson or ethical observation as part of the political function.

Nor was news defined parochially. The politics of socialists overseas, whether reports about the Hamburg City Council or long extracts from the American paper *Appeal to Reason*, were given great prominence, and foreign socialists such as Liebknecht and Bebel were lionized. At the same time, the bulk of the copy was made up of feature articles, essays, and, following contemporary practice, the serializations of contemporary novels ranging from those written by Jack London to those of H.G. Wells and approved classics from the past, including Carlyle and Emerson, of course, and the poetry of Whitman, Wheeler Wilcox, Ruskin, and socialist contemporaries such as William Morris and Edward Carpenter. The selection was governed above all by political considerations: Either the author was a socialist or the verse had political relevance, and this criterion often led to the inclusion of some rather dubious verse. Many of the novels and short stories too were stronger on moral message than either characterization or plot.

Nevertheless, some of the literary criticism was formidable indeed, notably, the regular columns in the *Labour Leader* from 1894-1898 of A.R. Orage who, as editor of the literary periodical the *New Age* from 1902 onward, became one of the most influential literary critics of his day.[9] And, of course, George Bernard Shaw and H.G. Wells wrote continually for socialist papers. Indeed, it might be argued that some socialist papers, notably, William Morris's *Commonweal*, are best remembered for their literary content and style than for any enduring political impact.

Moreover, because socialism was a movement of young people in this period, it is hardly surprising to find buried in the pages of obscure provincial socialist papers, names to reckon with such as the twenty-two-year-old film critic of the Bradford *Pioneer*, J.B. Priestley. Visual images, too, from the elaborate title pages of Walter Crane to the pungent cartoons of Will Dyson, a genre that has not yet been fully explored, were important in the socialist press. On the other hand, because it was an essentially amateur press that had few resources, copy was often a major problem; what else would have driven the editor of the *Bradford Labour Echo* in 1898 to publish forty incredibly tedious articles by E.D. Girdlestone on "Why I Am a Socialist"?

Central to the New Journalism was a new way of financing the press. Alan Lee has shown how the evolution of joint stock financing paradoxically loosened the ties of ownership but made monopoly easier.[10] One manifest change between the old and the new press was the degree of capitalization required and the role of advertising in bridging the gap between the cover price and the unit cost. The socialist press compares unfavorably with the commercial press both in the amount of capital deployed and in its ability to attract advertising.

Nevertheless, what is surprising is the extent to which the organizers of the socialist press were prepared to seek both capital and advertising revenue in order to develop their papers. In 1904, for example, the Independent Labour Party bought the title and stock of the *Labour Leader* from its own political leader by raising £10,000 in a private share issue to which members of the party could subscribe, using the procedures laid out by the Registry of Public companies.[11] In time this became a flourishing commercial business and remains the only surviving remnant of the party. The same can be said of Twentieth Century Printers, which began life as printers for the Marxist paper, *Justice,* or the Civic Press of Glasgow, once the Labour Literature Society. If the original notion was to serve the party, eventually the profit motive caught up with at least this end of the political world. Many years after the newspapers themselves had died, some of these printing businesses flourished. A good Welsh example is Swansea Printers, which began to help publish one socialist paper and ended up surviving four others during the ensuring sixty years.[12]

Socialists were not slow to seize any opportunity to promote their cause through commercial activities, as the registries of Public Companies, Provident Societies, and Friendly Societies testify, forming everything from boot and shoe companies to drinking clubs.[13] Somehow, a few socialists managed to combine a successful printing business with a flourishing paper. A few papers were fortunate in having a sympathetic printer, such as Wadsworths of Keighley and Peter Lindley of Pendlebury,[14] but the majority had to get the best price they could from local firms.

What then was involved in the economics of socialist publishing? In the first place, only a small income was generated from direct sales. The socialist press lived from hand to mouth to publish its editorial content. It had no room for maneuver at all in the management of distribution and in effective accounting. The national papers used major commercial distributors, including Wymans and W.H. Smith. Local papers had their own local outlets, but all of them, to a lesser or a greater degree, relied upon volunteer help to distribute the papers and collect any money due. In order to maximize circulation some papers resorted to the kind of inducements offered by Alfred Harmsworth, though never were they as lavish or as attractive. There is no evidence that this worked at all. The most ambitious scheme of this kind was launched by Keir Hardie in the *Labour Leader* in 1902. At that time he was facing considerable financial problems. An attempt to capitalize his paper through a share issue had been a miserable failure.[15] Now he offered a prize draw, with a free passage (presumably one way) to New Zealand as first prize and a free passage to South Africa for the first runner-up.[16] Considering that the Boer War was still continuing and the debate was raging over the use by the British of concentration camps and a scorched earth policy, one can only wonder at his sense of timing. Presumably, on this occasion, contestants must have been praying to win third prize – a return trip to Switzerland. They need not have worried. After announcing several postponements, to give the contestants in the remote Highlands of Scotland and Wales a fair chance to compete, a deathly silence fell. Much later the organizer, William Stewart, admitted that the contest had been a fiasco, though he never explained how the entrance fee was returned to those who presumably entered. Perhaps they were the ones who won the one-way trip to New Zealand.

Surprisingly, perhaps, advertising formed a substantial part of the income of socialist papers. Some even adopted a widespread commercial practice of issuing their papers free and relying on the income for advertising; one Leeds paper claimed to be able to distribute 50,000 free copies a month, though 3,000 a month was more typical. Such papers often contained as much as 50 percent of advertisement space, usually local services or business but also including a surprisingly eclectic range of brand names, though it has to be admitted that many of the companies involved, such as the Cadbury and Fry chocolate companies, Hudson's soap, Mother Seigel's syrup, and Fels' Naptha Soap, were well known for their radical views. Fels is, of course, pretty unique. This extraordinary American millionaire advertised his wares in socialist papers but also provided guns for the Irish Republicans and conference funds for Lenin's Bolsheviks.[17]

But why did advertisers bother, apart from those with an obvious interest in the movement? One explanation is that advertising was both new and relatively cheap and its impact was still largely unknown. In these early days before the development of the sophisticated techniques of targeting, it was tempting to go for blanket coverage, and this may explain why the same advertising appears in so many diverse publications regardless, it would appear, of political affiliation, locality, or any other factor. The object was to appear in as many papers as possible.

Despite strenuous efforts to raise shares, sell advertising space, and boost circulation, most socialist papers were thoroughly unprofitable. The exceptions are those that achieved the magic conjunction of good copy, reliable advertising, regular sales, and adroit accounting or papers that were able to command the loyalty of politically committed men and women over a prolonged period.

By far the most ambitious, expensive, and disastrous venture of the period was the attempt to establish a socialist daily newspaper.[18] It was ambitious because it sought to emulate the Fleet Street press by adopting its style and format, its organizational structure, and methods of production, distribution, and promotion. The *Daily Citizen* represented the first and only attempt to run a daily paper owned by the Labour movement itself. In theory the idea was sound enough, but in practice there was the major problem of reconciling people's willingness to join a trade union and vote for a left-wing politician with their inclination to buy and read right-wing papers. This is a problem that has never been enirely resolved. Despite the reservations of professional advisers, the labour movement set about trying to create a new daily from 1906 onward. It took six years, a great deal of infighting, and some very robust political tactics devised by Ramsay MacDonald (later the first Labour prime minister) before the paper reached the streets in October 1912.

But from the issuance of that very first copy the paper always lived under a cloud.[19] I shall briefly refer to my original three points.

In the first place, the paper never had a personality of its own. Its journalists were professionals but, one suspects, not very good professionals. In three years there was no equivalent of H.N. Brailsford, H.W. Massingham, or J.L. Garvin. The editor, Frank Dilnot, was appointed at the rather unsocialist salary of £1000 a year, but he lacked the flair of his best-known contemporaries.

Second, the content of the paper fell between two stools. Because the paper was owned by the labor movement, it came under the censorious scrutiny of activists and purists. Distasteful news was prohibited, racing and betting news banned, political comment carefully monitored and channeled. Whenever the paper tried to break free, there were outcries of indignation from party branches.[20] Eventually racing news had to be included because the paper needed to sell copies but not before some of the directors resigned. When the First World War broke out, the paper faced a colossal dilemma. Should it join the rest of the institutions of the movement and support the war or stay with the most loyal readers and resist it? The paper chose the line of least resistance; half-supporting the war. It thus lost support from both sides.

There was, however, a more fundamental problem. By choosing the Fleet Street version of the press, the paper was committed to joining a most expensive business, and the money was never sufficient to do so. By socialist standards, the *Daily Citizen* raised a fortune in investment—more than £150,000 in all. By Fleet Street standards it was not enough. The fifty journalists and sixty other employees constituted a staff that was tiny compared to that of the *Daily Mail* or the *Daily Express*. The paper had to rely far more than others on the wire services and could not support its own editorial and news-gathering service. There were, as a result, no scoops, no specials. Readers who wanted the conventional product were well catered to; the rest wanted something very different. Although the *Daily Citizen* fell neatly between two stools, it can be argued that had it been a full-fledged commercial paper, it could hardly have been a socialist paper. Does this lead us to the conclusion that it is impossible to run a socialist paper entirely on commercial lines?

It is clear that the socialist press is different from the conventional commercial press because its purposes are different and its audience is differentiated. Yet the history of the left-wing press in Great Britain and to an even greater extent abroad shows that there were elements in the New Journalism of the commercial press that were imported successfully. In this sense the New Journalism was not a monolithic whole but was divisible into portable components. A study of the socialist press in Great Britain in the years before the First World War suggests that although no paper could ignore the New Journalism, the requirements of socialism might have been very different. But then, it could equally be argued that the socialist press, like its radical predecessors, struggled on, surviving continuous crises but never developing a sound commercial base. Its survival depended on the energy of ambitious politician-journalists and the dedication of small groups of activists.

In this respect there was nothing very new about it at all. Besides, the capital supplied came with many strings attached. It was raised piecemeal from the labor movement, and it was to the trade unions and the political parties that the paper had to go for more funds. Each time there were new strings, new demands, new strictures. Nor were there enough readers. The first copy sold 300,000, but this quickly fell, and the average was closer to 120,000. Advertising was fair but inadequate so that when restrictions were imposed by the government on all papers in September 1914, the *Daily Citizen* had nothing to fall back on. Eventually a legal decision restricting trade union investment killed the paper in 1915.[21]

It has to be said that it was supremely ironical that at the moment that the *Daily Citizen* hit the streets in 1912, a second socialist daily also appeared. The *Daily Herald* was the product of a rank-and-file strike and remained a modest, unashamedly committed paper that appealed to a small but devoted readership.[22] It asked for and got little capital. It made no pretense at covering the news but gave robust, vigorous opinion. When war broke out in 1914, it remained vigorously opposed to the establishment and thus attracted many of the *Daily Citizen's* disenchanted readers. After struggling for four years as a weekly, it reemerged as the Labour Party's sole daily paper, which it remained until it eventually changed its name and its destiny, to the *Sun*.

It has to be said, however, that the failure of the *Daily Citizen* was of its own making. There were too few journalists to generate the necessary quantity and quality of ordinary news but too many journalists for a journal of opinion. Moreoever, the editor and the senior staff were not good enough. But above all, perhaps, the paper's fortunes demonstrate that a daily socialist paper run on New Journalistic lines had to be so.

NOTES

1. This point and many of the ensuing points of detail are more fully explored in Deian Hopkin, "The Newspapers of the Independent Labour Party, 1893-1906" (University of Wales Ph.D. thesis, 1980), pp. 123-127 inter alia.

2. For an overview of the socialist press in this period, see Deian Hopkin, "The Socialist Press in Britain, 1890-1910," in George Boyce, James Curran and Pauline Wingate (eds.), *Newspaper History: From the 17th Century to the Present Day (London, 1978), pp. 294-306.* There is some useful material in Stanley Harrison, *Poor Men's Guardians: A Record of the Struggles for a Democratic Newspaper Press, 1763-1963* (London, 1974). All the titles referred to in this chapter can be consulted in the left-wing newspaper microfilm collection at the Hugh Owen Building, University College of Wales, Aberystwyth.

3. For a near-complete checklist of such periodicals, see Royden Harrison *et al* (eds.), *The Warwick Guide to Labour Periodicals, 1790-1970* (Brighton, 1977).

4. The editorship of Robert Blatchford is discussed in Logie Barrow, "The Socialism of Robert Blatchford" (University of London Ph.D. thesis, 1975), and to some extent in Judith Fincher, "The *Clarion* Movement" (University of Manchester MA thesis, 1973). The best published biography of Blatchford is Laurence Thompson, *Robert Blatchford: Portrait of an Englishman* (London, 1951).

5. See Fred Reid, "Keir Hardie and the *Labour Leader,* 1893-1903," in Jay Winter (ed.), *The Working Class in Modern British History: Essays in Honour of Henry Pelling* (Cambridge, 1983), pp. 19-42.

6. Patricia Hollis, *The Pauper Press: A Study in Working-Class Radicalism of the 1830s* (Oxford, 1970); Joel H. Wiener, *The War of the Unstamped: The Movement to Repeal the British Newspaper Tax, 1830-36* (Ithaca, New York, 1969); Henry Weisser, *British Working-Class Movements and Europe, 1815-1848* (Manchester, 1975).

7. At least one newspaper, the *Southampton Labour Chronicle,* was foreclosed because of a libel action, but many others, including the *Labour Leader,* had to make provision for libel costs. See Hopkin, *"Newspapers,"* pp. 243-244.

8. For Boggart Ho' Clough, see Reid, "Keir Hardie," pp. 24-28. An interesting contemporary account is H.C. Rowe, *The Boggarthole Contest* (Glasgow, 1900).

9. For Orage's career, including his socialist activities, see Philip Mairet, *A.R. Orage: A Memoir* (London, 1936).

10. Alan J. Lee, *The Origins of the Popular Press in England, 1855-1914* (London, 1976), pp. 79 ff.

11. The sale of the *Labour Leader* is discussed in Kenneth O. Morgan, *Keir Hardie: Radical and Socialist* (London, 1975), pp. 137-142. The details of the new company can be consulted in the Registry of Public Companies, file N 106263 (National Labour Press Ltd).

12. For part of the story, see David Cleaver, "Swansea and District's Labour Press, 1888-1914," *Llafur: Journal of the Society for the Study of Welsh Labour History*, IV (1984), 35-42.

13. The relevant files can be consulted in the Public Record Office in BT (Board of Trade) 31. The range and character of some of these companies are discussed in Hopkin, *"Newspapers,"* pp. 238-290.

14. Peter Lindley's activities are briefly analyzed in John Smethurst, "The Pioneer Press," *Bulletin of the Society for the Study of Labour History*, no. 31 (1975), 59-62. An interesting account of a socialist publishing house is M.J. Harkin, "The Manchester Labour Press Society, Ltd," *Ibid.*, no. 28 (1974), 22-27.

15. Some indications of Hardie's problems are given in the Francis Johnson Correspondence (Harvester Microform: 1983, various references). The abortive company was the Atlas Press Society Ltd; Registry of Friendly Societies, Scotland, FS/5/192. Unfortunately, the files of friendly and provident societies are far less informative than those of public companies.

16. See William Stewart, *J. Keir Hardie: A Biography* (London 1921), pp. 194-197. See also issues of the *Labour Leader* for May, June, and July 1902.

17. Stewart, *Hardie*, p. 274. For Fels's sponsorship of Lenin, for example, see A.P. Dudden and T.H. Von Laue, "The RDSLP and Joseph Fels," *American Historical Review*, LXI (1955-1956), 1343-1364.

18. This is more fully discussed in Deian Hopkin, "The Labour Party Press," in Kenneth D. Brown (ed.), *The First Labour Party, 1906-1914* (London, 1985), pp. 105-128. The most comprehensive account of the history of the *Daily Citizen* is Tomoko Tchikawa, "The *Daily Citizen, 1912-15*" (University of Wales MA, 1984), on which the following account is primarily based.

19. For one thing, initial reactions to the first issue of the paper ranged from disappointment to ridicule. See, for example, Laurence Thompson, *The Enthusiasts. A Biography of John and Katherine Bruce Glasier* (London, 1971), p. 185, and R. Kenney, *Westering* (London, 1939).

20. See, for example, the various resolutions passed by ILP branches in South East London in the ILP collection at the British Library of Political and Economic Science; e.g., Misc 314, iv b.

21. *Bennett v. National Amalgamated Society of Operative House and Ship Painters and Decorators,* High Court, Chancery Division, 2 February 1915; *Weekly Notes,* 1915, 6 Geo V, p. 73.

22. For a broad comparison between the two papers, see R.J. Holton, "*Daily Herald* versus *Daily Citizen,*" *International Review of Social History,* XIX (1974), 347-376. An interesting inside account of the creation of the *Daily Herald* is George Lansbury, *The Miracle of Fleet Street* (London, 1925). The company records, such as they are, are contained in the files of the Limit Publishing Company, Public Record Office, BT 31 /21545/ 129717.

12
Rosemary T. VanArsdel
Women's Periodicals and the New Journalism: The Personal Interview

---

In 1881 Florence Fenwick Miller, age 27, was in the midst of her second three-year term as a member of the London School Board for Hackney, at that time the only position in Great Britain for which women could campaign to be elected and also cast their votes. Her term of service had been a stormy one for two reasons: her overt support for Charles Bradlaugh and Mrs. Annie Besant's republication of the birth control tract, *The Fruits of Philosophy; or, The Private Companion of Young Married Couples* by Dr. Charles Knowlton of Boston (1833), and her financial contribution to their defense fund; second, because she strongly supported the concept of secular education in the schools, which offended some of her constituents. For these reasons her day-to-day activities—her voting record, for example, and her board attendance records—were closely watched by her borough and reported in the local newspapers, the *Eastern Argus, Hackney and Kingsland Gazette,* and *Shoreditch*

Observer. [1] But as Fenwick Miller's reputation as a public figure grew, she became a candidate for another kind of reportage, the personal interview, then beginning what was to become a tremendous growth in popularity in the last two decades of the nineteenth century. The first interview of her, a long column and a half-piece with photograph, occurred in the *Lady's Pictorial* (17 December 1881) as part of a series titled "Ladies of the London School Board."

It is useful to pause to note not only why the interview was popular in its own day but also why it is enormously useful for the modern scholar. In addition to quoting Fenwick Miller's views on School Board questions, the article also gives details of her mannerisms while speaking, such as stabbing the air with her pen to drive home a point; her physical description ("her stature of middle height and her frame fully built") and her costume ("a plain black silk, and sometimes a drab cashmere surmounted by a plain collar"); and makes some attempt to follow her reasoning in debate ("a constant habit of searching for weak points in the advocacy of her opponents"). The contemporary reading public was whisked behind the scenes, so to speak, and given an inside peek at a public figure, a tantalizing prospect. The article also gives the modern scholar an invaluable record; it provides the only description extant, in minutest detail, of the chamber in which the meetings of the London School Board were held, of how the furniture was arranged, where the chairman and the press representatives sat, where the speakers stood during debate, and, finally, the accommodation for the visitors' gallery. It is a total re-creation of a nineteenth-century scene, which is of considerable importance in its own time and now because it has long since vanished. Finally, the reader is given a very strong indication in the last sentence of the interview of how Fenwick Miller's colleagues regarded her contentiousness in debate: "To borrow a simile from the history of Queen Boadicea, she drives a war-chariot with scythes projecting from the sides of the wheels."

There has been some difference of opinion over who was chiefly responsible for introducing the interview into the New Journalism of the 1880s and 1890s. Some claim it was W.T. Stead in the *Pall Mall Gazette*. Frederic Whyte, in his life of Stead, claims that the most telling part of his takeover from John Morley was an "increasing number of interviews—a novelty then in England...."[2] On the other hand, Joel Wiener asserts that "Edmund Yates is invariably considered to be among the pioneers of the 'New Journalism'.... he 'Americanized' the British press by introducing the interview to it."[3]

In any case, it is interesting to recall that earlier in the century, Harriet Martineau used extensively a form known as the biographical sketch, which she contributed to both the *Daily News* and *Once a Week* in a column titled "Representative Men."[4] There are differences between the two forms, the most obvious being that for a biographical sketch one need not talk personally with the subject; it can be a mustering of facts from any number of sources, much in the manner of an entry in a biographical dictionary. The second more subtle difference is in the tone; the biographical sketch is usually used for biographical record only, whereas the personal interview seeks to persuade, exemplify, illustrate, or hold up for emulation or example. Human beings, in general, are interested in reading about the lives and opinions of other human beings, especially if they are rich, famous, or noteworthy in some way, and in the 1880s and 1890s promoters of the New Journalism were alert to this fact.

Passing mention should also be made of a subspecies of the personal interview, known as the character sketch. This is similar to the personal interview; it differs only because the subject's words often are not quoted directly; however, because the author of the character sketch is usually a close friend of the subject and well acquainted with her views and habits, the portrait approaches the personal interview in intimacy and fidelity.

Women's journals in particular seized on the personal interview and the character sketch. It may in part have been a reaction to early periodicals such as the *Englishwoman's Review*, established in October 1866, a worthwhile but sober-minded quarterly devoted at first to promoting employment for women but soon to become one of the most important organs of the woman suffrage movement. The stark unattractiveness of its contents and appearance and the sharply didactic quality of its articles were not calculated to attract much of a general readership. The substitution of the sparkling and lively interview for the didacticism and factual grit was certain to attract new and enthusiastic readers.

Proprietors of new women's periodicals in the 1880s and 1890s were quick to see the appeal of Stead's and Yates's techniques and the potential of the personal interview for increasing journal sales. They also saw its potential for instructing and interesting women in the wave of new feminism of the time and for illustrating what women's places in the new society could and should be. There were at least five different reasons for the popularity of the personal interview: (1) to interest women in the accomplishments of other women; (2) to illustrate what women of determination could accomplish now that more horizons were opening; (3) to offer role models to emergent women; (4) to play upon the "human interest" element—showing Mrs. So-and-So "at home" and offering special, gossipy, behind-the-scenes glimpses of her private life to intrigue and to tantalize; (5) to sell journals while implanting the idea that "If she can do it, so can I!" Women's periodicals that specialized in the personal interview usually were instrumental in urging women of these decades to look beyond their traditional roles, to dare, to venture, to take risks, and the example offered in the interview provided one of the chief encouragements. The balance of the chapter will be organized around these five points.

In no sense is this survey intended to be a "bibliography" of personal interviews, nor an exhaustive listing; instead, it is a sampling from six selected women's periodicals, popular and well known in their own time, that made extensive use of the personal interview. The titles selected are *Hearth and Home; Lady's Pictorial; Ladies' Review; Woman's Signal; Woman's World; Young Woman.*[5] All of these journals were concerned with women's issues—suffrage, education, employment, legal and political rights—and gave ample play to them in their pages. They also favored interviews with women, a form of reportage that clearly flourished in the 1890s. The following discussion falls into three parts: the personal interview; the interview and the character sketch; and repeated personal interviews with one individual.

I

The *Young Woman,* a London monthly owned and edited by Frederick A. Atkins, which took as its motto "The sweetest lives are to duty wed," contained serial fiction, self-help, travel notes, and chats with famous ladies such as "Our Lady Hymn-writers," or, after the Columbian Exposition in Chicago in 1893, "Our Sisters Across the Sea." It enjoyed a large circulation from the first issue (October 1892), which was reprinted three times for a sale of 80,000 copies. The personal interview was very popular in its pages. One of the best, "Lady Henry Somerset," appeared in May 1893 and is a good example of the first category of interviews, "to interest women in the accomplishments of other women." Lady Henry, born to a prominent aristocratic family that embodied some of England's bluest blood, nevertheless, after a nasty fight to separate from her equally aristocratic but degenerate husband, turned her fortune and her energies to public works. She was a temperance leader, serving for nearly twenty years as president of the British Women's Temperance

Association. She was also a suffrage worker, a philanthropist for inebriate women and for underprivileged women and children on her own estates and a sometime editor and journalist. The portrait was written by her intimate friend, Frances E. Willard, long-time president of the World Women's Christian Temperance Union.

Lady Henry fascinated the public throughout her career because she owned magnificent castles and estates, had moved in the highest social circles in the land, and yet, at midlife, chose to spend her time on temperance and philanthropy. The reader of the interview is attracted by splendid pictures of her castles, by the romance of great wealth and power, and, presumably, by the goodness of her character. She was an *example;* and in closing her article, Willard frankly says of her subject that she hopes "her life [Lady Henry's] of tireless beneficence and Christian devotions may stir the holy emulation of some brave young heart." At least 80,000 readers had that opportunity.

Turning to the *Woman's World,* ably edited by Oscar Wilde from 1888 to 1890, there appeared in August 1890 a classic specimen of the personal interview titled "Mrs. Fawcett at Home." It is a fine example of the second category of interview, "to illustrate what women of determination could accomplish." Millicent Garrett Fawcett was, of course, the noted leader for woman suffrage. To pique reader interest, the reporter gives wonderful, chatty details of Mrs. Fawcett's life: One is given to understand that she is now a widow (her husband, Henry, the M.P., who was blind, having died in 1884), and lives "at a pretty house on Gower Street with her sister, Miss Agnes Garrett." She and her daughter, Phillipa, the senior wrangler in mathematics at Cambridge University, have been traveling on the Continent but have hurried home for the dedication by the prince and princess of Wales of a piece of Fawcett land for a public park in Lambeth. Pleasantries aside, the reader is led into the serious side of Mrs.

Fawcett's life: her work during twenty years as the leader of the woman suffrage movement; her deep involvement in lecturing and writing on political economy; her views on Ireland. Perhaps the most engaging quotation tells of her nervousness at her first public speech, in 1869, on suffrage: ". . . as I had prepared my speech and learnt it by heart, I succeeded in saying what I wished. A very slight error of judgment on my part would have been held to prove the unfitness of women for political responsibility. Even as it was, although I believe Mrs. [Peter] Taylor and I said nothing that could be used against us, the mere fact of our having spoken at all was referred to in the House of Commons, by a well known member, as a disgrace to our sex."

II

Testifying to the persuasive and instructive power of the personal interview were a whole series of interviews and character sketches that appeared weekly in the *Woman's Signal* during 1895 and 1896. These served to introduce readers to a group of powerful, dynamic women—not necessarily newsmakers but performing good and important work in the spheres in which they found themselves. There was no question that the interviews were designed to improve sales, but by the breadth of the experiences related, they spoke also to almost every one of the other four interview categories: women of accomplishment; women of determination; women as role models; and gossip.

Lady Laura Ridding (17 October 1895), an aristocrat in her own right, was married to the man who became bishop of the newly created diocese of Southwell in Nottinghamshire in 1884. Taking a bold and original view of the duties of a bishop's wife, she used her organizational and speaking skills to form a new "Woman's League" of approximately 6,000 women, "to give in all parishes and villages mutual support, assistance, and instruction from women to women." Lady Laura used her personal influence to channel their efforts toward the causes of temperance and suffrage. She was soon elected to public office in the diocese, and the interview concludes: "The actual work she will do will, doubtless, be of great benefit; but beyond the utmost possible direct good of such acceptance of public office by so honoured a lady will be the encouragement given to other women to follow the example." She became a role model!

The *Woman's Signal* of 24 October 1895 brought an article on an American lady, Mrs. Frank Leslie, obviously a born businesswoman. Although originally famous as a beauty and a social leader who thought of nothing but dinner partners and balls, on the death of her husband Mrs. Leslie took over his nearly bankrupt newspaper empire, repaid his debts, and expanded his enterprises beyond anything he had ever achieved. She was a woman of determination!

The issue of 7 November 1895 brought another look at Mrs. Henry Fawcett, obviously a popular and generous subject. This time the reporter focuses on the statesmanlike quality of her mind and the clarity of her powers of reasoning and speaking and complains that she will never be able to contribute these to the House of Commons because, as a woman, she is politically considered to be "only on a par with lunatics, infants, convicts who have not finished their sentences, and paupers still eating the bread they have not earned. What has this large and clear-brained woman done?"

The following week, 14 November, brought an interview with Dr. Annie Patterson of the Royal University of Ireland, the first woman in the United Kingdom to win a Musical Doctor's degree based on her own attainments. She was an accomplished woman!

Continuing week in and week out, readers of the *Woman's Signal* were bombarded with the personal stories of women of achievement, distinction, and outstanding personal characteristics. The next was a collective interview with five officers of the World Women's Christian Temperance Union (21 November), including the previously mentioned Lady Henry Somerset and Frances E. Willard, followed by an interview (5 December) with the queen's eldest child, the Empress Frederick of Germany, who was described as possessed of great mental ability. Also included was one with Mrs. Arthur Stannard (30 January 1896) who used the pseudonym "John Strange Winter" and published a journal by that title that added "Weekly" at the end. Mrs. Stannard startled literary London by publishing anonymously a book titled *Cavalry Life,* which critics received with "compliments, not only to the author's stories and literary art, but also to 'his' accurate descriptions of army life, and the manliness of 'his' mind." How could a woman possibly achieve such knowledge of the service and write so well of it?

Then followed Mrs. Dr. Maitland King (12 March 1896) who held a degree in homeopathy from an American institution; Mrs. L. Heaton Armstrong (11 June), second cousin to Frances Power Cobbe and "known as the greatest authority living upon those details of propriety and social conduct" [i.e., the Edwardian Emily Post]; Miss Alice B. James (25 June), "one of the greatest teachers of our time" and founder of a school and a kindergarden as well as a teacher's training college; and Mrs. Julie Salis Schwabe (16 September) who undertook to bring education to the poor in Italy after the Italian War of Independence and struggled for more than forty years to establish her school on a firm basis.

Before leaving this series of interviews in the *Woman's Signal,* it is worthwhile to pause over three very special ones because of the unusual nature of the work that the women did. Miss Agnes Weston, known as the sailors' friend, used her own capital to found a small Sailor's Home in Devonport and to provide wholesome shore-side accommodation for sailors between voyages (19 December 1895). Through her faculty for organization and tact in daily management the Sailor's Home grew to 400 "cabins" and provided reading and day rooms, bathrooms, and refreshment areas. The interview notes that her work received recognition from the queen and members of the royal family. She was a woman to be emulated!

The character sketch of Mrs. Marie Hilton describes a woman who founded what we would call today a day-care center for the children of the desperately poor in the East End of London, known as the English creche system (30 April, 1896), The reporter first describes the problems in graphic detail.

Away in the squalid, unlovely, dirty East of London there is a narrow, dingy street called Stepneycauseway. It abuts on that great riverside district, Ratcliffe, which is a by-word even in the East end for both poverty and vice. One of the great hardships of poverty is that it has to live side by side with wickedness. In the great crowd of closely-packed houses which cluster in Ratcliffe, there are to be found at least as many decent wives and mothers, and poor women living lives of utter hardship and incessant labour to maintain their essential respectability, as there are of the reverse class. Honest, industrious day-labourers, costermongers, and the like, crowd here with their families, mixed up amongst, yet keeping apart from, the criminal classes.

The problem of poverty is here in its most painful aspects, and one of the worst of them is the fate of the children born into the midst of this poverty.

The reporter takes the reader directly to the creche, as it was called, describes the open, airy facilities, the tiny cribs, childrens' toys, and the day-care system whereby Mrs. Hilton helped upward of 130 infants, to age five, daily. Anticipating modern sociological methods, Mrs. Hilton sent her assistant to call at the homes of the parents, to interview them, and to determine the worthiness of their needs. Such careful scrutiny, she said, saved her charity much grief and guaranteed sound organizational procedures. H.R.H. Princess Christian gave her patronage to the institution soon after it was founded, in 1868. The interviewer commented, "Mrs. Hilton's noble effort could touch but a few. The need is everywhere." She had become a role model for others to follow!

Finally, there is Priscilla Bright McLaren (2 January 1896), the sister of John and Jacob Bright, who provided a kind of divine inspiration to the women who worked with her. She was truly a matriarchal figure, then in her eighty-first year, who had championed the causes of both suffrage and temperance. She was the British counterpart of Susan B. Anthony. Her early experience in politics included observing the agitation for the first Reform Bill during the early 1830s. She also watched her brother John during the Anti-Corn Law struggle, and her husband, Duncan, during the Scottish Free Trade battle. These experiences strengthened her resolve to fight for woman suffrage. Although she was capable as a public speaker and, indeed, once addressed and presided over an audience of 6,000 women at the Free Trade Hall in Manchester, it was as an "inspirer and guide to others, rather [than being] herself a public worker" that she was most effective. "By conversation, by work on committees, by a widely extended correspondence, and by a quick appreciation and encouragement of the efforts of other women, she has exercised an influence which has made a mark on the progress of women during the las quarter of a century." She was one of the highest and finest representatives to be found of inspired leadership among women.

III

Attention now shifts to repeated personal interviews of the same individual, studied for variations in technique. Mrs. Fenwick Miller reappears with a record of at least eleven personal interviews during her active career days, roughly 1877 to 1902, ten of them in British journals and one in an American one.[6] She was, like Mrs. Fawcett, much in demand for interviews partly because she was a well-known public figure through her successful career in journalism and partly because of her vigorous and outspoken crusade for women's rights.

In analyzing Fenwick Miller's personal interviews one must remember that as a journalist herself, she was a master of the interviewer's technique and thus knew how to take charge and get her own message across. There is *always* mention of the time in her early twenties when she studied and practiced medicine in London. There is *always* mention of the nine years that she spent as a member of the London School Board. This is invariably followed by mention of her two subsequent careers of lecturing and journalism, and a note is made that when she married Frederick Alfred Ford she kept her own name because she was already famous. Finally, some aspect of the women's cause is *always* discussed: suffrage, women's legal rights, women's periodicals, or perhaps a discussion of the ideal, successful paper for women.

Analysis shows, however, that each interview came out differently, and each has a personality of its own. Noted earlier was the one in *Lady's Pictorial* (17 December 1881) that described the deliberations of the London School Board. Here Fenwick Miller comes across as tough, aggressive, spirited in debate, and "while she never loses temper, and generally wears a smile, her determination in denouncing what she believes to be wrong or fallacious could scarcely be surpassed."

Ten years later, in 1891, the journalist for *Hearth and Home* (23 July 1891) called at her home, "a handsome house in Ampthill Square." He describes her study "decorated in subdued tints of terra-cotta and light brown and the walls . . . lined with books," except for one wall reserved for pictures of famous leaders among women; and her "blue and gold drawing room;" the behavior of her children at tea. Finally, he emphasizes her personal magnetism:

Fair and comely, with great sweetness of expression, wedded to natural dignity of manner, Mrs. Fenwick Miller is the very antithesis of the typical idea of a person devoted to women's rights. There is immense magnetism about Mrs. Miller's personality, and she has a repose of manner which in itself amounts to a charm. But all her other attributes are forgotten when she speaks, her voice being so singularly clear and musical.

The following year, the *Ladies' Review* (1 October 1892), encompassing all the same biographical facts, emphasizes her "resolution of character." According to the periodical, her strength of will, her long-sighted persistency of purpose, speak eloquently to us all in whatever position in life we may be placed, and all the more eloquently because of the noble spirit by which they have been activated" [i.e., the women's cause]. The *Young Woman* (May 1893) stresses her writing and speaking capabilities, saying: "For, though she began her life as a medical student, passing her examinations with honours, and then stepped on to the public platform, where she still figures as an effective speaker and lecturer, Mrs. Miller is pre-eminently a writer. She understands the art and craft of journalism to perfection." The article ends by describing her useful participation in the Congress of Women at Chicago's Columbian Exposition of 1893. The *Woman's Signal* (3 October 1895) deals with her qualifications to become the new editor of that paper.

Finally, the *Woman's Journal* (4 January 1902), published in Boston, gives a good picture of Fenwick Miller as the British national representative of the Women's Suffrage Association of England to the National Suffrage Convention in Washington, D.C., and includes the predictable biography.

At the conclusion of this limited sampling of the personal interview in its several variations, one can readily see that it was definitely a lively addition to the New Journalism. It offered an intimate, close-up view of people, particularly of women, who were well known, whose careers were valuable, who were determined to succeed, who could be emulated; and its freshness and rather gossipy tone sold periodicals. Teamed with the cause of women's rights and suffrage, it was a powerful new tool to educate, to inform, and to move to action.

NOTES

1. *Eastern Argus; Hackney and Kingsland Gazette; Shoreditch Observer;* November 1876 to November 1885, *passim.*

2. Frederick Whyte, *The Life of W.T. Stead* (London, 1926) vol. I, 104.

3. Joel H. Wiener (ed.), *Innovators and Preachers: The Role of the Editor in Victorian England* (Westport, Connecticut, 1985), p. 259.

4. Valerie Kossew Pichanick, *Harriet Martineau: The Woman and Her Work, 1802-1876* (Ann Arbor, Michigan, 1980) pp. 204-205.

5. Titles selected for the sampling and their dates: *Hearth and Home* (21 May 1891-January 1914; merged with *Vanity Fair*); *Lady's Pictorial* (5 March 1881-26 February 1921; merged with *Eve*); *Ladies' Review* (9 April 1892-December 1908); *Woman's Signal* (4 January 1894-23 March 1899); *Woman's World* (1888-1890); *Young Woman* (October 1892-April 1915; merged with *Young Man*).

6. Interviews located in the following periodicals: *Hearth and Home; Lady's Pictorial; Ladies' Review; Woman's Signal; Women's Penny Paper; Young Woman* (British); *Woman's Journal* (American). Interviews not yet identified: *John Strange Winter's Weekly; Gentlewoman; Pearson's Monthly; London Daily Sun.*

13
Martha S. Vogeler
Pulling Strings at
Printing House Square

When Valentine Chirol resigned his post in Berlin as *The Times* correspondent in the spring of 1896, the paper's Foreign Department at Printing House Square wished to replace him with someone who would not alienate influential Germans and their government and thus dry up his sources of news, as Chirol had done. And, if possible, he should be familiar with Berlin society. Chirol convinced his superiors in London that the best person to fulfill both requirements was already on the spot — the Berlin correspondent for the *Morning Post.* [1]

The new man designated "Our Own Correspondent" by *The Times* (after an interim replacement) was George Saunders. Not yet forty years old, he had been in Berlin for nine years. A solemn, impressive-looking Scot who had an imposing handlebar mustache, he had taken his degree at Balliol in 1884, read law at Lincoln's Inn, and been drawn into journalism as the result of a chance meeting with W.T. Stead. Saunders had a bit of his mentor's puritanism; one historian speaks of him advertising his distaste for Berlin, "the city of the plain."[2] But he lacked Stead's political idealism. When Stead came to see him in Berlin while enroute to a peace mission to Russia, he seemed to Saunders "good-hearted" but "a little 'daft' of course."[3] Stead, he thought, failed to realize that it was "as dangerous to discuss peace as to discuss war, or more so."[4] And whereas Stead was a journalist entrepreneur, Saunders was the unquestioning employee. He took his responsibilities for *The Times* so seriously that when in London to report to Printing House Square, he refrained from going on to Dundee to see his parents lest he be thought to be taking a holiday.[5]

His appointment to *The Times*'s Berlin office marked a real advance in Saunders' career, but it may not have greatly increased his income. The paper was in the financial doldrums and cutting corners wherever it could. His rather pinched circumstances troubled him, but the important thing was maintaining *The Times*'s excellent reputation for foreign news, which was being challenged by other papers and by Reuters, the news agency. He was, therefore, disconcerted to learn in March 1898, after he had been in his new post only little more than a year, that his assistant was being transferred. Writing to his father, himself a well-known journalist, Saunders underlined the words about the change in his staff and noted that the vacant post would be filled by Austin Harrison, whom he identified as "the son of Mr. Frederick [sic] Harrison, the Positivist leader & friend of George Eliot."[6]

This, of course, did scant justice to Frederic Harrison. His promotion of Comte's Religion of Humanity had not prevented him from becoming a professor of jurisprudence and ubiquitous in political, educational, and social circles in late Victorian London. Now sixty-six years old, he had been writing about a staggering variety of subjects for monthlies and newspapers, including *The Times*, since before Saunders was born.[7] Indeed, it seems very likely that Austin Harrison was taken on by *The Times* because his father was known and respected by three senior men on the staff: the editor, George Earl Buckle; the subeditor, William Stebbing; and the assistant manager, Charles F. Moberly Bell. Austin's first position with *The Times*, beginning in mid-March of 1898, a few weeks before his twenty-fifth birthday, was on the London night desk, handling European telegrams. In mid-April came the appointment to be Saunders' assistant. The terms are not entirely clear, but a letter of Frederic Harrison's suggests that he and Bell arranged everything between them: Austin was to go to Berlin "to learn his trade (probably for a year)." That he apparently was to receive no regular salary seems not to have troubled his father, who had found Bell "exceedingly pleasant & friendly."[8] And why not, given Bell's need to cut costs?

To Austin the arrangement must have seemed providential. It enabled him to return to the Continent, where, after leaving Harrow in 1890 in his eighteenth year, he had studied on and off with private tutors and at various universities for seven years. He had learned French and German, acquired a taste for avant garde literature and drama, and, according to one contemporary, became a "Nietschean radical."[9] Ostensibly he was preparing for the Foreign Office examination. When he failed it in March 1898, his father was not only disappointed but embarrassed, having managed to get Austin on the list of candidates by making a request to the prime minister, Lord Salisbury, with whose politics he often had occasion to differ.[10] Austin "must look to another career," said his father, and it was that which had brought the young man to Printing House Square in the same month.[11] When after a few weeks of what must have been fairly routine work, he was assigned to the Berlin office, his father, apparently in all seriousness, told Mrs. Harrison that he thought their son had proved useful to Buckle.[12] Saunders, in Berlin, had not been consulted about the appointment of his new assistant, and the letter to his father in Dundee announcing it suggests his ambivalence. Saunders said that he believed Austin to be "a clever youth" and added, "So I am a kind of schoolmaster."

Saunders was to prove less considerate as a schoolmaster, or surrogate father, than he was as a son. Despite a crushing work schedule, he found time for long letters about his problems to his father. David Hogg Saunders, like Frederic Harrison, was a well-known contributor to the Liberal press, but whereas Harrison senior was an avowed agnostic, Saunders senior signed himself "Christian Democrat" and was active in Scottish Presbyterian circles. His son also held firm to the national religion, reading his Bible daily no matter what the distractions.[13] Is it reasonable to suppose that he would be entirely pleased to have a colleague whose father called Christianity an outmoded religion?

The arrival of Austin Harrison in Berlin came at a particularly trying time in Saunders' personal and professional life. Housing was expensive, and he had not yet found quarters he wanted, a place close to the center of town and large enough for both his office staff and family. Meanwhile, his flat in Königin Augustastrasse was uncomfortably small and could not accommodate an English governess for his children as well as the German governess that he and his German wife thought necessary. Both his physical and mental health were a worry; neuralgia and rheumatism plagued him, and his work for The Times seemed excessive. "I find it hard to keep up my general reading," he complained to his father. "If I read through the Times and some 15 or 20 German papers every day, manage my own household, the governesses, home, etc., I have hardly a minute left even for meditation." He therefore envied his successor at The Morning Post, who was leaving Berlin because he had grown tired of being so far from home.[14]

Saunders was also frustrated as a correspondent. Like Chirol, he deplored the hostility of the German press toward Britain and believed that Kaiser Wilhelm was fomenting it to prepare the German people for an expanded navy. Saunders once called German foreign policy "the negation of the Tenth Commandment."[15] Through his father-in-law, a prominent Berlin banker, he had come to know—and to dislike—many of the emperor's wealthy supporters. Yet he understood that he must not offend them. For doing so Chirol had lost access to news sources that were essential to his usefulness as a journalist and had felt obliged to return to the London office. The head of the Foreign Department there, Sir Donald MacKenzie Wallace, had warned Saunders upon his appointment to write nothing "unnecessarily irritating" to the emperor.[16] Plain speaking by nature, Saunders was oppressed by this restriction, which added to the difficulties of his post. He complained to his father about the weight of *The Times* on his shoulders: It was "heavier and more constant . . . than the weight on the shoulders of an Ambassador."[17]

In such a situation, a capable assistant could be of immense value, and both Saunders and Bell seemed ready to give Austin a fair chance. Saunders let him occupy one of the rooms used by *The Times* in a building at number 3 Köthener Strasse, and less than two months later Bell decided that when Saunders took his annual holiday in Scotland starting in mid-August, Austin would be in charge of the office. Explaining this to Frederic Harrison, Bell said that he would let Austin "do the best he can, watching closely to see what that best is." But Bell probably expected Austin's best to fall short, for he noted that when told about his defects in spelling, Austin had claimed "the excuse of heredity." This bordered on impertinence, but Bell said only that the excuse would not serve for the young man's more serious defects in style, and he urged Harrison to suggest his own lucid prose as a model to his son.[18]

Unintimidated by criticism, during the month that he was in charge, Austin boasted to his mother about having written a "very funny thing" in order to counteract the "ridiculously affected tone of purism" that was one of the "Scotch peculiarities" of the Berlin office. He did not expect the piece to be published, and apparently it was not. The reports in *The Times* with the Berlin dateline for this period are indistinguishable from Saunders' work except that they are headed "From Our Correspondent," whereas Saunders' byline is always "Our Own Correspondent." Like Saunders, Austin for the most part selected, translated, and interpreted items from the German press likely to interest British readers. Austin did not expect to be overly taxed because it was holiday time, and important people in the court and the Reichstag were away. And he was encouraged by having heard that Saunders was "very fond of him," though that did not change his own belief that the man was "selfish" and "scheming" and would do little to advance the careers of his "underlings," especially someone like himself, who lacked a proper university education.[19] Meanwhile, in early September Frederic Harrison wrote to Bell from Amsterdam, where he was attending the Congress of Historians, to say that he was going on to Berlin to see Austin and thought he had served *The Times* well during Saunders' absence and deserved a holiday.[20] To his wife, Harrison waxed ecstatically about an "excellent" telegram of their son's in the paper: "Really I think he has made a hit, & beats S[aunders] out of time."[21]

Berlin's "bracing" air and efficient sanitation momentarily banished Harrison's longstanding antipathy toward Germany. A lover of France—the home, after all, of his Positivist philosophy—he had come to despise Germany during the Franco-Prussian War and had refused to set foot in the country ever since. But he conceded that Austin seemed happy, comfortably lodged in *The Times*'s quarters in an airy room with a telephone that "went to anywhere." In his free time Austin fenced when the weather was not too warm and attended the theater.[22] During his five-day visit, Harrison wrote again to Bell about Austin's need for a holiday, and this time it was granted. In the same letter Harrison noted that *The Times* had not printed the long account he had sent from Amsterdam describing Queen Wilhelmina's enthronement, which he had witnessed as the Foreign Office's representative. The article in fact appeared on the day Harrison wrote, September 13, testimony to his connections in Printing House Square, for the paper had been covering the events adequately.[23]

Harrison's letter coincided with Saunders' return to his post. It is easy to imagine how he felt upon learning that his young assistant, after less than half a year, was about to enjoy a month's leave because his father had pulled strings. And the string puller was still on the scene, no doubt ready to discourse on his son's superior abilities. As luck would have it, there had been a remarkable series of developments for Austin to cover: the tsar's disarmament proposal; Anglo-German talks in London about Great Britain's desire to purchase Delagoa Bay; the arrest, confession, and suicide of a key witness in the Dreyfus case; the Sudan War and the expectation of a confrontation of the French and British forces; Turkish outbursts in Crete; the assassination of the empress of Austria; the German emperor's demand for antistrike legislation; and new details about the recent death of Bismarck.[24]

What Saunders thought of the way Austin had minded the store in his absence is not known, but he apparently felt obliged to help him entertain his father. Saunders took Harrison to see the emperor emerge from the studio of a Berlin sculptor whom he had been interviewing about a memorial to Bismarck,[25] and later Saunders dined with father and son, though there must have been a dozen things he would have preferred doing at home or at the office after a month's absence. Harrison, on the contrary, was delighted to see close up the emperor and his palace and government buildings and to have the chance to talk to Saunders about Austin's situation. It was, Harrison wrote to his wife, "rather complicated" and required "vigorous treatment." Austin "could get about £400 per ann. at once on another paper, but at present he is S[aunder]'s clerk (with 0). S[aunders] would like to keep him as he is." Harrison resolved to deliver an "ultimatum" to Bell, and before leaving did what he could to shore up Austin's position by taking him to call on a few prominent residents to whom he had brought introductions: a couple belonging to the noted Anglo-German Siemens family of engineers and Heinrich and Lily Braun who edited *Die Neue Gesellschaft* and were, because of their advanced opinions, the "Sidney Webbs of Berlin."[26] Just before his departure, Harrison learned that Bell had instructed Saunders to let Austin draw "£10 a month." It was "not enough," objected Harrison, writing to his wife. But Austin, who heard the news only weeks later when he came back from his holiday in Scandinavia, composed a most ingratiating letter to Bell, thanking him for the "regular salary."[27]

Because Austin's pay was to come out of the Berlin office allowance, Bell's decision no doubt vexed Saunders. The rent on the office space was costing him £200 a year, which was more than his operating budget allowed, and Austin was living there free. To make matters worse, Austin could "neither write correct English nor spell. He wouldn't do for a local reporter on the *Dundee Advertiser.*" Considering Austin "simply a drag," Saunders felt the pressure mounting and feared that he might "break down."[28] It is not surprising then that in December he sought once again to convince Printing House Square of his young assistant's incompetence. On the ground that the Berlin telegraph clerks were complaining about the illegibility of some of the copy coming from *The Times* office, Saunders ordered

Austin to talk to them and report their comments to Chirol, now Wallace's assistant at the Foreign Department in London. What Austin related—to Bell as well as to Chirol—was that the clerks all said that they could read *his* handwriting "straight off and correctly."[29] (If so, it must have improved since he took the Foreign Office examination, which, according to his father, Austin had failed because of bad penmanship.[30]) Austin explained the problem by pointing out that the illegible copy had come to the Berlin office of *The Times* for relay from St. Petersburg, where the clerks failed to adapt their penmanship to the German script.

Having dealt with one problem to his own satisfaction, Austin went on to describe another to Bell. Upon settling into his room in *The Times* office, he had put his books in an empty bookcase there only to be told later by Saunders to remove them to make room for certain office volumes. He had delayed, thinking to buy a bookcase of his own. Two days later Saunders angrily commanded George, the office servant, to carry out the order immediately. When Austin expostulated, Saunders, expressing long pent-up anger, informed him that he had been living on the premises only as his guest and should prepare to vacate his room at the end of the month. Austin assured Bell that he had not been aware of this indebtedness to Saunders and would, of course, find other lodging. What he wanted to know now was where he stood with *The Times* after what he ruefully suggested calling a Battle of Books.

His father, hearing from Austin of the episode, fired off a salvo of his own to Bell but this time was outmaneuvered. Bell defused the situation by presenting the facts. Saunders was paying the rent on the office, which had originally been taken by *The Times,* until such time as he could find one place to accommodate both his staff and his family. Austin was in fact his guest. He would have to move, but he would remain *The Times*'s assistant correspondent in Berlin.[31]

More skirmishing was to come. At the end of January 1899, Bell passed on to the anxious father the latest account of his son from Saunders: Austin's behavior was "all that he could have wished," but his work had been "deteriorating instead of improving." The evidence this time was a telegram that Austin had written at Saunders' request one evening after Saunders had left the office. A break in the wires had prevented it from being dispatched, and George had brought it to Saunders, who had sent it to Bell. To obtain an "impartial opinion" of the writing, Bell had shown the telegram to Chirol, who, Bell reminded Harrison, had been one of the best correspondents *The Times* had ever had, held no special brief for Saunders, and was "favourable to Austin." Indeed, Chirol's only fault was his "leniency." Yet he had passed a damning judgment on the telegram. "What more can I say?" asked Bell.[32]

Because to Harrison there seemed much more to say, he stalked Bell at Printing House Square. Later he reported to his wife that the interview had been "very friendly." Still it was necessary to write their son a "very long and careful letter to warn him, to give him my advice, my wishes."[33] Bell's next letter to Harrison, written a few days later, mentions an investigation under way and urges him for the time being to write nothing more to Austin about "the trap."[34] This is the term that Harrison had used for the incident of the telegram because he had been convinced by Austin that Saunders had maliciously given Austin the assignment in circumstances that would produce careless prose and then had retrieved the document from George and circulated it. Moreover, according to Austin, Saunders had actually dictated part of the "unlucky telegram" and was in fact responsible for some of the ungrammatical and inaccurate writing that he condemned as Austin's, a situation Harrison compared to recent accusations against Dreyfus by one of his most biased judges. But because Austin had said that he and Saunders were once more on friendly terms, Harrison asked Bell not to trouble himself further about the matter.[35]

Bell's loyalty to his senior man in Berlin and to *The Times* precluded his letting the matter rest there. Alarmed by Harrison's assertion that if he thought a trap had indeed been laid for his son, he would bring the matter "before the public and even to a court of law," Bell consulted Chirol. He in turn contacted George, the office servant in Berlin whom he knew from his own time there and learned from him that before leaving the office on the evening in question, Saunders had discovered that the wire service had been interrupted but told Austin that *The Times*'s telegram would have to go "somehow." Austin could not have found out until after he had written it—that is, until just before ten o'clock in the evening—that it would definitely not be transmitted. Because Austin acknowledged that he had telephoned the telegraph office at eleven o'clock to ask whether the line was open yet, he had obviously not been sure until then, and by that time it would have been too late to improve a carelessly composed text. George's account convinced Bell that Austin must have written the telegram with the understanding that there was a chance that it would be transmitted. In spite of this latest contretemps, Bell was prepared to let Austin stay at his post for the two weeks remaining till the end of February, at which date his departure, which had already been fixed with Saunders, would become effective.[36]

Strangely enough, Harrison, who, after all, was a lawyer accustomed to examining evidence, seems not to have asked some reasonably pertinent questions. Why, if Austin's work was so flawed, had he been left in charge of the office for the month Saunders was away? And if his performance during that month had been deemed unsatisfactory, why had nothing been said of this? Did it not seem odd that Saunders would take the trouble to send to London the incriminating telegram, written as it was in such exceptional circumstances, if he had other, less questionable evidence of Austin's deficiencies at hand? Instead of posing such queries, Harrison sought to find a way of prolonging his son's association with *The Times*. He suggested to Bell that Austin be sent on a roving commission to Spain as a political correspondent.[37] Harrison was probably remembering and hoping Bell would remember his own commissioned political articles from France for *The Times* in 1877 and 1888. But Bell did not rise to the bait. Harrison, perhaps trying to suggest that Austin's usefulness to the paper need not be confined to political journalism, also called Bell's attention to a review of a new drama by Hermann Sudermann that Austin had sent to *The Times* on his own initiative and which had been published.[38] Finally, seeing the handwriting on the wall, Harrison contritely attributed Austin's "want of discretion" to his "unlucky training" in youth, when he had been a "wanderer in foreign countries & his own master so many years."[39] The implication was that Austin had missed the good influence of a Positivist home. Harrison did not balance this disadvantage against Austin's enormous advantage in having a father who could pull strings for him in Printing House Square. Of course, when Harrison penned this explanation, the pulled strings had already snapped.

That Saunders might have pulled some strings himself is possible. Even if innocent of setting a trap for his young assistant, he had ungenerously, perhaps spitefully, seized every opportunity to present him as incompetent and seems not to have permitted him to send any telegrams under his own byline except in the four weeks when he was in charge of the office. Saunders' rancor was still apparent eight months after Austin had left *The Times*. The Boer War had just begun. Writing about it from Dorotheenstrasse, where he had finally found a house suitable for both his family and office, Saunders mentions Austin as someone he had "shovelled out of *The Times*" but who was "still hanging about . . . talking of the 'rights of humanity' and British tyranny" in South Africa.[40]

Saunders had once more done less than full justice to a Harrison. Within a few months of leaving *The Times*, Austin was sent by the *Manchester Guardian* to the Hague to help Stead cover the peace conference convened by Russia. He struck that experienced journalist as "pretty bright" but "rusty in his shorthand," lacking in initiative and punctuality in taking orders, and conceited.[41] When directly afterward he was taken into Reuters' Berlin office, he did better. He soon became chief and held the post five years. His father's influence might have brought him both assignments, for Frederic Harrison was on friendly terms with C.P. Scott, editor of the *Manchester Guardian*, and had known Baron Paul Julius Reuter, founder of the news agency.[42] Among the scoops mentioned in the centenary history of Reuters is one credited to Austin. Defying the German government's attempt to censor reports of a particularly bellicose speech of the emperor's in July 1900, Austin had telegraphed the complete exhortation in which the emperor urged his marines, who were setting out to avenge the murder of the German minister in Peking, to "give no quarter, make no prisoners," and to behave like "the Hun under their King Attila."[43] Austin's courage in reporting these now notorious words gave Reuters the kind of edge over newspaper correspondents that it cherished. To be able to show English readers the fanaticism of the German emperor was no doubt personally gratifying to Austin as well. He published *The Pan-Germanic Doctrine* in 1904 and *England and Germany* in 1907, both warning about the "German menace." The first book brought him to the attention of Alfred Harmsworth (soon to be Lord Northcliffe), for whom he briefly edited the *Observer*. In 1910 he took over Ford Madox Ford's *English Review*, which until 1923 gave him a platform for his political and literary opinions and the opportunity to publish many important writers. Then he returned to journalism.[44]

If Saunders had followed his former assistant's prewar writing, he should have commended at least his Germanophobia. His own was intensified by his move to the Paris office of *The Times* in 1908 and informed his only book, *The Last of the Huns,* published in 1914. By then, of course, the Allies were using the term "Huns" for Germans pejoratively. Explaining that the rubric derived from the emperor's "excited speech . . . to a body of German troops about to embark for China," Saunders quotes the relevant words but, understandably, does not cite their first appearance in the British press.[45] During and after the war, Saunders held several government posts, the last one in the Foreign Office, where Austin Harrison had once hoped to have a career.[46]

Saunders died in 1922, four months before Frederic Harrison (then in his ninety-second year); Austin Harrison died in 1928. All three obituaries were published in *The Times.* Frederic Harrison's, the longest, mentions his numerous contributions to the paper but says nothing about his having pulled strings at Printing House Square.[47]

NOTES

1. *The History of The Times.* vol. III; *The Twentieth Century Test, 1884-1912* (London, 1947), pp. 270-80.

2. A.J.A. Morris, *The Scaremongers: The Advocacy of War and Rearmament, 1896-1914* (London, 1984), p. 25.

3. Saunders to "Dear Papa," 13 November 1898, George Saunders MSS, Box 2/1/132, Churchill College Archives, Cambridge (hereafter cited as "GS/1/folio number, CCA").

4. Ibid., 3 January 1898, GS/1/128, CCA.

5. Ibid., 28 February 1898, GS/1/129, CCA.

6. Ibid., 26 March 1898, GS/1/130, CCA.

7. See my *Frederic Harrison: The Vocations of a Positivist* (Oxford, 1984).

8. FH to John Morley, [12 April 1898], Frederic Harrison Collection, Library of Political and Economic Science, London School of Economics (hereafter cited as "LSE").

9. Joseph McCabe, "Austin Harrison," *A Biographical Dictionary of Modern Rationalists* (London, 1920), p. 325.

10. Schomberg K. McDonnell to FH, 3 July 1895, and Eric Barrington to FH, 5 July 1895, LSE.

11. FH to John Morley, 10 March 1898, LSE.

12. Frederic Harrison to Ethel B. Harrison (hereafter "EBH"), Tuesday [12 April 1898], also mentioning Austin's expected departure on Saturday [14 April], LSE.

13. Box 10, SFM 1/27, CCA (obituaries of D.H. Saunders); *History of The Times*, vol. III, p. 295.

14. Saunders to "Dear Papa," 3 January and 28 February (quoted), 1898, GS/1/128, GS/1/129, CCA.

15. Ibid., 13 November 1898, GS/1/132, CCA; Morris, the *Scaremongers*, chapter 2; *History of The Times*, vol. III. chapter 11.

16. *History of The Times*, vol. III, p. 300, footnote 1, citing Sir Donald MacKenzie Wallace to Saunders, 27 January 1898.

17. Saunders to "Dear Papa," 13 November 1898, GS/1/132, CCA.

18. Moberly Bell to Harrison, 7 June 1898, Letter book #18, folio 151, *The Times* Archives.

19. Austin Harrison to EBH, 20 August [1898], LSE.

20. FH to EBA, Wednesday 7 September [1898], LSE (mentioning the letter).

21. FH to EBH, Thursday 1 September [1898], LSE.

22. FH to EBH, 14, 17, 18 (quoted) September 1898, LSE; on the visit see also his *Autobiographic Memoirs*, 2 vols (London, 1911), vol. II, pp. 160-161.

23. FH to Bell, 13 September 1898, *The Times* Archives; *The Times*, 13 September 1898, 11 ef (headed "From a Correspondent in Holland"); rpt. in *Autobiographic Memoirs*, vol. II, pp. 154-159; FH to EBH, Thursday 8 September [1898], LSE.

24. See *Poole's Index to "The Times"* under "Germany" for the period; columns from "Our Correspondent" (Austin Harrison) begin 13 August 1898 and end 12 September 1898; columns before and after are from "Our Own Correspondent" (Saunders).

25. FH to EBH, 16 September 1898, LSE; "Our Own Correspondent" (Saunders), *The Times*, 16 September 1898, 4a (on the emperor's visit to the studio).

26. FH to EBH, 14, 16, 17 September 1898, LSE.

27. FH to EBH, 18 September 1898, LSE; Austin Harrison to Bell, 12 October [1898], *The Times* Archives.

28. George Saunders to "Dear Papa," 3 January 1898, 19 January 1899 (quoted, italics added), GS/1/128, GS/1/133, CCA.

29. Austin Harrison to Bell, 7 December (quoted) and 14 December 1898, *The Times* Archives; but see Bell to Austin Harrison, 2 September 1898, Letter Book #19, folio 48, granting his request for a "type-writing machine."

30. FH to John Morley, 10 March 1898, LSE.

31. Bell to FH, 10 December 1898, Letter Book #19, folio 892, *The Times* Archives; FH to Bell, 17 December 1898, *The Times* Archives, thanking Bell for the information.

32. Bell to FH, 26 January 1899, Letter Book #20, folio 205, *The Times* Archives.

33. FH to EBH, Saturday [28 January 1899], LSE.

34. Bell to FH, 3 February 1899, Letter Book #20, folio 270, *The Times* Archives.

35. FH to Bell, 6 February 1899, *The Times* Archives.

36. Bell to FH, 15 February 1899, *The Times* Archives.

37. FH to Bell, 3 and 21 February 1899, *The Times* Archives.

38. FH to Bell, 3 February 1899, and Bell to FH, 3 February 1899, Letter Book #20, folio 270 (sending the original of Austin's article), *The Times* Archives; "Sudermann's New Play," *The Times,* 3 February 1899, 13b.

39. FH to Bell, 17 February 1899, *The Times* Archives; cp FH to Bell, 21 February 1899, Ibid., assuming the blame for misinterpreting Austin's account of the telegram incident.

40. George Saunders to "Dear Papa," 8 November 1899, GS/1/137, CCA.

41. EBH to Godfrey Harrison, 12 May 1899, LSE; W.T. Stead to C.P. Scott, 22, 26, 28 May 1899, 122/37, 122/340, 122/45, *Manchester Guardian* Archives (references I owe to Joseph O. Baylen).

42. Baron Reuter's death on 25 February 1899 might not have precluded Harrison's trading on the old friendship, which probably extended to the Second Baron Reuter; but see Michael Palmer, "The British Press and International News, 1851-99: of Agencies and Newspapers," in George Boyce, James Curran and Pauline Wingate (eds.) *Newspaper History: From the 17th Century to the Present Day* (Beverly Hills, California, 1978), p. 218, on the demand of British papers in 1899 that Reuters employ British nationals in its world agencies, which perhaps created an opening for Austin Harrison in Berlin.

43. Graham Storey, *Reuters' Century,* (London, 1951), p. 146, probably referring to "Speech by the German Emperor (through Reuters' Agency), *The Times,* 10 July 1900, 5c."

44. Obituary, *The Times,* 16 July 1928, 19c; *World,* 22 April 1913, copy in *The Times* Archives.

45. *The Last of the Huns* (London, [1914]), p. 92.

46. Obituary, *The Times,* 11 September 1923, 10c, 13e: *History of The Times,* vol. III, pp. 643-653; *Who Was Who, 1916-1928* (London, 1947).

47. See footnotes 44 and 46; for Frederic Harrison, see *The Times,* 15 January 1923, 11c, 12cd.

PART FOUR

AN ASSESSMENT

14

James D. Startt

Good Journalism in the Era of the New Journalism: The British Press, 1902-1914

Between the South African War and World War I, the British press experienced a transformation that appeared as capable of impairing its stature as it altered its form.[1] Too frequently, however, historians perceive that transformation in the stereotyped terms of the New Journalism—narrowly conceived. Both the New Journalism and Edwardian journalism were more diverse than such interpretation allows. The New Journalism, for instance, involved more than sensational news, and it formed only one element, albeit a vital one, of the Edwardian press. Many historians, in fact, have failed to provide an adequate explanation either of Edwardian journalism or of the nature of its transformation in their accounts of the press of that age.[2]

The New Journalism did, of course, change older journalistic practices. Its combination of commercial success and popular appeal made it a formidable communications force, and its critics were persistent in articulating their apprehension about it. They claimed that it featured magazinelike entertainment in its too sensationalized columns and articles. It catered to the emotions, to triviality, and to public whim and lacked persuasive political commentary, the critics said. Thus they thought that it reduced the effectiveness of the press as a political instrument—especially an instrument to be mobilized in behalf of political parties. Moreover, because the New Journalism resembled American journalism, critics considered it an insidious import from the United States, one that was destructive of British life and traditions. This line of criticism, correct though it might have been in part, fails to convey the actual nature of the occurring press transformation. The element of "good journalism," journalism respectful of traditional canons of the press and honestly and effectively engaged in the public life of the times, is missing in this kind of critique. It is also a missing element in many historical accounts involving the Edwardian press. Yet the leading journalists of the times were conscious of "good journalism" and tried to incorporate it into their various enterprises. The purpose of this inquiry is to demonstrate that "good journalism" did exist both in the thought and work of leading Edwardian journalists. In the process it will endeavor to provide a realistic perspective on the nature of the transformation of the Edwardian press—especially the political press.

I shall begin with the case of Lord Northcliffe, who as Alfred Harmsworth had made his name as the leading practitioner of the New Journalism. Known as the Napoleon of Fleet Street, he was a genius at making the New Journalism work, a fact verified by the place and popularity achieved by the *Daily Mail*, the core publication of his vast press enterprises. Although a man of many quirks and personality complexities, he once explained: "My chief ambition—though I fear a hopeless one—is to be the maker of perfect newspapers. . . ."[3] No one who has studied his voluminous correspondence with his staff at the *Daily Mail* or his many and at times irritating communiqués to the leading figures at *The Times* after he became chief proprietor of that paper and tried to give it a sound financial base can doubt that he was serious about that contention—even if one must admit that his definition of perfection might not have been that held by all of his professional contemporaries.

The *Daily Mail*, of course, was the most Harmsworthian of all of his papers, and it was the vanguard of the New Journalism after 1896. Moreover, as a commercially successful, popular morning paper, it was a direct challenge to Britain's quality morning dailies. Northcliffe tried as the years went on to have the *Daily Mail* reach its potential as a popular journal of importance. He wished it to be of influence in the affairs of political parties and to be quoted for its opinion by other parties. In the process he forged that paper into a publication that combined many attractive features of popular journalism and more of the vestiges of a quality press than one might suppose. The front page of a typical issue of the paper, like that of the quality dailies, was devoid of headlines and was usually devoted to a variety of announcements about business, shipping, and entertainment matters. Sometimes illustrated advertisements covered it completely. That was followed by several pages of news articles and additional announcements. Then came the leader page containing more theater announcements, an editorial article or two that might be three-fourths of a column (16-17) inches) in length, letters to the editor, several signed articles about current topics, and a review of the world's press. Next came a page of articles on foreign news. The final three pages contained more shipping news, advertisements (some addressed especially to women), sporting news, miscellaneous items, and part of a continuing fictional story. Interesting? Yes. But it was also newsworthy.

As to the charge of sensationalism, a quality that Northcliffe himself came to dislike, there is both truth and error in it. It is important to remember that sensationalism neither began nor ended with him.[4] After his time it grew as a vice of modern journalism. Moreover, most of the critics of popular journalism were admirers of quality journalism and tended to hold the former to the standards of the latter. But although quality and popular journalism share many things, their responsibilities are different. The one cannot be judged simply by the other's standards. Northcliffe knew that the heavy language and limited news appeal of the quality press would lose rather than gain and keep readers for his papers. His *Daily Mail* was highly readable, and that made it sensational in the opinion of some critics. Sensationalism, in fact, can be either a matter of style or of content, but neither type need be disreputable, though either can be. Especially as the *Daily Mail* matured, Northcliffe sought to make it a respectable paper that would have popular appeal. In terms of style, he tried to tone down its language, though he continued to appreciate a sharp turn of phrase. He disallowed any vulgar reference and crude or offensive expression from its columns and even purged it of Americanization of language. Sometimes his staff thought that he went too far in his insistence on purity of language.[5]

The strength of the charge of sensationalism against Northcliffe dealt with content, with news selection.[6] In the *Daily Mail* one would find not only political, foreign, domestic, and financial news but also reports on fashion, travel, sport, and always something for women. Its leading articles addressed major political issues, but interspersed among them were ones on citizenship, adventure, notable people, and, of course, on aviation, a development that Northcliffe closely followed. He also insisted that his reporters find news in "human interest" areas of life to which the quality press gave little publicity. Such news, he believed, should be displayed prominently and not be tucked away in a corner of a dull page. Moreover, to enliven the paper even more, he added serial stories and an occasional journalistic stunt (e.g., a competition). Did he thus make the unimportant important? The question, of course, elicits a subjective answer, but, to a degree, the answer is yes. That answer, however, needs qualification. Northcliffe's own journalistic policy "was to do big things big and little things little."[7] A survey of the paper's leading articles proves that such a policy was implemented.[8] By 1909, for instance, only occasionally would a leading article be devoted to a topic such as "Adventure" or the "Best Age for Marriage." Important national and international topics dominated those articles. Regardless, features other than editorial commentary established the popular tone of the paper. It used a broader definition of news than the traditional morning daily, and it contained items of entertainment value. The paper had popular appeal, which, in turn, attracted readers to its more serious news and opinion.

Other aspects of Northcliffe's popular journalism need to be grasped. Again, the *Daily Mail* can be used for purposes of demonstration. That paper reflected his hovering scrutiny as it did his concept of modern journalism. "The paper is getting long, flat and perfunctory," he told its editor, Thomas Marlowe, in a typical communiqué. "I am not fond of flaring headlines, but they are getting more and more deadly."[9] He wanted moderate, not dull, headlines for columns. Northcliffe in matters of attitude was, in fact, the embodiment of middle-class respectability, and he wanted the paper to reflect that attitude. He wished it to be an effective disseminator of political, foreign, and imperial news, and he demanded that it be a paragon of accuracy in news reporting. If it was the champion of popular cases, it also usually took an orthodox Conservative line on major political issues. The use that Northcliffe made of cabled news was unprecedented, aside from the services provided by those two stately papers, *The Times* and the *Daily Telegraph*. He assembled a brilliant staff and worked with it to match each member with the area of his greatest expertise. By such means he strove to make the *Daily Mail* a paper efficiently produced, trustworthy in its news, and attractive in appeal. That combination made the *Daily Mail* the most successful paper of its type in Britain. As we have seen, it had popular appeal, which was enough to justify the charge of sensationalism made by some critics. But the paper had its defenders too, and as one of them observed: "The *Daily Mail* is as sober, moderate and as responsible as the *Daily Chronicle* or the *Daily News,* the chief Liberal journals of London, but apparently it has a criminally larger circulation."[10]

The *Daily Mail,* in fact, strengthened its position with the passing of years. It maintained its position against competition by other halfpenny papers, and it attempted to prove itself, as its editor, Thomas Marlowe, explained, "equal to and if possible better than those [newspapers] of a higher class." "I should like to see," Marlowe said, "the *Daily Mail* enjoying the literary reputation of the 'Figaro,' the commercial prosperity of the 'Daily Telegraph,' and the prestige that still in some degree clings to the 'Times.' Here is work to keep us all busy for years to come.[11]

Before leaving the *Daily Mail* and Northcliffe, a final facet of his journalism must be considered, his insistence that the paper be politically independent. By that he meant that it should be free from political party control, free to offer its support when and to whom it pleased. The practice of that kind of independence provides one reason why political leaders despaired of his fluctuations, even when he supported them. "We do not want any bowing down to officials. . . . I have a natural horror of that sort of Journalism, . . ." he told Marlowe. "My views on this matter are those of Delane; that a Newspaper is meant to publish news, and not to please highly placed people."[12] Northcliffe based his authority on "the great outside public" and, as he told Bonar Law, the leader of the Conservative party after 1911, he believed that such knowledge would "do our party great good in the country."[13] J.L. Garvin, who knew Northcliffe well and understood him, explained in retrospect:

The 'Daily Mail' was the great adventure of a man who was both a democrat and an idealist. He allowed the public to set the tone of his paper. Since they were to read it they must themselves determine the sort of reading they desired. But the matter was his affair. By his will a topic became of public interest, and his will was expressed in small things as in great. He understood his public, allowed for its immature and unstable qualities. . . . He entered, in fact, into a sort of partnership with it, but he was himself the senior partner. . . . He wielded a unique public influence; and he exerted that influence to the uttermost.[14]

Northcliffe, indeed, considered himself in partnership with the readers whom he attracted in unprecedented numbers. He aimed his papers at the expanding middle class. By attracting them he knew that he would also gain the attention of some of the lower class.[15] That readership served as a magnet for advertisers, who, in turn, helped to provide financial independence for the paper. Such independence allowed him to be free of party control. He played his own type of role in political affairs, and political leaders valued his support, although they wished it were more dependable.[16] Although they did not consider him an original or deep political thinker, they respected him for his knowledge of and special relationship with the "great outside public."

The case of Northcliffe and the *Daily Mail* reminds one that at the center of the journalistic revolution there existed a quest for good journalism. Accurate news reporting, comprehensive coverage, journalism that was of political consequence while it was in touch with the public's interest and alive to its causes were qualities that most journalists would acknowledge as sound. It can be argued, therefore, that Northcliffe sought to improve journalism as he transformed it. Can vestiges of a search for a better journalism be found elsewhere in the Edwardian press?

Part of the answer to that question can be found by considering that citadel of traditional journalism, *The Times*. In its own cautious way it was improving its format and service in the years before Northcliffe became its chief proprietor, although its circulation and financial position remained precarious.[17] *The Times* "has seen the wisdom of bringing itself into line with . . . up-to-date methods which ten years ago would not have been deemed worthy of a moment's consideration," wrote Northcliffe several years before he began his association with that prestigious paper.[18] After Northcliffe gained control of that paper in 1908, one would expect to find it improving in format, organization, and management. These things Northcliffe accomplished as he continued and accelerated the reform of that paper.

Important as Northcliffe's efforts were to the rehabilitation of that paper, it is easy to overstate, as many accounts do, his role in saving it. The senior staff at *The Times*, men such as Moberly Bell, its managing director; G.E. Buckle, its editor; and Valentine Chirol, its foreign editor, also played a role as they interacted with their new dynamic chief proprietor. Northcliffe's much quoted references to them as the "Old Gang" and "Ye Black Friars," are misleading. Even before he took over the paper, they knew that changes were needed. After his arrival, they recognized and even welcomed many of his innovations.[19] They were concerned, however, about the pace of change and the preservation of traditions associated with that paper. The resulting "conservative revolution" at *The Times* reflected their caution and willingness to change, as it did Northcliffe's force and drive. When the rift between the senior staff and Northcliffe occurred, it was not so much a result of institutional changes as the product of his abrasive ways and his effort to exert his influence over the editorial policy of the paper.[20] Regardless, after 1912, when Northcliffe appointed Geoffrey Robinson, an editor of his own choice, the reforms continued, culminating in 1914 in the reduction of the price of the paper to one penny. On that occasion *The Times* explained in elaborate detail to its "new readers" that despite its coverage of subject, which was more exhaustive than the other papers, it was "MORE EASILY READ THAN ANY OTHER NEWSPAPER IN THE WORLD."[21]

That was an exaggeration. Nevertheless, *The Times* had become a well-organized and an attractive paper. It compared favorably with rivals such as the *Morning Post* and the *Daily Telegraph*. *The Times,* in fact, now could be contrasted favorably with its Victorian predecessor. For the sake of comparison consider a typical *Times* leader page from the 1880s and one from 1914. Intended only for the well-informed reader, the former was a hallmark of Victorian journalism. Its first column, which had no masthead, contained a partly paginated index to the paper's contents and a few pieces of Parliamentary news. The remaining five columns were composed of several leaders; all were sober, untitled, and broken only by paragraphs at half-column intervals. Filled with facts and figures and with references to people, problems, and circumstances that only the politically astute could know, it had a crowded if not forbidding appearance. By contrast, the typical *Times* leader page of 1914 was attractive. In its first column was a small masthead followed by a full column-long and well-paginated index of the paper's contents. Then came "TO-DAY'S NEWS," a column and a half of well-delineated and comprehensive news items. The leading article itself was a column long, and it was followed by several shorter ones. All were clearly headlined. Following that was a long article, "Cynicism Old and New," a witty and tantalizing piece for readers who possessed knowledge of the literary giants of the past. A column from a special correspondent completed the page.[22] Taken as a whole, its layout was clear, dignified, and attractive. Its content, wider in scope than its 1880s counterpart, had strength of phrase, and its arguments conveyed the weight of authority. Thus *The Times* kept most of its old readers and attracted new ones as well.

The quality press of the Edwardian era was actually quite diverse. Although *The Times* was the acknowledged leader, there were other influential quality papers such as the *Daily Chronicle,* the *Daily News,* the *Daily Telegraph,* the *Morning Post,* the

Westminster Gazette, and a number of other morning, evening, and weekly publications. Modernizing tendencies such as we have observed in *The Times* were, in greater and lesser degree, present in many of these publications too. For instance, when A.G. Gardiner became the editor of the *Daily News* in 1903, he immediately introduced a bolder typography for the paper, expanded its literary section, and added features that were designed to appeal to the cause of labor.[23] Or take the case of the *Speaker.* In the words of Frank Swinnerton, the old *Speaker* "looked dull."[24] Then in 1907 it was renamed the *Nation,* and H.W. Massingham became its editor. No stranger to the New Journalism, Massingham had a reputation for making the papers he served more readable and interesting.[25] As the editor of the *Nation,* he introduced features such as "The Diary of the Week" and "A London Diary" that made the journal livelier. In fact, Massingham's blend of features of the New Journalism and his radical passion made the *Nation* one of the most "significant weeklies of the twentieth century."[26]

Perhaps the best example of the combination of political passion and journalistic skill was that of the Conservative J.L. Garvin. In 1908 he became the editor of the *Observer,* England's oldest Sunday newspaper, and was immediately successful not only in rehabilitating that languishing paper but also in converting it into a major political force in the country. It took him only eighteen months, with the cooperation of Northcliffe who owned the paper, to increase its circulation 185 percent and its revenue 162 percent while holding increased expenditure to 50 percent.[27] Garvin had definite journalistic goals. He labored to "give the public what they don't want," his way of saying that he wished to entice them into reading about and contemplating serious subjects in depth.[28] For a few years, before his affiliation with the *Observer,* he was the editor of the *Outlook,* which he tried to make the "best weekly in the world of its kind."[29] The same quest for journalistic excellence characterized his editorship of the *Observer*. Once, when asked to summarize his intentions in journalism, he provided this answer. They were, he said, based on three principles: (1) to give the paper above all, "character," (2) to restore in an age of tabloid journalism the full treatment of important subjects, (3) to give the public what it, at first, did not want—the only real path to moral influence.[30] Accordingly, he wanted his paper to have character, depth, and influence.

Garvin fulfilled those journalistic goals. Consider the *Observer*, his masterpiece. His powerful editorials were truly the soul of the paper. They made the *Observer* compelling reading, and they remain to this day fascinating examples of informed and persuasive political commentary. Displaying a broadness of mind, they carried contemporary politics into the realms of history and literature, subjects that Garvin knew well. To read them, even when disagreeing with them, was an exercise in studied argumentation that, in the process, seldom failed to provide an insight into life. In an age of great writing editors, his prose style, which manifested character and compassion and love of langauge, was unique. Moreover, his understanding of newspaper organization format and page makeup was distinctly modern. The *Observer* engaged people's attention. It created interest. On the editorial page, for instance, along with those masterful leading articles, the reader encountered a column on the week in review, another on "Sayings of the Week," a paragraph of news from the *Observer* published a century ago, a verse or two of doggerel poetry, and a column of theater notices. One takes no license with the truth in saying that Garvin created "a new pattern of Sunday newspaper for the educated reader."[31]

The abundance of favorable contemporary opinion about him provides another indication of his journalistic achievement. A few examples will suffice. "My generation is passing away, yours is taking possession of the stage," Valentine Chirol, the foreign editor of *The Times* and a stalwart defender of traditional journalism, told him. "I look upon you as the inheritor of whatever was best in the journalistic generation with which I have been . . . associated, with an added brain-power which is recognized alike by friend and foe."[32] Lord Grey, the governor-general of Canada and a man in touch with the British press, spoke of Garvin as "far and away the most brilliant journalist in England."[33] When in 1912 Garvin assumed the editorship of the *Pall Mall Gazette* and quickly energized that evening paper, Winston Churchill wrote, congratulating him on his success. "I relish equally good journalism and a personality that dominates the mechanics of a paper," he said.[34] No small compliment for the Liberal Churchill to pay to the Conservative Garvin.

It is clear that among the editors of prestigious publications of the time there were men of outstanding journalistic ability. They were also men who valued the principle of a "free press in a free society." More precisely, they believed in editorial independence. This helps to explain the tension that sometimes erupted between editors and proprietors. The principle was by no means new in English journalism, but the frequency with which it was mentioned in the private correspondence of the editors indicates that they felt compelled to defend it against proprietary and political pressures.

Men such as Gardiner, Massingham, and Garvin wrote as they wished, sometimes to the regret of the political leaders and parties they supported. The principle of editorial independence also had long been a tradition at *The Times,* and as the correspondence of its editor, G.E. Buckle, shows, it continued to be one.[35] That principle was a guide for editors in their relationship with parties, proprietors, and readers. For instance, when Geoffrey Robinson became the editor of *The Times* in 1912, the editor and proprietor of the *Spectator,* St. Loe Strachey, wrote to Northcliffe.

I feel sure you have got a good man in Geoffrey Robinson. . . . When I wrote to congratulate him I told him I hoped he would soon get an opportunity to stand up to his public over some matter, as in the end nothing helped a newspaper more than a sense that its editor was independent and quite prepared to say unsmooth things to his readers if necessary.[36]

As for Strachey himself, he revealed his own attachment to editorial independence many times in his correspondence. In a comment typical of that expressed commitment, he told Garvin on one occasion: ". . . I cannot wholly trust any politician when it comes to the question of buying votes [here he was referring to party appeals for Irish support]. Both sides must be watched in the matter and this, in my opinion, is one of the most important functions of an independent press."[37]

Traditional political journalists previously took pride in their independence, and they continued to do so. In most cases they thought of independence as the freedom to choose between political parties, parties to which they offered their support and intelligent criticism. It was independence within party, not independence of party that they prized. During the Edwardian era some editors of the political party press, such as J.A. Spender, continued to practice and value this traditional kind of independence. Others, however, men such as Garvin, Massingham, and even Strachey, were capable of creating irritation within a party context or in some cases of arguing against a party positon. They were hardly, to use T.H.S. Escott's term, "conventionally partisan" journalists.[38] Such independence made a number of political journalists of the quality press less dependable in terms of consistent and reliable support for party doctrines, but it placed them in the good graces of the canons of modern journalism. The trend was even more pronounced among the popular morning newspapers produced by the promoters of the New Journalism.

These papers championed an even broader kind of independence. A man such as Northcliffe, as we have seen, thought
of independence in a nonpartisan way. He considered his independence a reflection of his attachment to the wider public, to
the public in general. He considered himself a champion of the
public interest, not the interest of a political party. Such a concept
of independence was a product of the long development of
modern, scientific, industrial culture in the West, and it
manifested itself in many social, political, and economic meanings – all of them positive. Papers produced with this principle in
mind could not be subservient to any political party, though it
must be added that the new press barons were themselves deeply
involved in party politics. Moreover, the popular press of the
New Journalism regularly addressed itself to many matters other
than the dominant political party issues of the day. As R.D.
Blumenfeld once observed, "at the best of times the issues of
political parties cover only a small portion of the public issues affecting the great mass of people in their daily lives. . . . It [the
popular press] has made it its business to air popular grievances
however small they may appear to be to the national legislators."
In doing so it performed a political function and broadened its
political base but in the process also made party efficiency more
difficult. Blumenfeld maintained that "this important result of the
movement of modern journalism away from political parties must
not be overlooked."[39] The trend of which he spoke was well
under way in the years before World War I. All things considered, it is difficult to see how the expanded press of the Edwardian era could have remained as effective an instrument of
political parties as it had been previously. Growing democratization and commercialization created conditions different from
those in which political party journalism had flourished.

Indeed, when some Edwardians spoke of the decline of the
political position of the press, they had in mind the press as an

instrument of political parties. In fact, though a lively political party press vitalized Edwardian public life, the press itself became more commercial as the political community became more democratic. Both circumstances reduced the potential influence of the party press and enhanced the position of proprietors—and proprietors like Northcliffe were more independent than an editor like J.A. Spender. It is clear that political journalism was expanding beyond strict party lines.

Nevertheless, as the political press expanded in terms of independence and audience, the idea of the "influence of the press" retained its mystique. "The fact remains," as Stephen Koss observed, "that readers and writers alike believed not only that such influence existed, but also that it was pervasive. . . . Mistaken or not, this conviction created its own reality."[40] Abundant evidence exists to prove this observation. Not only the new press barons and the prominent editors of the political press but also the politicians themselves assumed that the press was a factor of consequence in the political equation of the day. The latter often expresses their appreciation of press support received or anticipated and communicated their concern for press backing in a number of ways. For example, Joseph Chamberlain told Garvin on one occasion, "In answer to your question, I shall be glad to do everything I can to assist the 'Outlook.' I will see you whenever you want to give you as much information and suggestions as I can with regard to policy."[41] Such exchanges might have been mere rhetoric, a politician's attempt to encourage support. One cannot discount such motives. But they are more than balanced by other considerations. The correspondence between the leading political journalists of the day conveys the assumption of a belief in their influence. That comes as no surprise. There is, however, a more revealing form of correspondence to consider—that among politicians containing references to the press and to journalists. As an example, consider: "Yes, I saw the article in the

'Spectator.' Austin [Chamberlain] was furious about it and told me that he thought of writing a counterblast, but [the] 'Westminster Gazette' of the following day contained an article on the same subject which knocked the bottom out of Strachey completely." So commented Lord Lansdowne to Bonar Law in a letter typical of much of the political correspondence of the day.[42] Moreover, lively press campaigns punctuated Edwardian politics. It is difficult to imagine that issues such as tariff reform or the demand for a larger navy would have reached the levels they did if the press had accorded them only scant space and comment.

Despite the dominant belief in the influence of the press, some doubt was expressed about the validity of that idea. Had not Liberal and Labour politicians succeeded in disproportion to the number of papers supporting them in the election of 1906? That was only the most apparent example of the failure of majority press support to produce the desired results. The journalists were worried that their craft was losing political influence. ". . . Grave men throughout the world," wrote St. Loe Strachey, "are beginning to doubt whether the tremendous claims which we at one time put forward on behalf of The Press as the beacon lights, or, to change the metaphor, the watch dogs of the world, do not in truth rest upon mere rhetoric or even imposture."[43] Even if one makes allowance for the tendency among journalists to overstate the Victorian status of the press, Strachey's comment is an important one, for it captured the Edwardian apprehension about the possible waning influence of the press in political life. In every generation, however, opinions about the effectiveness of any institution are mixed. Those who generally appreciate the successful functioning of an institution may have reason to lament or even to despair of its performance in a particular instance or series of instances.

The political influence of the press, moreover, has always been a relative element in politics. It varies according to time and circumstances. In the Edwardian age, for instance, more people read newspapers than ever before, but many people read them for news rather than views. Thus the press was not exactly the marketplace for political opinion that it had been in Victorian times when there was a better defined and smaller governing class and when there were fewer papers than in the early twentieth century. Moreover, one can also reason that many people who could be counted as part of "the new reading public" were little interested in political content. Then as later they were attracted to their favorite daily by features that had little to do with political commentary. Moreover, in the case of the portion of the public that was attentive to the political content of the press, it must be admitted that they had an abundance of confusing political problems to digest. The issues of the day were divisive, and that fact was of consequence for both the press and the public. Neither the Conservative nor the Liberal press was consistently of one mind on the major issues of the day. Partly this was due to the nature of the issues (e.g., tariff reform, social reform, the budget) and partly it was due to the growing political independence of the press.

It can still be argued that press support did not always produce the desired number of voters and that it preached to the converted. But even in this case, there are counterbalancing arguments. It is, after all, important to buttress the beliefs of the converted, and the press was reaching and influencing a political public of growing diversity. The press influenced that public to some degree in many matters ranging from purchasing habits to entertainment preferences. It is reasonable to assume that the press also influenced this wider public in its political perceptions and thinking. True, it did not have the power to control how someone voted. It never did. But power and influence should not be confused. The press had influence, which by nature is suggestive. Politicians appreciated that fact, as we have seen, and accordingly when war began in 1914 took immediate steps to control the nation's news publications.

The press was a source of pride among the leading practitioners of the craft. In their formal public statements one can find, as would be expected, a defense of all that was best in the British journalistic tradition.[44] It is, however, surprising to observe the way in which several of these editors treated the New Journalism. Because J.L. Garvin best combined the old and the new in his journalistic style, I shall turn to him for an example. In a speech he gave in 1910, he addressed himself to the question of why contemporary journalism appeared more "clamorous and sensational" than it did in previous times. Partly, he said, it was due to a tendency in the British press to copy the blare of its American counterpart, a tendency, he said, that had gone too far but was not being arrested by public opinion. He also attributed it to the increased use of headlines, but he added that was merely another manifestation of the "law of increasing classification . . . which had given us chapters and paragraphs, and shorter sentences in books and better indexes to them." In his opinion, if the critics who then complained about the "decadence of the press" troubled themselves to examine the press as it existed forty or fifty years before, they would have found it tedious. Garvin, in fact, took this opportunity to defend much of what was new in journalism. The press, he said, had been invigorated, and it was sound in its treatment of news. As for the charges of sensationalism, they were "to a large extent indictments of life itself, . . ." and "if journalism is to fulfill its function it must reflect the life that is, not the life that was." All these things considered, he concluded that "There . . . [was] as much fibre and ability in the profession as at any previous time and these qualities . . . [were] able to make as deep a mark upon affairs" as they ever did.[45]

Garvin was by no means alone in his defense of the Edwardian press. Let us consider the reflections of a few other noteworthy journalists on the subject. The respected Liberal editor Robert Donald, for example, reviewed some of the changes that had occurred in journalism in the last twenty years and noted that many old journals had been transformed, that the commercial side of journalism had grown and was able to support more editorial enterprise, and that contemporary journalists compared favorably with their Victorian predecessors. "The journalist of today," he said, "shows more originality and initiative, possesses greater literary ability than his prototype of any generation."[46] Or consider Northcliffe. In 1905 he put into writing some of his thoughts about the press of his time. As one would expect, he found it superior to the older press. It was, he said, better able to gather and distribute news, commercially sounder, more independent, and more professional. ". . . I am profoundly convinced," he wrote, "that it is no mere optimism to state that the future of the daily newspaper grows brighter every year."[47]

During the era of the New Journalism, "good journalism" remained alive. There was, of course, truth in the charges leveled against the popular press of the time, but they can be carried too far. The press, for instance, had become more commercialized and consolidated, but given the economic, political, and social conditions of the time, one must question whether there were alternatives to such realities. Besides, commercially sound papers had much to offer journalism—not only better means of production and distribution but also the means to attract fresh talent. Financial well-being provided the means to be independent and to develop or retain high quality but expensive types of news gathering and presentation such as foreign news services. One must admit also that reckless, sometimes disgraceful, elements could be found in the popular press, but as any history of the press in previous centuries will show, that was not new.

The Edwardian press was an exciting institution. It was an influential factor in the public debate of the times, and the vigor of its political editors justifies the descriptions of them by some historians as part of "a golden age of editors."[48] The press, moreover, gained in journalistic effectiveness. A new engaging format appeared in the popular press that added sharpness to the presentation of news and opinion. Serious political news and commentary were by no means absent from the best of these papers. Many people today would be surprised at the amount of space devoted to such matters in such newspapers. Furthermore, some of the stylistic innovations in layout and format were embraced by the quality press without damage to its reputation. All papers and journals, of course, could not be saved. Each, then as always, had its particular problems to confront. But those quality organs that remained alive and vigorous found some of the stylistic innovations and management techniques of the popular press useful tools in their own survival. They became more vivid, better organized, and more attractive—even to "the educated reader." The Edwardian press gained in diversity and appeal, widened its definition of news, and addressed itself to an expanded public. As a vehicle of political communication, it was a more comprehensive public institution than its Victorian predecessor. All things considered, it is possible to see in the press of this age not so much the triumph of the New Journalism as a constructive germination combining the new and the old. In that process concern for "good journalism" was a factor of consequence.

NOTES

1. The term "the press" needs explanation. No attempt is made to examine all the parts that compose the British press. That, of course, would be a gigantic undertaking. The focus of this paper is on that portion of the press that addressed itself regularly to large affairs of state and tried to be a significant element in shaping them. Stephen Koss's term "the political press," therefore, seems to apply. In the case of the journalists studied here, it can be assumed that the papers

and journals with which they were associated have been investigated. Regarding the representatives of the quality press included, I selected representatives of both Liberal (including Radical) and Conservative persuasions who were acknowledged by their peers as men at the head of their profession. Regarding the popular press, I chose to concentrate on Alfred Harmsworth (Lord Northcliffe). Others might have been selected, either C.A. Pearson or Max Aitken (Lord Beaverbrook). But Pearson was really an imitator of Harmsworth, and besides, blindness ended his career as a journalist in 1908. Aitken, the classic example of a journalist as a political intriguer, did not emerge as a major figure in British journalism until the Edwardian era was nearing its end.

2. See, for instance, David Thomson, *England in the Nineteenth Century: 1815-1914* (Baltimore, Maryland, 1961), p. 176; T.L. Jarman, *Democracy and World Conflict: A History of Modern Britain, 1868-1970,* 3d ed., rev. (London, 1970), pp. 80-83; and R.C.K. Ensor, *England, 1870-1914,* (Oxford, reprinted 1963), pp. 532-536. General textbooks on modern England scarcely mention the topic. See, for instance, Clayton Roberts and David Roberts, *A History of England, 1688 to the Present* (Englewood Cliffs, N.J., 1980); R.K. Webb, *Modern England: From the Eighteenth Century to the Present,* 2d ed. (New York, 1980); and David Harris Willson, *A History of England,* 2nd ed. (New York, 1984). Historians of journalism provide a fuller account in their general treatment of the subject but little in the way of either interpretive challenge to the stereotyped picture or new argumentation based on archival research. See, for instance, two books by Harold Herd, *The Making of Modern Journalism* (London, 1927), pp. 9-91; and *The March of Journalism* (London, 1952), pp. 222-252; and the best work in the field, Francis Williams, *Dangerous Estate: The Anatomy of Newspapers* (London, 1957), pp. 129-183. Particular aspects of the subject are covered in two excellent recent studies: Stephen Koss, *The Rise and Fall of the Political Press in Britain,* 2 vols. (Chapel Hill, North Carolina, 1981 and 1984) and Alan J. Lee, *The Origins of the Popular Press in England, 1855-1914* (London, 1976).

3. Northcliffe to Richard Haldane, 5 June 1911, Lord Northcliffe Papers, vol. III, British Library. Hereafter cited as Northcliffe Papers.

4. An examination, for instance, of either the cheap magazine press or the radical press in the nineteenth century easily verifies the previous presence of sensationalism in the British press.

5. Hamilton Fyfe, *Northcliffe: An Intimate Biography* (New York, reprinted 1969), p. 107.

6. Philips Gibbs, *The Journalist in London* (London, 1952). p. 102.

7. Fyfe, *Northcliffe*, p. 80.

8. The survey covered six separate months spaced throughout 1908 and 1909.

9. Northcliffe to Thomas Marlowe, 30 June 1911, Northcliffe Papers, vol. XLVI.

10. J.S. Willison, "An Answer to Critics," *The News* (Toronto), 2 February 1910, p. 1. Clipping found in Earl Grey Papers, 4th Earl, University of Durham, Department of Palaeography and Diplomatic. Hereafter cited as Grey Papers.

11. Memorandum by Thomas Marlowe, 1911-1912, Northcliffe Papers, vol. XLVI.

12. Northcliffe to Thomas Marlowe, 12 July 1911, Ibid.

13. Northcliffe to Andrew Bonar Law, 12 July 1911, Andrew Bonar Law Papers, House of Lords Record Office, London 24/5/114. Hereafter cited as Bonar Law Papers.

14. J.L. Garvin, "Lord Northcliffe, the Life-Work of a Great Man," Corrected proofs for an undated article [but clearly written after Northcliffe's death], J.L. Garvin Papers, Works, Humanities Research Center, University of Texas at Austin. Hereafter cited as the Garvin Papers.

15. Thomas Marlowe, Memorandum, 1911-1912, Northcliffe Papers, vol. XLVI.

16. The record is extensive on this point. The following two references are offered merely as evidence that figures in both the Unionist and Liberal parties were sensitive to positions taken by the *Daily Mail*. Joseph Chamberlain to Harmsworth, 20 November 1905, Northcliffe Papers, vol. CXLI; and Winston Churchill to Harmsworth, 22 September 1903, Ibid., vol. IV.

17. *The Times*, for instance, introduced headings in the leading articles on 15 July 1907, considerably before Northcliffe became chief proprietor.

18. Alfred Charles William Harmsworth, "The Making of the Modern Newspaper," *World Today*, December 1905, p. 1281.

19. See, for instance, G.E. Buckle to Northcliffe, 12 July 1908, Buckle Papers, Archives of *The Times*. Hereafter cited as Buckle Papers. Also Valentine Chirol to Northcliffe, 12 September 1908, Northcliffe Papers, vol. XCIX, and Buckle to Northcliffe, 7 February 1911, Northcliffe Papers, vol. XCI.

20. Buckle to Geoffrey Robinson, 23 December 1912, Buckle Papers; Valentine Chirol to Cecil Spring Rice, 19 August 1909, Sir Cecil Spring Rice Papers, Churchill College, Cambridge, 1/12; and Valentine Chirol to Buckle, 8 August 1911, Sir Valentine Chirol Papers, Archives of *The Times*, Box. 2.

21. *The Times*, 17 March 1914, p. 1.

22. See *The Times*, 16 February 1888, p. 9, and 8 January 1914, p. 7.

23. Stephen Koss, *Fleet Street Radical: A.G. Gardiner and the "Daily News"* (Hamden, Connecticut, 1973), p. 50.

24. Quoted in Alfred Havighurst, *Radical Journalist: H.W. Massingham, 1860-1924* (Cambridge, 1974), p. 143.

25. Ibid., pp. 118 and 144. Massingham, who was well known among Edwardian journalists for his caustic commentary, served earlier as assistant editor of T.P. O'Connor's *Star*, one of the chief organs of the New Journalism. His work was readable and interesting. His "Pictures in Parliament," the feature he

contributed to the *Daily News* during his association with that paper from 1901 to 1907, was brilliant in its engaging language. It broadened parliamentary comment to include the impact of what was said and how the words spoken reflected the character of the speaker and the tone of the moment.

26. Ibid., p. 2

27. David Ayerst, *Garvin of the Observer* (London, 1985), p. 70.

28. Linton Andrews and H.A. Taylor, *Lords and Laborers of the Press: Men Who Fashioned the Modern British Newspaper* (Carbondale, Illinois, 1970), p. 83.

29. Garvin to Leopold Amery, n.d. [March 1905], Garvin Papers.

30. Quoted in Koss, *Rise and Fall*, vol. II, p. 170.

31. Andrews, *Lords and Laborers*, p. 84.

32. Valentine Chirol to Garvin, 5 February 1908, Garvin Papers.

33. Lord Grey to Henderson, 20 January 1908, Grey Papers.

34. Winston Churchill to Garvin, 27 January 1912, Garvin Papers.

35. See, for instance, Buckle to Northcliffe, 1 March 1911, Northcliffe Papers, vol. XCI; Buckle to Reginald Nicholson, 23 June 1911, Buckle Papers; and Buckle to Geoffrey Robinson, 23 December 1912, Ibid.

36. Strachey to Northcliffe, 20 September 1912, John St. Loe Strachey Papers, House of Lords Record Office. Hereafter cited as Strachey Papers.

37. Strachey to Garvin, 16 February 1909, Ibid., 7/1/1.

38. T.H.S. Escott, *Masters of English Journalism: A Study of Personal Forces* (London, reprinted 1970), p. 337.

39. R.D. Blumenfeld, *The Press in My Time* (London, 1933), p. 125.

40. Koss, *Rise and Fall*, vol. II, p. 7.

41. Joseph Chamberlain to J.L. Garvin, 22 February 1905, Joseph Chamberlain Papers, University of Birmingham Library, 20/4/26. Here are a few other examples. "Really your papers have been . . . good to us and . . . fair to the Admiralty all the year" (Winston Churchill to Lord Northcliffe, 15 October 1912, Northcliffe Papers, vol. IV). "If you and the other editors will kindly do all you can to enlighten the public to the necessity for our having a proper national army, all will go well, otherwise the country will get into serious trouble" (Lord Roberts to R.D. Blumenfeld, December 15, 1911, R.D. Blumenfeld Papers, House of Lords Record Office, London, Box O-S).

42. Lord Lansdowne to Bonar Law, 23 December 1913, Bonar Law Papers, 31/1/51.

43. Strachey to John Buchan, 19 June 1908, Strachey Papers, 3/2/35.

44. For example, see Robert Donald "The Future of the Journalist," 1913, in H.A. Taylor, *Robert Donald* (London, c. 1934), pp. 271-277; J.L. Garvin, "Journalism of Today," Garvin Papers, Works; and St. Loe Strachey, "The Ethics of Journalism," *Educational Review*, XXXVI (1908), 121-131.

45. Garvin, "Journalism of Today," pp. 3, 4, 5, and 7.

46. Donald, "Future of the Journalist," p. 271.

47. Harmsworth, "Making of the Modern Newspaper," p. 1282.

48. The phrase, "a golden age of editors" is taken from Havighurst, *Radical Journalist,* p. 2, and refers to the years 1900-1925.

Joel H. Wiener
Bibliographical Essay

Victorian and Edwardian journalism has attracted increasing attention from scholars in recent years. The Research Society for Victorian Periodicals (RSVP), founded in 1969, sponsors an annual conference, promotes significant projects dealing with the press, and publishes a quarterly journal, the *Victorian Periodicals Review*. In London, the *Journal of Newspaper and Periodical History*, founded in 1984, is published three times a year, and a monthly seminar on Newspaper History meets at the University of London. Both the *Victorian Periodicals Review* and the *Journal of Newspaper and Periodical History* compiles useful annual bibliographies of work done on journalism that supplement more general bibliographies published in *Victorian Studies* and elsewhere. This scholarly activity has made it easier to investigate aspects of the press, including the New Journalism, in part because it has encouraged publishers such as Harvester Press to reissue on microform many of the key newspapers and magazines. Still, as this book emphatically attests, considerable work remains to be done on the history of the press, and many bibliographical gaps are yet to be filled.

One starting point for a study of the New Journalism is the recently published *The Newspaper Press in Britain: An Annotated Bibliography*, edited by David Linton and Ray Boston (London: Mansell Publishing, 1987). This impressive reference work contains about 1,000 entries, many of them annotated. Unfortunately, because of publishing constraints, the editors have had to exclude magazines and journals from their purview. The *Wellesley Index to Victorian Periodicals, 1824-1900*, edited by Walter E. Houghton, 4 volumes (Toronto: University of Toronto Press, 1966-1988), is a mine of information in this as in so many other areas of journalism. It identifies the authors of many contemporary articles dealing with aspects of the New Journalism. The completion of this landmark work in 1988 has eased further the task of the historian of the New Journalism. Among other recent books, two bibliographical studies are particularly useful: J. Don Vann and Rosemary T. VanArsdel, eds., *Victorian Periodicals: A Guide to Research* (New York: The Modern Language Association of America, 1978), and Lionel Madden and Diana Dixon, *The Nineteenth Century Periodical Press in Britain: A Bibliography of Modern Studies* (Toronto: Victorian Periodicals Newsletter, 1975). In the former volume an essay on "Histories and Studies of Individual Periodicals" by Joanne Shattock is especially useful. The *Journalism Studies Review*, edited by Ray Boston and published from 1976 to 1983 at the University of Cardiff, contains several interesting brief articles on aspects of the New Journalism. Volumes three and four of *British Literary Magazines*, edited by Alvin Sullivan (New York: Greenwood Press, 1984, 1986), has some material on popular journalism, although its emphasis is on the better-known literary magazines.

As is true of every aspect of Victorian and Edwardian journalism, the standard biographical and press directories yield nuggets of information. Many prominent journalists put in cameo appearances in the *Dictionary of National Biography* or Frederic Boase, *Modern English Biography,* 6 volumes (1892-1921). Among the leading press and advertising directories dating from the nineteenth century, *Sell's Dictionary of the World's Press* and *Mitchell's Newspaper Directory and Advertisers' Guide* contain the most information about popular journalism. Newspapers of the period are also likely to repay a close search. An outstanding example is the *Sketch,* which features more than 75 pictorial interviews with leading editors and proprietors in a series titled "Journals and Journalists of the Day" (1893-1896). The *Review of Reviews,* founded by George Newnes in 1890 and edited by W.T. Stead for the first 22 years of its existence, presents in capsule form a summary of all the leading articles published in Great Britain and other countries. It is an important source for understanding the impassioned contemporary response to the New Journalism.

The standard histories of the press are less helpful for the New Journalism than might be assumed. Several of them were written in the nineteenth century, and they lack both information and perspective on the subject. This is true of the histories by James Grant, Joseph Hatton, Alexander Andrews, and, to some extent, H. R. Fox Bourne, although the latter's *English Newspapers: Chapters in the History of Journalism,* 2 volumes (London: Chatto and Windus, 1887), remains the best history of the British press. It was written during the transitional period between the old and the new journalism, and its mostly negative perception of the latter primarily reflects the changes initiated by Stead. T.H.S. Escott, *Masters of English Journalism: A Study of Personal Forces* (London: T. Fisher Unwin, 1911), has the advantage of a longer view and a great deal of firsthand information by its author, who was one of the leading journalists of the age. Escott's biographical approach, however, distorts the proper view of journalism in the midst of a process of change. Another comparatively early study of the press, H. Simonis, *The Street of Ink: An Intimate History of Journalism* (London: Cassell, 1917), continues to be an underestimated source. Published originally in the *Newspaper World* as a series of articles and based on considerable personal knowledge, it is insightful in its description of the changes effected in newspaper offices as a result of the New Journalism. Also stimulating are two books by Edward Raymond Thompson ("E.T. Raymond"): *Portraits of the Nineties* (London: T. Fisher Unwin, 1921) and *Portraits of the New Century (The First Ten Years)* (London: Ernest Benn, 1928). The former includes a chapter titled "Old and New Journalists," and the latter contains an essay on "Press Magnates." In both books, Thompson criticizes the "Newest Journalism" (his term for the innovations brought about by Northcliffe and other press magnates) for imposing commercial values upon the press.

Among more recent histories of the New Journalism, two stand out: Alan J. Lee, *The Origins of the Popular Press in England, 1855-1914* (London: Croom Helm, 1976), and Piers Brendon, *The Life and Death of the Press Barons* (London: Secker and Warburg, 1982). Lee's scholarly analysis of the commercial changes in the popular press in the half century after the repeal of the newspaper tax is persuasive. He takes the view that the liberal ideal of an independent press broke down in the late nineteenth century when confronted with an attack by capitalism. The effect was to create an "intellectually more passive (and) morally less confident readership." Brendon's book is less serious, though entertaining to read. It is replete with anecdotes and hard information about the press barons in Britain and the United States who transformed the landscape of journalism, only to be overrun in turn by twentieth-century "media conglomerates."

Harold Herd, *The March of Journalism: The Story of the British Press from 1622 to the Present Day* (London: George Allen and Unwin, 1952), also offers a solid analysis of the New Journalism, as does Francis Williams, *Dangerous Estate: The Anatomy of Newspapers* (London: Longman, Green, 1957, reprinted in 1984 with an interesting foreword by Michael Foot). Herd is more dispassionate than Williams, who asserts that the New Journalism was responsible for, among other things, the dichotomy in the British press between "quality" and "popular" newspapers. Stanley Morison, *The English Newspaper: Some Account of the Physical Development of Journals Printed in London between 1622 and the Present Day* (Cambridge: Cambridge University Press, 1932), is an illuminating study of typographical changes in the press, and it also contains a lot of material about the New Journalism. Morison is generally on the side of the latter because of its innovations and because it helped to create a lively press. Allen Hutt, *The Changing Newspaper: Typographic Trends in Britain and America, 1622-1972* (London: Gordon Fraser, 1973), is a useful updating of Morison. There are important articles on the New Journalism by Joseph O. Baylen ("The 'New Journalism' in Later Victorian Britain," *Australian Journal of Politics and History,* 18 (1972), 367-385) and Harold Perkin ("The Origins of the Popular Press" in *The Structured Crowd: Essays in English Social History* (Brighton, Sussex: Harvester Press, 1981), pp. 47-56). Baylen maintains that the New Journalism was defined primarily by Stead, who employed popular methods of journalism to achieve moral goals. Perkin attacks as "almost pure myth" the alleged link between the Education Act of 1870 and popular journalism and argues for a long view of the press in which many factors helped to give it shape.

Finally, there are specialized histories of aspects of the press that shed light on the New Journalism. Stephen Koss, *The Rise and Fall of the Political Press in Britain,* 2 volumes (London:

Hamish Hamilton, 1981, 1984), makes the point that the New Journalism represented the end of an old tradition rather than the beginning of a new one. Cynthia White, *Women's Magazines, 1693-1968* (London: Michael Joseph, 1970), cogently discusses the emergence of mass periodicals for women in a chapter titled "An Industry Is Born: 1875-1910," and Tony Mason, "Sporting News, 1860-1914," in Michael Harris and Alan Lee (eds.), *The Press in English Society from the Seventeenth to the Nineteenth Centuries* (London: Associated University Presses, 1986), is a pioneering analysis of an important area of journalism. In *The Long Revolution* (London: Chatto and Windus, 1961), Raymond Williams explores the cultural ramifications of change in the popular press. Also worth consulting is Lucy Maynard Salmon, *The Newspaper and Authority* (New York: Oxford University Press, 1923). Salmon analyzes in considerable detail thematic subjects such as interviewing and pictorial journalism.

Personality was a conspicuous feature of the New Journalism, which was built in part around the successful treatment of "human interest" stories. Innovative editors, such as Stead and T.P. O'Connor, marketed themselves aggressively before an eager public. The lives of both men have been studied in detail, though neither is as yet the subject of a satisfactory biography. Until the publication of Joseph O. Baylen's definitive study of Stead, the interested reader must make do with lesser goodies. These include several stimulating articles by Baylen ("W.T. Stead and the 'New Journalism'," *Emory University Quarterly*, XXI (1965), 196-206, and "The Press and Public Opinion: W.T. Stead and the 'New Journalism'," *Journalism Studies Review* no. 4 (July 1979), 45-49); Frederic Whyte, *The Life of W.T. Stead*, 2 volumes (London: Jonathan Cape, 1925), a pedestrian account based on Stead's correspondence; and Raymond L. Schults, *Crusader in Babylon: W.T. Stead and the Pall Mall Gazette* (Norman, Oklahoma: University of Oklahoma Press, 1972), an illuminating summary of an important aspect of Stead's career. The best accounts of O'Connor's life are Hamilton Fyfe, *T.P. O'Connor* (George Allen and Unwin, 1934) and L.W. Brady, *T.P. O'Connor and the Liverpool Irish* (London: Royal Historical Society, 1983). The latter book is a well-documented study of the Irish question in O'Connor's career, both in relation to his journalism and his political activities. O'Connor's *Memoirs of an Old Parliamentarian* (London: Ernest Benn, 1929), written late in his life, contains little about his great career in journalism.

There is not much published material about other leading New Journalists. Frederick Greenwood, who badly deserves a biography, is reasonably well served in J.W. Robertson Scott, *The Story of the Pall Mall Gazette, of Its First Editor Frederick Greenwood and of Its Founder George Murray Smith* (London: Oxford University Press, 1950), an impressionistic account focusing on Greenwood's editorship of the *Pall Mall Gazette* from 1865 to 1880. Scott presents a convincing case for Greenwood as a pioneer of the New Journalism. Edmund Yates and George Augustus Sala do not fare as well as Greenwood, although both men have left behind fascinating memoirs: Edmund Yates, *His Recollection and Experiences*, 2 volumes (London: Richard Bentley and Son, 1884) and George Augustus Sala, *The Life and Adventures . . . Written by Himself*, 2 volumes (London: Cassell, 1895). On Yates's career, see Joel H. Wiener, "Edmund Yates: The Gossip as Editor" in Wiener (ed.), *Innovators and Preachers: The Role of the Editor in Victorian England* (Westport, Connecticut: Greenwood Press, 1985), which delineates that journalist's interest in gossip from the days of the *Illustrated Times* in the 1850s to the *World* in the 1880s. Ralph Straus, *Sala: The Portrait of an Eminent Victorian* (London: Constable, 1942), is an ineffective biography of a great journalist who deserves to be treated more seriously by historians of the press. On Ernest Parke, who edited both the *Star* and the

Morning Leader with a blend of panache and moral fervor, there is only a detailed account in J.W. Robertson Scott, *'We' and Me: Memories of Four Eminent Authors I Worked With . . . .* (London: W.H. Allen, 1956). Parke, notwithstanding his importance, does not rate even a line in the *Dictionary of National Biography.*

Two other leading New Journalists have left memoirs to posterity. Clement Shorter was an innovator in pictorial journalism, particularly as editor of the *Sketch* in the 1890s. *C.K.S.: A Fragment of Himself,* edited by J.M. Bulloch (London: privately printed, 1927), is a brief, informative reminiscence by Shorter that covers these years. Henry Lucy, who virtually created the art of Parliamentary sketch writing, published six volumes of journalistic reminiscences: *Sixty Years in the Wilderness* (London: Smith, Elder, 1909, 1912), *Nearing Jordan* (London: Smith, Elder, 1916), and *The Diary of a Journalist,* 3 volumes (London: John Murray, 1920, 1922, 1923). Lucy's autobiography is not as revealing as might be hoped, but it helps to flesh out the picture of a journalism in transition. Edmund Garrett worked with Stead on the *Pall Mall Gazette* and assisted him in the development of interviewing as a popular technique of journalism. He is the subject of a brief memoir by Edward T. Cook, who edited the paper after Stead: *Edmund Garrett: A Memoir* (London: Edward Arnold, 1909). The contributions of a more prominent New Journalist, W. Robertson Nicoll, are largely overlooked in T.H. Darlow, *William Robertson Nicoll: Life and Letters* (London: Hodder and Stoughton, 1925). Nicoll wrote a gossip column for the *Sketch* for twelve years and helped to advance women's journalism, but his biography is largely taken up with his more conventional editorship of the *British Weekly.* Finally, two other biographies of journalists are worth noting. Algar Labouchere Thorold, *The Life of Henry Labouchere* (G.P. Putnam's Sons, 1913), contains information about Labouchere's editorship of *Truth,* a weekly magazine that specialized in financial gossip and exposures. Lawrence Thompson, *Robert Blatchford: Portrait of an Englishman* (London: Victor Gollancz, 1951), is a solid account of the life of a socialist journalist who made effective use of the techniques of the New Journalism as editor of the *Clarion* (1891-1895). Blatchford's well-known autobiography, *My Eighty Years* (London: Cassell, 1931), is, surprisingly, unenlightening on this subject.

Although inadequate attention has been paid to many of the key personalities of the New Journalism (including Thomas Marlowe, who edited the *Daily Mail* for 27 years), the "great editors" of the Victorian and Edwardian years continue to fascinate historians. These men attempted to uphold a tradition of independent political journalism and to resist the pressures of a mass market and proprietorial interference. Yet their careers illustrate how they were forced to accommodate themselves to changes in the press. Two editors who were reasonably successful at resistance were John Morley and Edward T. Cook. Morley edited the *Fortnightly Review* for fifteen years before preceding Stead as editor of the *Pall Mall Gazette* (1880-1883). He has not yet received the journalistic biography that is his due, and his *Recollections*, 2 volumes (London: Macmillan, 1917), reveal little about his contributions to the press. J. Saxon Mills, *Sir Edward Cook, K.B.E.: A Biography* (London: John Constable, 1921), is an informative account of a man who edited successively three great newspapers: the *Pall Mall Gazette*, the *Westminster Gazette*, and the *Daily Chronicle*. More forthcoming on the subject of the New Journalism is Stephen Koss, *Fleet Street Radical: A.G. Gardiner and the "Daily News"* (London, Allen Lane, 1973). Koss relates how Gardiner conceived of journalism as a public service while, at the same time, introducing many popular features into the *Daily News* (1902-1919), including a bold typography and columns of chitchat. C.P. Scott, who edited the *Manchester Guardian* from 1872 to 1929, was a representative of the "old school." But he too responded to change, as is made clear in J.L. Hammond, *C.P. Scott of the Manchester Guardian* (London: G. Bell and Sons, 1934), especially the illuminating chapter written by W.P. Crozier titled "C.P.S. in the Office."

John A. Spender was another self-described "political journalist of the old sphere," and in his absorbing autobiography, *Life, Journalism and Politics*, 2 volumes (London: Cassell, 1927), he makes clear his dislike of the New Journalism. Yet his tenure of the *Westminster Gazette* (1896-1922) was marked by concessions to popular journalism. Unfortunately, the only published biography of Spender-Wilson Harris, *J.A. Spender* (London: Cassell, 1946) – is inadequate to its subject. There are satisfactory studies of two other leading editors. Alfred Havighurst, *Radical Journalist: H.W. Massingham (1860-1924)* (London: Cambridge University Press, 1974), discusses Massingham's revitalization of the *Daily Chronicle* while he was its editor from 1895 to 1900. Alfred M. Gollin, *"The Observer" and J.L. Garvin, 1908-1914: A Study in a Great Editorship* (London: Oxford University Press, 1960), lucidly discusses Garvin's transformation of the *Observer* into a "quality" Sunday newspaper while making full use of sporting news and other popular features. Finally, mention should be made of the fine study by F.M. Leventhal, *The Last Dissenter: H.N. Brailsford and His World* (Oxford: Clarendon Press, 1985), which shows how Brailsford, a Liberal journalist, adjusted to the demands of popular journalism in the twentieth century.

The leading press magnates also stamped their personalities upon the age, and above them all strode the imposing figure of Lord Northcliffe (Alfred Harmsworth), who introduced so many changes into British journalism that he has been described by friends and detractors alike as "Northoleon." There are numerous biographies of Northcliffe as well as impressionistic recollections of him by people who knew him well and others who knew him hardly at all. The best biography is Reginald Pound and Geoffrey Harmsworth, *Northcliffe* (London: Cassell, 1959), a massive, uncritical, though indispensable, study based on extensive use of the Northcliffe papers. Also worth reading is Tom Clarke, *Northcliffe in History: An Intimate Study of Press Power* (London: Hutchinson, 1950). Clarke was a reporter for the *Daily Mail* before he became the editor of the *News Chronicle,* and he provides fascinating glimpses into Northcliffe's mind. J.A. Hammerton, *With Northcliffe in Fleet Street* (London: Hutchinson, 1932), is a favorable memoir of Northcliffe by a newspaperman who worked in his organization for many years.

The other leading press proprietors have, understandably, attracted less attention than Northcliffe. George Newnes, who has some claim to be the true founder of the New Journalism with his launching of *Tit-Bits* in 1881, is the subject of a workmanlike biography by Hulda Friedrichs, *The Life of Sir George Newnes, Bart.* (London: Hodder and Stoughton, 1911). Newnes subsequently published three of the most innovative journals of the period: the *Review of Reviews* (1890), the *Strand Magazine* (1891), and the *Westminster Gazette* (1893). Like Northcliffe, he was a prolific "ideas man" who extended journalism into new areas, including publications for boys and women. Arthur Pearson was the least important of the trinity of prewar press barons, although his founding of the *Daily Express* (1900) is a milestone in popular journalism. Sidney Dark, *The Life of Sir Arthur Pearson* (London: Hodder and Stoughton, 1922), is an exercise in hagiography that recreates little of Pearson's energy. The most penetrating biography of a press lord is A.J.P. Taylor, *Beaverbrook* (London: Hamilton, 1972). Beaverbrook, however, did not take effective control of the *Daily Express* until 1916, by which time most features of the New Journalism had taken root.

There is no biography of Sir Edward Hulton, who founded several important popular newspapers in Manchester, including the *Manchester Evening Chronicle* (1897) and the *Daily Sketch* (1909). An impressive general book on newspaper ownership is Viscount Camrose, *British Newspapers and Their Controllers* (London: Cassell, 1947). Camrose was himself a proprietor of the *Daily Telegraph*. He knew many of the personalities involved, and his analysis of the intricacies of financial control is authoritative.

Newspapers are the essence of the New Journalism, the product of human experience. And yet we know relatively little about many of them. A few excellent histories of individual newspapers have been published; but, for the most part, the task of studying newspapers has proved unattractive to scholars. How badly needed, for example, is a history of the *Daily Mail,* the *Evening News,* or the *Daily Graphic.* The best starting point in this area is probably H.W. Massingham, *The London Daily Press* (London: The Religious Tract Society, 1892), a concise account of the London newspapers, including the penny and halfpenny papers, written at a time when the New Journalism was taking shape. The *Star* was the most exciting daily newspaper of the early 1890s, and it has been decently served by its official historian, W. Pope, *The Story of "The Star," 1888-1938: Fifty Years of Progress and Achievement* (London: "The Star," 1938), a rambling if knowledgeable account of the newspaper. John Goodbody, "*The Star:* Its Role in the Rise of Popular Newspapers, 1888-1914," *Journal of Newspaper and Periodical History 2* (Spring 1985), 20-29, is a scholarly treatment of the paper's early days, which makes the case for it as a serious political newspaper. The most influential popular newspaper of previous decades was the *Daily Telegraph,* which was founded in 1855 and boasted the largest daily circulation in the world prior to the advent of the *Daily Mail* in 1896. Little of the paper's greatness, however, is evident in Lord Burnham, *Peterborough Court: The Story of the "Daily Telegraph"* (London: Cassell, 1955), a study that is strong on gossip and short on interpretation. More lightweight is R. Allen, *Voice of Britain: The Inside Story of the "Daily Express"* (Cambridge: Patrick Stephens, 1983), an illustrated account of the paper that makes the point that from the beginning it aimed at a readership somewhere between quality and downmarket.

There are several histories of the *Daily Mirror,* which in 1904 made the decisive breakthrough in news photography and was the first daily newspaper to secure a regular circulation of more than one million. Hugh Cudlipp, *Publish and Be Damned!: The Astonishing Story of the "Daily Mirror"* (London: Andrew Dakers, 1953), is the best of these histories, but it is a rather breathless romp and should be supplemented by *The Romance of the "Daily Mirror," 1903-1924: An Illustrated Record of the Enterprise of "The Daily Mirror" in the Twenty-One Years of Its Eventful Career* (London: Daily Mirror Enterprises, 1925). For the *Pall Mall Gazette,* the only attempts at a history (albeit impressionistic) are to be found in two books by J.W. Robertson Scott: *The Story of the Pall Mall Gazette* (1950), previously cited, and *The Life and Death of a Newspaper: An Account of the Temperaments, Perturbations and Achievements of John Morley, W.T. Stead, E.T. Cook, Harry Cust, J.L. Garvin and Three Other Editors of the "Pall Mall Gazette"* (London: Methuen, 1952). There is no history of *Tit-Bits,* but its partner in the Newnes stable, the *Strand,* is the subject of an excellent account by its last editor: Reginald Pound, *The Strand Magazine, 1891-1950* (London: Heinemann, 1966). A fine essay by Virginia Berridge, "Popular Sunday Papers and Mid-Victorian Society," in George Boyce, James Curran and Pauline Wingate (eds.), *Newspaper History: From the Seventeenth Century to the Present Day* (London: Constable, 1978), deals with several popular newspapers of an earlier period. It is based on her important doctoral thesis, "Popular Journalism and Working Class Attitudes, 1854-1886: A Study of *Reynolds's Newspaper, Lloyd's Weekly Newspaper* and the *Weekly Times,*" Unpublished Ph.D. thesis, University of London, 1976. And although neither *The Times* nor the *Manchester Guardian* can be regarded as examples of the New Journalism, both newspapers were affected by the changes in journalism. Their excellent histories illustrate the impact of the New Journalism: *The History of "The Times": The Twentieth Century Test, 1884-1912* (London: "The Times," 1947) and David Ayerst, *"Guardian": Biography of a Newspaper* (London: Collins, 1971).

What was it like to be a journalist during a time of such rapid change? How deeply was the New Journalism permeated by commercial values? To what extent did its success depend upon innovations in style and content? For answers to these and related questions about the texture of journalism, it is advisable to turn to memoirs and recollections by journalists who themselves participated in the changes. In this category, two books stand out: Kennedy Jones, *Fleet Street and Downing Street* (London: Hutchinson, 1919), and R.D. Blumenfeld, *The Press in My Time* (London: Rich and Cowan, 1933). Jones collaborated with Northcliffe on the *Evening News* and the *Daily Mail,* and his dictum was "Don't forget you are writing for the meanest intelligence." His penetrating analysis focuses especially on the interstices between journalism and politics, about which he is unfailingly informative. Blumenfield was an American journalist who began his career in Fleet Street as London correspondent of the New York *Herald* and then edited the *Daily Express* from 1902 to 1932. He excels at describing the "psychological raison d'être" of the press, which in his terms signifies the personal needs of its readers. Another excellent firsthand study of the New Journalism is Hamilton Fyfe, *Press Parade: Behind the Scenes of the*

Newspaper Racket and the Millionaires' Attempt at Dictatorship (London: Watts, 1936). Fyfe worked on the *Daily Mail* and other papers and knew the London press intimately. He is critical of the commercial side of journalism, though in a discerning way. His anecdotal memoir, *Sixty Years of Fleet Street* (London: W.H. Allen, 1949), also helps to record the shift from an old to a new journalism.

There are other absorbing personal accounts of the changes in popular journalism. Among the best of these is Aaron Watson, *A Newspaper Man's Memories* (London: Hutchinson, 1925), by a pressman whose multifaceted activities in journalism illustrate many of the changes taking place. Notwithstanding its obsession with the author's sexual affairs, Frank Harris, *My Life and Loves*, 4 volumes (New York: Grove Press, 1963; first published in 1923), contains some revealing passages about his editorship of the *Evening News* in the 1880s. J. Hall Richardson, *From the City to Fleet Street: Some Journalistic Experience* (London: Stanley Paul, 1927), is an account by a crime journalist who worked on the *Daily Telegraph* for forty years. It provides an illuminating account of how "descriptive reporting" was affected by the New Journalism. Bernard Falk's two volumes of reminiscences, *He Laughed in Fleet Street* (London: Hutchinson, 1933), and *Five Years Dead* (London: Hutchinson, 1937), are amusingly written and informative about the "storm, rush and excitement" of Fleet Street journalism in the early twentieth century. Two other interesting memoirs are Raymond Blathwayt, *Through Life and Round the World: Being the Story of My Life* (London: George Allen and Unwin, 1917), and Sidney Dark, *Not Such a Bad Life* (London: Eyre and Spottiswoode, 1941). Blathwayt concentrates on the development of interviewing in the 1880s and 1890s, whereas Dark vividly recollects his early years on the *Daily Mail* and particularly the *Daily Express*. Frederick J. Higginbottom, *The Vivid Life: A Journalist's Career* (London: Simpkin,

Marshall, 1934), recounts interesting material about the *Pall Mall Gazette,* which he edited from 1909 to 1911. Wareham Smith, *Spilt Ink* (London: Ernest Benn, 1932), is fascinating on the subject of newspaper advertising, and Francis Gribble, *Seen in Passing: A Volume of Personal Reminiscences* (London: Ernest Benn, 1929), describes his eventful experiences on the *Daily Graphic* and the *Sun* in the 1890s. In *Adventures in Journalism* (London: William Heinemann, 1923), and *The Pageant of the Years: An Autobiography* (London: William Heinemann, 1946), Philip Gibbs writes charmingly about his work as a journalist on the *Daily Mail,* which he characterizes as "the great school of the new journalism." Max Pemberton, *Sixty Years Ago and After* (London: Hutchinson, 1936), is a somewhat disappointing account by a man who was involved in the press revolution from the outset and who later became a director of Associated Newspapers, the Northcliffe organization.

Changing modes of news production and distribution are a crucial aspect of the New Journalism, and a recent study—Lucy Brown, *Victorian News and Newspapers* (Oxford: Clarendon Press, 1985)—presents an excellent analysis of late-Victorian news gathering. Among the book's many virtues is its examination of how the concept of "news" came to be redefined under the impact of technological and economic change. Three earlier books provide essential background reading for Brown's study. William Hunt, *Then and Now: Or, Fifty Years of Newspaper Work* (Hull, 1887), and George Scott, *Reporter Anonymous: The Story of the Press Association* (London: Hutchinson, 1968), deal with the origin and history of the Press Association, the organization that was founded by provincial newspaper proprietors in 1868 for the collection of domestic news. Graham Storey, *Reuters' Century, 1851-1951* (London: Max Parrish, 1951), is a satisfactory history of the great Reuters News Agency, which includes a useful section on the impact of the New Journalism on agency reporting.

Finally, there are the "hidden" changes that laid the foundation for transformations in journalism. The best history of the new printing technology, without which an expansion of the press could not have taken place, is Ellic Howe, *Newspaper Printing in the Nineteenth Century* (London: privately printed, 1943). Unfortunately, the crucial revolution in pictorial journalism is badly served by scholars. Jackson Mason, *The Pictorial Press: Its Origin and Progress* (London: Hurst and Blackett, 1885), written before the days of news photography, is still the best general history of the technical side of press illustration. The only scholarly supplement available at present is Jeffrey A. Wright, "The Origins and Development of British Press Photography, 1884-1914," Unpublished Msc. Econ Thesis, University College (University of Wales), Swansea, 1982. Fortunately, there is an outstanding study of advertising: T.R. Nevett, *Advertising in Britain: A History* (London: Heinemann, 1982), which documents the link between technological change and the expansion of newspaper advertising after 1855.

Index

Notes on Contributors

J. O. BAYLEN, regents' professor of history emeritus, Georgia State University, has published extensively on nineteenth-century journalism and the press and is coeditor of the *Biographical Dictionary of Modern British Radicals, 1770-1914* (1979-1988), 3 volumes. His biography of W. T. Stead is scheduled for publication in 1988, and he is presently engaged in a study of Dr. E. J. Dillon, long-time *Daily Telegraph* correspondent in pre-1917 Russia.

RAY BOSTON, former director of the Centre for Journalism Studies, Cardiff University, retired early in 1985 to complete an annotated bibliography, *The Newspaper Press in Britain* (with David Linton), published in March 1987. His labor history monograph, *British Chartists in America*, appeared in 1971. He was the founder-editor of *Journalism Studies Review*, which was published from 1976 to 1983. He has published many articles in the field of journalism history.

LAUREL BRAKE is lecturer in English, University College of Wales, Aberystwyth. She is the editor of *Year's Work in English Studies* and coeditor of the *The Pater Newsletter*. She has published articles on Victorian biography, criticism, the periodicals, and Walter Pater. Presently she is editing a volume of Pater's journalism in the collected edition of his work.

B. I. DIAMOND is currently a doctoral student at Georgia State University. Over the past decade, he has been employed as both a reporter and editor on weekly and daily newspapers in Florida and Georgia. At present he is a public affairs officer for the Georgia Department of Defense. He has published several articles on Victorian journalism.

KATE FLINT is fellow and tutor in English at Mansfield College, Oxford. A graduate of Oxford and the Courtauld Institute, London, she previously taught at Bristol University. *Dickens* was published in 1986, and she has edited *Impressionism in England: The Critical Response* (1984). A study of the language and function of late nineteenth-century art criticism is forthcoming, and she is writing *The Woman Reader, 1830-1920*. She has written numerous reviews and articles on nineteenth- and early twentieth-century fiction and painting.

JOHN GOODBODY is a journalist with *The Times* of London. He has Master of Arts degrees from Trinity College, Cambridge, where he read English, and Birkbeck College, London University, where he studied economic and social history. He is currently researching the history of London evening newspapers in the late nineteenth century.

DEIAN HOPKIN is senior lecturer in History, University College of Wales, Aberystwyth. He is founding editor of *Llafur* and author of papers and articles on labor history and the left-wing press. He edited with Peter Denley the volume *History and Computing* (1987) and inaugurated in 1986 the International Association for History and Computing.

ALED JONES is a lecturer in history at the University College of Wales, Aberystwyth. He has published articles on the history of journalism and nineteenth-century labor and is coeditor of *Llafur,* the journal of the Society for the Study of Welsh Labour History. He is currently completing a book on the newspaper industry in Wales since 1830.

JOHN M. ROBSON is a university professor and professor of English at the University of Toronto and honorary editor of the Royal Society of Canada. General and textual editor of the Collected Works of John Stuart Mill (25 volumes to date), he has written widely on nineteenth-century authors and themes. Currently he is working on a book developing the themes of "Marriage or Celibacy?" and on a biography of Mill.

HARRY SCHALCK is professor of history at Westchester University. He has written articles on the Victorian press and on planned English and American garden suburbs of the late nineteenth and early twentieth centuries. Presently he is at work on a comparative study of several of these garden suburbs.

JAMES D. STARTT is professor of history at Valparaiso University where he teaches British history, twentieth-century European history, and journalism history. He is the author of *Journalism's Unofficial Ambassador: A Biography of Edward Price Bell, 1869-1943* (1979), as well as a number of articles in journals and other scholarly publications and is an associate editor of *American Journalism.* Presently he is working on a study of Edwardian journalists and the problems of empire.

ROSEMARY T. VanARSDEL, distinguished professor of English emerita, University of Puget Sound, is coeditor, *Victorian Periodicals: A Guide to Research,* volume I, and the forthcoming volume II in that series, and of *George Eliot: A Centenary Tribute.* A past president of the Research Society for Victorian Periodicals, she is the author of numerous articles on Victorian and Edwardian studies.

MARTHA S. VOGELER is professor of English at California State University, Fullerton. She has published *Frederic Harrison: The Vocations of a Positivist* (1984), a centenary edition of Frederic Harrison's *Order and Progress* (1975), and articles on other Victorians and Edwardians.

JOEL H. WIENER, professor of history at the City College of New York, has published widely on nineteenth-century British history. His books include *The War of the Unstamped* (1969), *A Descriptive Finding List of Unstamped British Periodicals* (1970), and *Radicalism and Freethought in Nineteenth-Century Britain* (1983). He has edited several books, including *Innovators and Preachers* (1985). His biography of William Lovett is to be published in 1989.

CPSIA information can be obtained at www.ICGtesting.com
Printed in the USA
LVOW10*1625170714

394810LV00008B/100/P